Citizenship and Community

Citizenship and Community

Civic Republicanism and the Modern World

Adrian Oldfield

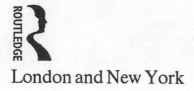

London and New York

First published 1990
by Routledge
11 New Fetter Lane, London EC4P 4EE

Simultaneously published in the USA and Canada
by Routledge
a division of Routledge, Chapman and Hall, Inc.
29 West 35th Street, New York, NY 10001

Typeset by
NWL Editorial Services, Langport, Somerset TA10 9DG

Printed in England by Clays Ltd, St Ives plc

British Library Cataloguing in Publication Data
Oldfield, Adrian, 1939–
   Citizenship and Community: Civic Republicanism and the
   Modern World.
   1. Republicanism
   I. Title
   321.86

   ISBN 0–415–04875–3

Library of Congress Cataloging in Publication Data
Oldfield, Adrian, 1939–
   Citizenship and Community: Civic Republicanism and the
   Modern World / Adrian Oldfield
      p.   cm.
   Includes bibliographical references.
   ISBN 0–415–04875–3
   1. Political obligation—History. 2. Political
   participation—History. 3. Citizenship—History.
   4. Political science—History. I. Title.
   JC329.5.043   1990   90–32351
   323.6'5'01—dc20   CIP

To the memory of Der
(John Stephenson Spink)

Contents

Contents

Preface

I began teaching the history of political thought at a rather advanced stage in my academic career and was struck, as I suspect only a novice can be, by affinities between what Machiavelli and Rousseau had to say both about citizenship and about what constitutes a political community. Hegel and Tocqueville came later. This book has its origins in that early study. Later on, and as modern democratic theory burgeoned, I was struck again, and this is the second source of what follows, by the relative neglect by that theory of the civic-republican tradition of political thinking. Few had taken up the gauntlet thrown down by Bernard Crick in his Sheffield inaugural lecture.[1] It seems appropriate, in this bi-centennial year – of the French Revolution, and of the ratification by the states of the United States constitution – to remind people that citizenship has as much to do with the practice of civic virtue in a political community, as it does with the rights of man: indeed, that civic virtue has a much more ancient connection with citizenship than has the heady appeal to the sanctity of the individual.

Politicians, in Britain at least, are currently searching with a certain air of desperation for a viable conception of what is called 'active citizenship', to bring individuals to a recognition of the duties they owe to their community. Some of them look to the church for a restoration of moral values – they mean, of course, the Church of England. They could do worse than glance at Aristotle and his successors. But they should beware, for civic republicanism carries with it some rather uncomfortable implications for the holders of political power. It holds out the prospect of introducing – one hesitates to say *re*-introducing – some element of honour and responsibility into political life, but it is unsettling for those who believe that freedom exists only to the extent that human beings are left undisturbed by public bodies. This book is an exploration of what it would mean to take civic republicanism seriously in the modern world.

The four political theorists whose ideas are examined in Part II

ix

have largely selected themselves. They are all in the mainstream of undergraduate courses in the history of political thought, and part of the purpose of this book is to locate their thought firmly within civic republicanism, rather than have it continue to be seen either as an aberration in the progressive triumph of liberal political thinking, or as a foreshadowing of Marx. They are all, too, continental Europeans, and it is interesting that English-language political thought has not produced a civic republican to rank with the greatest. My understanding of Machiavelli, Rousseau, Hegel and Tocqueville has been much assisted by the many secondary commentaries on their thought. That these are acknowledged largely in the bibliography rather than in the notes does not diminish my debt to that scholarship.

I thank the University of Salford for granting me study leave during the early part of 1989, and my colleagues in the Department of Politics and Contemporary History there for enabling me to pass the Spring 1989 semester with the Department of Political Science at Texas A & M University. I was made most welcome in College Station, and my time was both productive and enjoyable. My thanks to Bryan Jones and his colleagues there.

I thank the following for reading and commenting on parts of the manuscript, for being willing to discuss its ideas with me, or, more generally, for my education as a political theorist: Bernard Crick, Art DiQuattro, Mike Goldsmith, David Jary, Eric John, Peter and Sue Johnson, Dorothy Knowles, David Linley, Andrew Lockyer, David McAvoy, Herbert McCabe, David Marquand, Howard Mason, Jeff Porter, Ed Portis, Ian Smith, Chris Taylor, Roberto Vichot and Geraint Williams. None of them is responsible for the substance of what follows, but they are all responsible, in various ways, for the fact that there is a book at all, and for their encouragement that the project was, in the words of one reader, 'not obviously foolish in conception or incompetent in execution'. My greatest debt is to the dedicatee who, more years ago than I care to remember, first stirred my interest in political theory.

Graciously, and with unfailing patience and good humour, Miss Joan Cooper typed successive drafts of the manuscript, and Mrs Kath Capper revealed to me, at a late stage, the secrets of the word-processor. I thank them both, as I do Mrs Marcia Bastian, who typed the first draft of Chapters 6 and 7.

Acknowledgements are due to the following for permission to quote from material to which they own the copyright: to Collins and to Harper & Row for Alexis de Tocqueville, *Democracy in America* (ed.) J. P. Mayer and Max Lerner, 1968; to Oxford University Press for G. W. F. Hegel, *The Philosophy of Right* (ed.) T. M. Knox, 1967;

and to Penguin Books for Niccolo Machiavelli, *The Discourses* (ed.) Bernard Crick, 1970, and for Jean-Jacques Rousseau, *The Social Contract* (ed.) Maurice Cranston, 1968.

Adrian Oldfield
Radcliffe
November 1989

Chapter one

Introduction: Status or practice, rights or duties?

The political mind in Britain and the United States has, in recent years, been much exercised by talk of citizenship. The issue of citizenship has been addressed from a variety of perspectives and with different questions. For some, the issue has been citizenship as entitlement, where the question has been how the material benefits of prosperity can be more equitably distributed, in recognition of the dignity of human life. For others, the issue has been citizenship as need: how to provide people with the resources thought to be necessary for effective human agency. For yet others, the issue has been citizenship as admission: how can groups suffering the prejudice against some kind of social stigma have the stigma removed and be admitted to the human world that everyone else lives in? And for still others, the issue has been citizenship as self-government, where the question has been how to widen the opportunities for popular participation in political life. What all these perspectives share is the assumption that individuals *are* citizens, and that, as such, they have certain requirements. In both literature and rhetoric, these requirements are typically referred to as 'rights'.

Such an emphasis on rights is not surprising given the presence of a common element in the political and cultural traditions of American and British society, namely, liberal individualism. Though liberal individualism is only one strain of liberal thought, it has, since the seventeenth century, roughly from Hobbes on, been a dominant one in Anglo-American political thinking. Liberal individualism accords the individual not only ontological and epistemological priority, but moral priority as well. Individuals as citizens are sovereign, not in the sense that they are sufficiently in control of their lives in significant and relevant ways, but in the sense that they ought to be. And the threat to their sovereignty comes just as much from society, and especially the state, as it does from other individuals. Thus to insist upon the rights of citizens is to endorse their claims to protection from threatening forces. As human beings, individuals require the

1

freedom and security to pursue their lives unhindered. Hence the term 'liberal individualism'.

Within this way of thinking, citizenship is a 'status', a status to be sought and, once achieved, to be maintained. One major difference between the modern western world and earlier times is in the definition of who may be legitimately accorded the status of citizen. There is some distance between the world of Hobbes and Locke (when, arguably, citizenship was confined to certain male property-owners) and our world where, at least in rhetoric, all human beings – men, women and children – have the rights of citizenship, though the latter do not have the full exercise of their rights until they reach adulthood.[1] Many of today's political debates and movements are directed towards fulfilling the promise of the rhetoric: that is, towards making the status of citizenship, and the possession of the rights which belong to that status, meaningful in terms of empowering individuals to exercise their rights, of creating opportunities for them to do so, and in terms of placing curbs on political authorities to prevent them encroaching on individual rights. In this discourse, political authorities are regarded with the same suspicion that Locke had for civil government – and that some of the framers of the United States constitution had for a central executive – for it is human beings who act in the name of the political authorities and human beings are not to be trusted, especially when they have power.

The function of the political realm is to render service to individual interests and purposes, to protect citizens in the exercise of their rights, and to leave them unhindered in the pursuit of whatever individual and collective interests and purposes they might have. Political arrangements are thus seen in utilitarian terms. To the extent that they afford the required protection for citizens and groups to exercise their rights and pursue their purposes, then citizens have little to do politically beyond choose who their leaders are to be. The duty of citizens is to abide by the authoritative decisions made by political leaders. When otherwise satisfactory political arrangements come under threat, the duty of citizens will extend to defending them. Should political arrangements fail, for whatever reason, to provide freedom and security then citizens claim the right to change them, with the ultimate right of resistance being held in reserve. One of the rights of citizens within this framework is the right to be active politically: to participate, that is, in more substantial ways than merely by choosing political leaders. Because it is a right, however, citizens choose – on the assumption that they have the resources and the opportunity – when and whether to be active in this way. It is no derogation from their status of citizen if they choose not to be so active.

For its proponents, a major advantage of liberal individualism – a rights-based account of the relationship between individuals and the wider society – is that it does not postulate any one conception of the good life. It advocates the procedures and rules, and the maintenance of an institutional framework, within which individuals – with their given or chosen interests and purposes – pursue their own versions of the good life for themselves. Justice is required as a 'remedial' value,[2] in order to ensure that each individual's pursuit of his or her own good life does not prejudice in certain unacceptable ways the pursuit by others of their own good lives.

Behind such an argument is a view of the individual as autonomous. Largely unaided, individuals choose their own life projects, and ask the state to be allowed to follow them and to be protected accordingly. This individual responsibility for both the choice and the pursuit contributes to the necessary moral development of individuals. Rights-based accounts of the relationship between individuals and society are predicated, therefore, upon the autonomous and responsible moral agent. Followed through consistently, they sustain that agent's autonomy and responsibility. But unless forms of collective life – for example, devotion to a neighbourhood, a class, a nation – constitute a substantive part of the good life of the agent, then such forms are conceived by the agent as instruments assisting pursuit of whatever good life is chosen. Nothing is enjoined upon the individual beyond a respect for the autonomy of others and the minimal civic duties of keeping the state in being – voting, paying taxes and, when the state itself is under threat, a readiness to come to its aid in some form of military service.

This account of the relationship of individuals to the wider society fits in well with many of the important features of western liberal democracies. If, in some, the rights of individuals are imperfectly realized and secured, then at least it is not difficult, in principle, to devise laws, policies and institutions that will guarantee their more effective security. Neither should it be difficult to identify those individuals and institutions who might be expected to act accordingly, or who can be pressed into appropriate action. It is, in other words, an intelligible aspiration in such societies to seek to secure the rights of individuals more effectively. This does not mean that even if rights are entrenched, in constitutions or bills of rights, there are no further difficulties – either in interpretation as to what may be properly inferred from them, or in adjudication when it is a question of whose rights are involved (as, for instance, in the recent American controversy over abortion, where the rights at issue are those of the mother and those of the unborn child[3]). What entrenchment does, however, is to reinforce individuals' conception of themselves as bearing rights, and to stimulate a demand for entrenchment else-where. Hence the current British debate about the desirability or otherwise of a bill of rights.[4]

Any alternative account of the relationship between individuals and society must, if it is to be taken seriously, accommodate itself to the fact that, in the western world, individuals do conceive of them-selves as possessing rights and as being autonomous, in the sense that they are in some ways both independent of the society in which they live, and responsible for their own lives. Autonomous individuals *are* the subject-matter of any social and political theory, but they are not its only subject-matter.

There are a number of reasons why some alternative account is re-quired. The first and most obvious one is that the rights-based account does not exhaust all that can be said – and that is in fact true – of the relationship between individuals and society. Individuals do not only conceive of themselves as bearing rights, nor is their posture to forms of collective life solely instrumental. In particular, individ-uals recognize that they have duties, duties which extend further than the minimally civic and respect for others, and which are associated with the fact that they identify themselves socially – as parents and children; as members of a class, a religion, or a race; as neighbours and friends; as carrying on a trade or profession; as acknowledging a common nationality. Some of these social identities are no doubt chosen by individuals, but many are the 'givens' of their very exist-ence: acknowledged certainly, but acquired involuntarily, and often imperishable. Apostasy is sometimes simply not an option to be con-sidered without profound personal unease, as, for instance, in renouncing one's family, one's faith, or one's country. These social identities are expressive of many forms of collective life and many carry explicit duties with them; as such, they make it impossible for individuals to regard collective life purely instrumentally.[5]

If one of the social identities to which duties are attached is that of citizen, then one of the forms of collective life is the political com-munity. This is the second reason for an alternative account: the revival of interest in the idea of community. There is a lively debate between liberals and communitarians,[6] and there have at times been penetrating discussions of whether there is any meaningful concep-tion of community in the modern world which is consistent with the continued autonomy of individuals.[7] The theme of community has been addressed in many and different ways, and often by the same people who have expressed concern about what they consider to be the relative emptiness of liberal individualism's conception of citizenship. One consistent thought in the literature has been the idea that the modern world lacks, or has lost, any sense of community. For some this lack is not loss at all, but palpable gain especially when they have reflected on the closed, hierarchical communities of the preindustrial world. Escape from the stultifying deadness of such communities could only benefit the individual in terms of gain to his or her autonomy and freedom. Others, however, have regretted the decline in the social solidarity and cohesion which past communities were alleged to possess, such a decline being simply the corollary of the triumph of the individual. Still others have looked back, sometimes with sweet and undisguised nostalgia, to the political communities of the ancient world where life was lived 'whole', as it were, and individual freedom co-existed with social solidarity. They have, however, quickly shaken themselves out of this nostalgia, dusted themselves down, and concluded that they were dreaming. Such *rêveries* have nothing to do with the modern world. But they have been too precipitate, for if there is one place in western political thought where one might expect the themes of citizenship and community to be considered together, then it is in the civic-republican tradition that has its beginnings in the ethical and political thought of Aristotle. This tradition, reinforced and modified by a succession of subsequent thinkers from Machiavelli to Rousseau and beyond, via seventeenth-century English and eighteenth-century American republican thought, is at least as resilient a strain in western thinking as liberal individualism, and it addresses much more cogently the twin themes of citizenship and community.

It is the contention of this book that the civic-republican tradition repays study in two important respects. The first is its test of full membership of the political community. This test, by which the individual becomes a citizen, is performance of the duties of the practice of citizenship. Within civic republicanism, citizenship is an activity or a practice, and not simply a status, so that not to engage in the practice is, in important senses, not to be a citizen. Second, civic republicanism recognizes that, unsupported, individuals cannot be expected to engage in the practice. This means more than that individuals need empowering, and need to be afforded with opportunities to perform the duties of the practice: it means, further, that they have to be provided with a sufficiency of motivation. Civic republicanism is a hard school of thought. There is no cosy warmth in life in such a community. Citizens are called to stern and important tasks which have to do with the very sustaining of their identity. There may be, indeed there ought to be, a sense of belonging, but that sense of belonging may not be associated with inner peace and, even if it is, it is not the kind of peace that permits a relaxed and private leisure, still less a disdain for civic concerns.

Communitarian writing today largely fails to address these issues.

The reason is not hard to find. Whilst communitarians are perfectly willing to acknowledge that individuals have a more than instrumental attachment to collective forms of life, they are extremely reluctant to abandon what they see as the central importance of the rights-based account of the autonomous individual. Any attempt to provide such an individual with a motivation to engage in civic duties is held to undermine that individual's autonomy – and autonomy is important because, without it, the individual is not a moral agent. The argument of this book will be, following in the civic-republican tradition, that the misgivings of communitarians are unfounded: far from undermining the individual's autonomy, those institutional supports that motivate individuals to engage in the practice of citizenship enable them to reach a degree of moral and political autonomy which a rights-based account cannot vouchsafe. Citizens govern themselves.

Communitarians hope that if individuals are empowered and given the opportunities they will come to participate politically, and will continue to do so as a result of the perceived benefits to themselves that follow. This is an important starting point – not just because others may then come to follow their example, but also because the appeal is to individual interest, a factor fully recognized in civic republicanism. If it remains at this level, however, such participation is insufficient to generate commitment to the practice of citizenship as a duty. To endorse the civic engagement of individuals for instrumental reasons is to reveal oneself still beholden to the rights-based account of the individual. The strongest form of political community that arises from such considerations is one that individuals with antecedently-given or chosen interests or purposes constitute with others when they discover that others share some of their interests. If such a community is not in fact established on the basis of contract, it is sustained by an implicit contract, and the interest shared is the freedom and security to pursue other, and private, interests and purposes.

We do not ask within this account – an account from which communitarians, for the most part, find some difficulty extricating themselves – how individuals come to have the commitments to the social identities to which duties are attached. They simply have the commitments, and perform the duties. It is a further – and for some, no doubt, a sad fact – that most individuals have little or no civic commitment. Civic republicanism does ask just how this commitment might be generated, and it asks this question because it holds that political life – the life of a citizen – is not only the most inclusive, but also the highest, form of human living-together that most individuals can aspire to. I shall not argue this moral point. It has in any case been argued many times within the corpus of civic-republican writing far more eloquently than I could hope to do. I shall simply seek to follow the implications of accepting it.

The argument that follows does not depend upon a change in human nature. Citizenship may be an unnatural practice for human beings – it is part of the purpose of this book to discover just how unnatural – but it is not thereby one for which they are congenitally unfitted. Furthermore, and in case the following discussion appears fanciful if not hopelessly utopian, what is put forward here is more than an ideal to which we can aspire: it is a standard against which we can measure the institutions and practices of our societies, and with which we can guide our own political activity. In this, the concepts of 'citizenship' and 'community' share important characteristics with other terms of political discourse – like 'justice' and 'freedom', for instance. We aspire to be just and free, even though we know we shall never be perfectly just or free. But that knowledge neither prompts us to abandon the ideals, nor does it dispose us to discard the concepts as inappropriate or irrelevant to the world in which we live. We judge that world in terms of how just and free it is. The suggestion advanced here is that we should also judge our world in terms of how far it realizes the ideals of citizenship and community.

In a political community what is shared is identity, born in part from self-determination, and in part from a common history, or language, or continued occupancy of the same territory. Political solidarity and cohesion result from the equality of a shared identity, which is at least in part self-determined and chosen. In other words, political solidarity and cohesion do not follow from the sharing of a history or a language, and so on. When we describe ourselves as American, Canadian or British, or as Lancastrian, Quebecois or Texan, we do not necessarily identify ourselves politically. We may be expressing something about our roots, or about our cultural inheritance, but because roots are experienced differently, and cultural inheritances variously interpreted, we do not thereby say anything about the commitment which a political identity involves as it is self-consciously recognized, acknowledged and taken on. It is this choosing of a political identity that gives rise to the solidarity and cohesion of a political community. And it is as 'active citizens' that we choose.

Now of course it is true that we are all born into networks of social, economic and political relationships that we do not choose. Therein lies a large part of the difficulty of any attempt to make the practice of citizenship in a political community meaningful in the modern world. Yet, over the past two hundred years or more, many peoples have – by revolutions, rebellions, wars of liberation or independence – sought to forge new identities for themselves, or to give political expression to identities that they already possessed. In almost no country in the western world – apart from Britain, if one conveniently forgets what for the Irish is 'the British problem' – has this not occurred. This is one of the subversive lessons of history for the project of a political community. It is not that revolution and war have always, or even often, resulted in the practice of citizenship. Clearly they have not. It is rather that war or revolution may be necessary to the very choosing of a political identity. This is also one of the subversive lessons of many writers in the civic-republican tradition: it is a point which is made forcefully by both Machiavelli and Rousseau, for instance.

We cannot expect a practice of citizenship to grow merely because politicians and political thinkers wish it, and exhort their populations to effort. It is not, as again the civic-republican tradition makes clear, a natural practice for human beings, or one that they would spontaneously choose. 'Natural' human beings, or 'non-civic' or 'pre-civic' ones, have to be moulded and shaped for their role as citizens. In part this is the task of education in its broadest sense, but education needs to be supported and reinforced by a prevalent set of mores and practices conducive to sustaining the civic ideal. This may entail a civil religion, a profession of faith in the community. The practice of citizenship means that much more of one's life is lived publicly than is the case in the modern world. It is not that one has no private life; it is rather that to be a citizen is to be politically active, and political activity takes place in the public domain.

It is important, further, to distinguish between the bonds which tie citizens to each other and altruism. There is no doubt a reservoir of altruism in many people which compels them to give blood, donate to worthy causes, or to spend time, effort, and money in organizing the disadvantaged. But citizenship is not about altruism: it is about acknowledging the community's goals as one's own, choosing them, and committing oneself to them. Altruism is the response of one human being to another. Citizenship is exclusive: it is not a person's humanity that one is responding to, it is the fact that he or she is a fellow citizen, or a stranger. In choosing an identity for ourselves we recognize both who our fellow citizens are, and those who are not members of our community, and thus who are potential enemies. Citizenship cuts across both religious and secular universalism and involves recognising that one gives priority, when and where required, to one's political community. This does not entail an aggressive posture towards strangers. It simply means that to remain a citizen one cannot always treat everyone as a human being. Again, this is a thought which lies at the heart of the civic-republican tradition.

This book is in three parts. In the first part, the concepts of citizenship and community are examined. The discussion is necessarily stipulative, but it is intended to be consistent with the civic-republican tradition of western political thinking. An assumption is made that the individuals with whom one has to deal are autonomous: that is, that they are capable of authentic choices about the ways of life they wish to follow. The discussion then proceeds to examine what it is that makes the autonomous individual a citizen. The argument here is that a particular form of moral bond must exist between autonomous individuals before they become citizens. This bond is identified by Aristotle as 'concord', or that form of friendship which is appropriate to citizens. It is this bond which motivates individuals to performance of the duties of citizenship. Finally, the discussion considers what it is that autonomous individuals do when they act as citizens: they make judgments about their identity and about the common purposes they wish to pursue. In doing so, they identify themselves as members of this political community rather than any other. Most of the argument in Part I is conducted at a fairly abstract level. In particular, the implications for political practice are not explored there, though they are indicated briefly: a more detailed appraisal comes in Part III.

In Part II (chapters 3 to 6) the political thought of Machiavelli, Rousseau, Hegel and Tocqueville is discussed from the perspective of what they have to say about citizenship and community. These are not marginal concepts for them, but ones that occupy the centre of their political thinking. For all except Tocqueville, the civic-republican inheritance is an important benchmark or starting point, but each of them looked differently at the ancient world. They perceived the modern relevance of this world in divergent ways, in part because they looked at different places in different times. Machiavelli's model was the Roman republic before it became a personal imperium, and he thought its experience replicable in sixteenth-century Italy if only his contemporaries would make the effort. Rome, too, inspired Rousseau – as did Sparta – but he was too conscious of how the human individual had changed over the centuries to think it possible simply to reproduce ancient practices and institutions, and, anyway, he believed he had a model closer to hand, in Geneva. For Hegel, the beautiful harmony of Athens was irrecoverable, but he drew from the experience of Athens a vision of the kind of harmonious life which he believed was waiting for modern man, should he have the wit to recognize it. Tocqueville avoided consideration of the ancient world; in fact, he dismissed it as irrelevant. Nevertheless, since he acknowledged Montesquieu as his mentor, he may be said to have had contact with that world at only one remove, though he drew from it no direct inspiration.

The contexts in which Machiavelli, Rousseau and Hegel write about the connected themes of citizenship and community reflect, in part, their different approaches to the ancient world. In writing about the expansionary Roman republic, Machiavelli makes the military dimension an essential ingredient in his discussion of citizenship, and thus of the political community in which citizenship is practised. Though Rousseau is alive to the political arrangements necessary to the large state, his prescriptive argument is concerned with those appropriate to the small, inward-looking, face-to-face political community. The arena for Hegel's thinking is the highly-differentiated modern nation-state, in which there are ascending levels of approach to that harmonious ethical life which is the goal of human history. Tocqueville saw the early nineteenth-century American experiment in republican politics as a possible version of Europe's future, in which an informed and enlightened ethos of citizenship served to counter what he saw as the dangerous tendencies of democracy.

Central to the thinking of all four is a consideration of what it means for human beings to be free. Without anticipating the following discussion, it is here that they perhaps most obviously part company with those liberal-individualist political thinkers, from Hobbes on, who perceived human freedom to lie in that area of life where individuals are not interfered with by society or state.

Each of the chapters in Part II has the same formal structure. They begin with a statement of the problem faced by each thinker, and go on to discuss the proposed solutions. Finally there is an examination of the implications for political practice identified by each writer. These implications are taken up again in Part III, where they are related to the late-twentieth-century world and especially to communitarian writing of the 1970s and 1980s. At this stage it will be made plain precisely what can, and what cannot, be gleaned about any modern practice of citizenship in a political community from discussion of thinkers in the civic-republican tradition. It will be claimed that, at the least, such a discussion provides us with relevant meanings for the concepts, and that many of the implications for political practice drawn by contemporary writers have, in fact, been prefigured by Machiavelli, Rousseau, Hegel and Tocqueville. It will not be forgotten that they were addressing their problems, and not ours, but it will be argued that their problems and solutions are connected to ours. In his *Autobiography*, R. G. Collingwood – the English philosopher and archaeologist of the inter-war years – had this to say about the nature of political theory:

Anybody would admit that Plato's *Republic* and Hobbes's

Leviathan are about two things which are in one way the same thing and in another way different.... The sameness is the sameness of an historical process, and the difference is the difference between one thing which in the course of that process has turned into something else, and the other thing into which it has turned. Plato's *polis* and Hobbes's absolutist State are related by a traceable historical process, whereby one has turned into the other; ... the history of political theory is not the history of different answers given to one and the same question, but the history of a problem more or less constantly changing, whose solution was changing with it.[8]

We can make sense of our own problems by seeing how they are related to and grow out of the problems faced by the past. This book is intended as a contribution to that project.

Part I

Citizenship and community: an analytical statement

Chapter two

The citizen in the political community

One of the grander themes of nineteenth-century sociological writing was based upon an observation that the two revolutions of the late eighteenth and early nineteenth centuries – the French and the Industrial – had so changed the nature of the relationships between individuals, and between individuals and society, that a new social order existed. The history of this change has been differently told, its starting point and seminal influences differently identified, and indeed the nature of the change itself differently described and accounted for. The two revolutions themselves, for instance, were taken by some as seminal influences, and by others as catalysts for changes which were already happening. In whichever way the histories were written, though, the story was one of a transition from the 'traditional' to the 'modern', from 'community' to 'society' – each of these terms indicating different ways in which individuals related to each other and to the larger social groupings of which they were part.

There is no need to review this nineteenth-century literature, for the job has already been done by writers such as Nisbet, Plant and Gusfield,[1] nor is there any need to assess the historical accuracy of the different accounts which were offered. Two aspects of this literature, however, do require comment. The first relates to the nature of the 'community' which was, at some point, superseded by 'society'; and the second, to the nature of the 'individual' who is supposedly typical of modernity.

The concept of community, which found a place in the writings of people as various as Burke, Comte, Tönnies, Durkheim and Weber, and whose passing they noted, was overwhelmingly a conservative one. If there was an archetype, it was the medieval community – the guild, the village, the church, the monastic order – and the qualities which these communities possessed, and which were stressed in the nineteenth century, were those of order and stability, consensus and integration. They would not change during a lifetime: neither would the places in them occupied by each individual. It was above all a hierarchical world, but the hierarchy – and the authority that went with it – were accepted. It was this which constituted that cohesion which made such collectivities 'communities'. Each person occupied a particular station within the hierarchy, and with that station went duties which were thought essential to the survival of the community. They were secure places, self-sufficient and relatively isolated. For those in the nineteenth century who reflected on the medieval communities, social relationships were characterized 'by a high degree of personal intimacy, emotional depth, moral commitment, social cohesion and continuity in time'.[2] The men and women who populated this world were 'heteronomous': that is, they accepted and internalized uncritically the social roles into which they were born, and the customs, traditions and moral codes of their society. They lacked any alternative view of the world against which they could measure the experience of that in which they lived.[3]

The historical accuracy of this portrait of the medieval world can, no doubt, be questioned, but this is not the issue. The issue, rather, is that such communities did not exist in the nineteenth century, or if they did, then they did so as relics of a past age which would soon pass. In the nineteenth century, a century now disturbed by the French and Industrial revolutions, social relationships were not suffused with the warmth and depth that went with the kinship, neighbourhood and friendship of the traditional community. Social relationships were different because the parties to the relationships had changed their character as well. Exogenous factors – economic, political, military, religious – provoked simultaneous, and mutually reinforcing, changes in both individual character and social relationships. Individuals were now no more than atomized units in an amorphous aggregate, rather than the integrated members of an organic whole. Among such individuals, social relationships were impersonal, mechanical, instrumental and competitive, for it was 'the individual' that now had prior ontological status.

The place that individuals have in contemporary public discourse – and have had for some three to four centuries – is underpinned by developments in thinking in the sixteenth and seventeenth centuries, developments which established their priority against both Church and state. First, there was the overthrow in large parts of northern Europe of the hegemony of the Catholic Church. The Church, in its Protestant, reformed state, no longer occupied the same kind of authoritative position in matters of individual thought and conduct: it was ceasing to be the exclusive intermediary between the individual and God. The intermediary now became the individual conscience: this was the supreme arbiter of how individuals led their lives and of how they related to their fellows. This conscience was no doubt guided by Church elders and other acknowledged and respected luminaries, but it could no longer be commanded by them. Before God, in this life and on judgment day, the individual stood alone.

The second change in thinking which secured a privileged position for the individual was the development of the language of natural rights. Richard Tuck notes that it was in the early and high Middle Ages that this language first appeared. Natural rights to property were given papal blessing in John XXII's bull *Quia vir reprobus* of 1329. Such language and thought did not, however, survive the Renaissance. What was important for Renaissance humanists was not natural law, but humanly-constructed law, in which all rights were civil rights. Natural-rights' language and thought had to be painfully reconstructed in the late sixteenth century, issuing in the great texts of the seventeenth.[4] Natural rights, being natural, existed prior to society and the state, the main purpose of which thus became to secure and protect them. Even for Hobbes, the authority of the sovereign over his subjects is conditional upon his securing to them their natural right to life; in Locke, natural rights are used as the basis of the theory of resistance to government. It took less than a century after Locke for this theory to be translated into action in the American and French revolutions.[5] Since society and the state existed to secure and protect natural rights – and since rulers were just as human as those over whom they ruled and could not thus be trusted – individuals, by virtue of their natural rights, acquired rights against society and the state. Thus was the moral primacy of the individual enshrined, and the claims of the community to loyal service devalued. Society and the state were now instruments for the furtherance of individual wills and purposes.

Autonomy

What this amounted to was the assertion of the 'autonomous' individual. Such an individual would clearly be out of place in the traditional communities which so exercised the minds of nineteenth-century social theorists. The question is whether there is any form of community in which such an individual would feel at home. 'Is there some way', Raymond Plant asks, 'of understanding community which will enable the freedom of the individual and the cooperation and fraternity of the community to be meaningfully held together?'[6] Plant's answer to this question is considered below, but his formulation can stand to indicate the parameters of this inquiry. We need first to say something about 'autonomy'. What does it mean?

The assumption is that autonomous individuals exist; the question is, what does their autonomy consist in? The concept of 'action' is a starting point here – action, as distinct from 'behaviour', draws attention to reasons, to motive, purpose and will.[7] It thus refers to two further, closely-related concepts: self-determination and authenticity. To say that someone's actions are self-determined is to say that they are a product of his or her will. Following Rousseau and Kant, this means that the self's will is not subject to, or constrained by, that of another. To say that a person's actions are authentic is to say not only that the will which wills them belongs to the self, and not to somebody else, but that it belongs to the self in some special way because the self has chosen it, or has at least rationally assented to it. The autonomous individual's actions, therefore – to the extent that they are self-determined – are expressions of that individual's authentic self. All this, however, is to beg a large number of questions.

Three major objections can be made to autonomy. First, it can be argued that inequality in the distribution of economic, political and social resources seriously limits the opportunities for self-determined actions available to the majority of men and women. In large parts of their lives, they do what they do because they have to. They are either subject to other people's wills, or constrained to act in particular ways by the exigencies of the institutional structures of which they are a part. It should be noted that this objection does not destroy the principle of autonomy. It says simply, and only, that the opportunities for autonomous action are open solely to a few. No political community, however, can be constructed – let alone justified – on the basis of such inequality. The task thus becomes one of redistribution – a large task, and not one to be minimized. How redistribution is effected is another question, and is not one which will be extensively discussed.[8]

The other two objections are more philosophically weighty, for they question the possibility of autonomous action for anyone and everyone: they question the authenticity of the self that wills. One objection derives from Marx, to the effect that ideology imprisons people within a particular way of thinking, so that what they will serves to sustain, or at best not to disturb, a particular set of economic, political and social arrangements. As Marx and Engels remarked, 'the class which has the means of material production at its disposal, has control at the same time over the means of mental production'.[9] Yet this cannot be the whole story. Even for Marx, there was the inevitability of eventual escape from ideological servitude into the communist society of free, autonomous individuals; the escape to be effected by a class-conscious, and therefore authentic, proletariat through revolutionary action. Furthermore, the objection, again, does not destroy the principle of autonomy. True, for the vast majority of men and women it is arguably the case that in the existing circumstances of capitalist society, the spell of ideology does deny autonomy, in the sense of authenticity. But presumably those who control the means of mental production are authentic: they know what they are doing. Indeed, it is a commonplace among a large body of historians, not all of them Marxists, that the most class-conscious class in nineteenth-century England was the middle class, which – though it did not for most of the century occupy high political office – ensured that what the state did served its interests. Were it to be the case that the controllers of mental production were also the unwitting servants of ideology, then the prospect of historical change as the result of autonomous action on the part of anyone would of course be unimaginable. This would seem to be the view of some, contemporary, structural Marxists, such as Althusser and Poulantzas,[10] but they are not the only legatees of Marx's inheritance. It may be enormously difficult for the mass of men and women to unmask ideology by their own unaided efforts. Lenin, as is well known, gave up at this point, arguing that the highest level of consciousness that the proletariat could reach on its own was what he called 'trade-union consciousness'. True 'social-democratic' or revolutionary class-consciousness had to be brought to the mass by a disaffected intelligentsia.[11] The mass had to be taught the ways of autonomous action. But unless everyone is a prisoner of ideology, the principle of autonomy remains intact against this objection. It can, thus, be a plausible aim to wish to extend, in both scope and numbers, the opportunities for men and women to 'be themselves' and act, accordingly, autonomously.

The final objection to authenticity, and thus to autonomy, derives from elaboration upon the fact, already noted, that human beings are social beings. The argument is that men and women are born into a pre-existing social world, that they are 'socialized' into a variety of roles, and that these roles provide them with such identity as they have. There is nothing in the 'self' apart from internalized codes of conduct in relation to the roles which that self occupies. If this is so, it is difficult to see what space authenticity can occupy. Each individual may be unique, in the sense that he or she is a particular amalgam of an infinite variety of roles, but this is not the same thing as saying that the self involved is in some way authentic. We are back with the heteronomous person. If the self finds its identity in and through membership of family, city, tribe, nation, and is not 'detachable from its social and historical roles and statuses', as Alasdair MacIntyre argues,[12] then it is difficult to see how this self can 'act' in any intelligible sense, rather than just behave. Certainly, unless there is something in the self – apart from the identity provided by social roles – which will enable it to make choices, then all possibility of moral action is foreclosed. It is, first of all, not the case that the roles

19

one occupies will always provide a unique course of action. It is, further, not the case that conflict between roles can be ruled out as a possibility: this is one aspect of the tragedy of life to which MacIntyre draws our attention in his discussion of Greek theatre.[13] The self may not be 'detachable' from its social and historical identity, but, unless it can distance itself from its social roles, it has no hope of making choices when the conduct required by different roles conflicts. And, of course, we do choose, and not necessarily in accordance with some pre-ordained hierarchy of roles. This 'choosing', this capacity for choice, indicates that there is something in the self which is not accounted for by referring to the social roles we occupy. This something constitutes the distance between the self and its roles, and creates the space for authenticity. If we grant that people can some of the time act autonomously, and not unreflectively in response to the injunctions of a social role – or blindly in accordance with an ideology, or submissively in terms of the hierarchical ascription of a status – and if we are trying to find a place for autonomy within some conception of community, then it matters not just that people act, but how they act. Not all forms of conduct will be compatible with community life. Autonomous conduct requires some kind of affective or moral dimension.

Friendship

The starting point is that autonomous individuals are social beings. This means more than that they derive part of their identity from the social roles they occupy. It means, further, that living itself is a shared venture. Chance, circumstance, and sometimes choice, have placed particular men and women in some kind of contiguity with each other, whether functional or geographic. If this contiguity is to be the basis of a community, then relationships between the individuals so placed have to be informed by certain characteristics. I can find no other word than 'friendship' for the relationship that must exist between individuals for community to work.

To state the conclusion of the argument before the steps have been taken to justify it: it is 'friendship' – rather than some other characteristic such as 'civic virtue', or 'civility' – which must obtain if there is to be such a thing as community, for it is the bond between individuals that creates the community itself. It is not a matter of each individual being bound separately to the community. This latter type of bonding can all too easily lead to the position where the community has a life of its own, over and above the lives of those who are its members. It is friendship which moralizes the actions of the autonomous individual, and which creates citizens.

Here, the reference point is Aristotle's discussion of friendship in Books VIII and IX of the *Nicomachean Ethics*. In order to place this discussion in an appropriate context, however, it is necessary to examine briefly what kind of association the *polis* is, and what constitutes its unity. In the *Politics*, Aristotle describes the *polis* as an association of men, but an association of different *kinds* of men. It is 'by its nature ... some sort of aggregation',[14] and not a total unity. It requires different and complementary capacities among its members if both it and they are to attain a better and higher form of life: 'A real unity, such as a polis, must be made up of elements which differ in kind.'[15] And this 'real unity' is founded on justice and friendship. It is justice and friendship which create the bonds between members of diverse capacities, and which thus constitute the unity of the *polis*. To be just, Aristotle comments in the *Ethics*, means to be 'lawful and fair':[16] lawful, 'because the law directs us to live in accordance with every virtue, and refrain from every kind of wickedness'.[17] 'Fair' in this context refers to both distributive and rectificatory justice, and requires that we take no more than our share, and accord others their proper share:

> a just act necessarily involves at least four terms: two persons for whom it is in fact just, and two shares in which its justice is exhibited. And there will be the same equality between the shares as between the persons, because the shares will be in the same ratio to one another as the persons; for if the persons are not equal, they will not have equal shares, and it is when equals have or are assigned unequal shares, or people who are not equal, equal shares, that quarrels and complaints break out.[18]

It is justice which constitutes the spirit of friendship. 'Friendship', he remarks in Book VIII of the *Ethics*,

> seems to be the bond that holds communities together, and lawgivers seem to attach more importance to it than justice, ... but people who are just still need the quality of friendship; and indeed friendliness is considered to be justice in the fullest sense.[19]

There are different kinds of friendship, however. Friendships differ, first, in their foundation, according to whether they are based on utility, pleasure or goodness. Perfect friendship is based on goodness:

> For these people each alike wish good for the other *qua* good, and they are good in themselves. And it is those who desire the good of their friends for the friends' sake that are most truly friends, because each loves the other for what he is, and not for any incidental quality.[20]

But such friendships are rare. Friendships differ also, as does justice, according to the nature of the parties to the relationship. The friendships between parents and children, between brothers, between comrades, and between fellow-citizens all differ, and so too does the justice appropriate to the different friendships. Thus 'the duties of parents to children are not the same as those of brothers to one another, nor are the duties the same for comrades as for fellow-citizens'. Hence the wrongs committed vary with the type of friendship: 'it is more serious to defraud a comrade than a fellow-citizen, and to refuse help to a brother than to a stranger, and to strike your father than anybody else'.[21]

In all these relationships there is both friendship and justice, 'because in every community there is supposed to be some kind of justice and also some friendly feeling'.[22] The term friendship, thus, is a generic term including love, affection, and what we, in the twentieth century, call 'friendship'. For Aristotle, friendship also includes the relationship between fellow-citizens, which is not love or affection, but 'concord'. In Book IX of the *Ethics*, he distinguishes 'goodwill' from friendship: 'Goodwill resembles friendship but is not identical with it, because goodwill can be felt towards people that one does not know, and without their knowledge, but friendship cannot.'[23] Between fellow-citizens, and thus as the basis of political association and action, friendship takes the form of concord – '*homonoia*':

> There is said to be concord in a state when the citizens agree about their interests, adopt the same policy, and put their common resolves into effect. Thus concord is concerned with practical ends, and among these only with such as are important, and can be achieved ... by the whole body of citizens .... Thus concord is evidently ... friendship between the citizens of a state, because it is concerned with their interests and living conditions.[24]

Such a relationship of concord can only exist between good men,

> because they are in accord both with themselves and with one another, having (broadly speaking) the same outlook. For the wishes of such people remain constant and do not ebb and flow like the tides: and they wish for what is just and advantageous, and also pursue these objects in common.[25]

Concord is, thus, that friendship which exists between citizens as members of a political community. It is a relationship between people who know each other; they are not strangers, between whom goodwill is possible, but not friendship. It is a relationship between people who differ in their talents and capacities. It is a relationship based on respect for such differences, and on concern for others' interests: each, thus, acknowledges the other's autonomy. It is above all a relationship based on recognition that living is a shared venture, that can only be successfully engaged in if there is commitment. The commitment, however, is to the fellow citizens, who – in choosing amongst themselves how to conduct their shared lives in the spirit of justice – create and sustain a community.

The community is prevented from becoming an entity that is somehow outside, above, or other than, the individuals who compose it – such that it could make demands on its members against their wills – by adopting democratic procedures. It is only in such procedures that the implications of community membership can be explored. Furthermore, and given that no set of public purposes may exist waiting to be discovered, democratic procedures are necessary for creating such purposes, which in part identify the community as this community rather than any other. It is the fellow citizens of the community who collectively, through democratic procedures, are the guardians of the community's identity and ethos, so that the only claims that are made upon the members are self-assumed. A spirit of 'concord', thus, allied with such procedures, creates the possibility – though it does not guarantee – that the outcome from democratic procedures will be socially acceptable.

Aristotle, of course, was writing about the Greek *polis* – a political community, geographically defined. That the possibilities for autonomous action by individuals in a spirit of concord are not exhausted in such communities is indicated by Raymond Plant's analysis of community in the modern world. Plant's argument is that it no longer makes sense to think of community in geographical terms.

Any search for a community appropriate to the modern world cannot be bound up with nostalgia for a lost rural ethos, with its emphasis on fixity of place and role, for the simple reason that such an ethos has become progressively weaker with the passage of time. It is possible to think of community, however, in functional terms, and trade off the very division of labour thought by other theorists actually to be destructive of community. The professions, he suggests, can be seen as functional communities in which there is common identity, stable membership, shared values, a common language and acknowledged authority: 'These seem to be criteria enough for agreeing that the notion of functional community makes sense.'[26] It makes sense, moreover, from 'some overall liberal view of man', for it takes 'into account the values of autonomy and freedom realised as a result of the decline of the traditional community'.[27] Any coherent view of community must, however, Plant claims, recognize the notion of authority as a necessary condition. In the traditional community, authority was customary, but social mobility has destroyed this idea of authority. How then can authority be compatible with an idea of community which does justice to individualism? Plant's answer is that authority is a necessary condition of any form of social life. Following Winch,[28] he argues that social life is rule-governed; there are right and wrong ways of doing things which do not depend on one's own caprice, and these rules are intrinsically linked with the idea of authority. In the functional community what has importance are social roles, which have norms and expectations built into them implying how relevant activity ought to be carried on: 'It is these rules attached to social roles, which have this normative force which constitutes the source of authority in the functional community.' The authority of the traditional community was unitary and pervasive; that of the functional community is not unitary or pervasive, abecause it does not cover the whole of a person's activity. Moreover, unlike traditional authority, that of the functional community is something the individual can, on the whole choose to assent to. Thus can justice be done, Plant concludes, both to the role of authority in community, and to the liberal view of the person: 'To define community functionally is to recognize a plurality of communities, thus a plurality of roles and functions, hence a wide range of rules and authorities.'[29]

Plant's case for the functional community draws attention to Hegel's analysis of the Corporation in what he calls 'civil society', where it is given an important role both in the integration of society into a cohesive political whole, and in the education (*Bildung*) of the citizen into his civic duties.[30] This is one answer to the question posed by the scale of the modern world to any attempt to make the idea of community meaningful. A geographically-defined community may not, however, be quite the anachronism Plant thinks it is, for it is possible to think of the federal state – or a decentralized one – as a further answer to the question of scale, in which the idea of community could also find a place. This was one aspect of early nineteenth-century American politics which fired the enthusiasm of Tocqueville.[31]

It is in Plant's argument that authority is a necessary condition of any form of social life, and thus of any community, that he directs attention to what it is that members of a community do when they contemplate their lives in friendship – in 'concord' – as autonomous beings. They establish the rules that are for them going to be authoritative and, in this, they exercise their judgment. Together with the ideas of autonomy and friendship, judgment is the third term denoting what is constitutive of a political community. With the exercise of political judgment, we come to the major duty of the practice of citizenship.

24

Judgment

'Judgment' typically has two senses: first, that judgment follows the object of judgment – it is made after the fact; second, that judgment (in the sense of deliberation) precedes a course of action – it is practical wisdom.[32] In both cases, judgment would seem to be something that individuals are naturally capable of, and thus that all can share in. As practical wisdom, judgment occupies that space (if that metaphor is appropriate) within autonomous individuals which allows them to distance themselves from their social roles, and to choose – both within a specific role and between roles – what conduct is appropriate and proper for them. Judgment, thus, is not a capacity or ability possessed by the fictional, completely heteronomous individual. It depends upon some measure of autonomy. Finally, though judgment is not rule-governed, it is something which one can expect to be supported publicly, with reasons.

Judgments in political communities entail an implied responsibility for the assumption of a shared way of life. They are judgments about the form of collective life it is desirable to pursue. The substantive judgments that a political community has to make concern that which is to be authoritative within the community. In relation to rules of procedure, for instance, the judgment would presumably be that, for autonomous beings, such rules should be democratic. There are other judgments to make which relate to the survival of the community as this community rather than any other. Judgments are needed, first, about the kind of conduct which is constitutive of that collective life in which members of a community undertake to share. It is not a question, here, of a community setting itself some overriding purpose, or of establishing one exclusive path towards the good life. The community, after all, is composed of diverse autonomous beings, different in their capacities, talents and functions. The good life for one is not necessarily the good life for another, but the good life for each must include activity which sustains the political community. It is thus a question both of establishing rules or norms of conduct in accordance with which each citizen will pursue his or her own independently determined good life, and of specifying those activities which are necessary to make the individual pursuit of the good life possible.

The survival of a community depends both upon its ability to protect itself, and upon the education and training of the young. Citizens have duties and responsibilities in these areas, which are thus a proper object of political judgment. Further, the community would cease to be a community if its citizens did not also recognize duties and responsibilities to those who, in some way – from old age or sickness, for instance – were incapacitated.

It is not supposed that the practice of citizenship in the political community, as so far defined, is 'natural' to individuals as autonomous – or, indeed, any other – beings, in the sense that they will spontaneously and necessarily conduct their relationships with their fellow members in ways conducive to the community's survival. To live as a member of a political community is a highly artificial form of life. It is not so much that citizens would be malicious, as that they would be ignorant both of the conditions necessary to sustain that life, and of conduct inimical to its survival, until they had engaged with their fellow citizens in political judgment about such matters.

All such judgments identify a community, and authorize a way of life appropriate to it. The authority possessed both by the rules and norms of conduct, and by the substantive purposes of the community, derives from the public judgment of its citizens. Since they remain autonomous beings, it is open to them to reconsider the desirability of the rules and norms, and of the purposes they once established.

This exercise – of providing a community with its identity – is one in which members of the community attempt to answer the question posed by W. J. M. MacKenzie: 'In what context do "I" properly use the word "we"?'[33] It is concerned with the shift from individual identity to a particular form of social or collective identity. Many aspects of social or collective identity constitute the 'givens' of any individual's life: nation, race, religion, class, language, history. These 'givens' can be approached by the individual in a number of ways. They can form part of the unconscious background against which the individual says 'we'. They can on the other hand be passively endorsed, self-consciously and enthusiastically affirmed, and sometimes repudiated. In other words, choices can sometimes be made about which 'we' to belong to, or not. To be self-conscious about the contexts in which 'we' is used, may or may not add strength to the collectivity so identified, but *political* identity, in the context of the community under consideration here, must result from self-conscious deliberation and judgment, and must also be expressive of an ethical commitment. Only such an identity is one which will reflect the spirit of autonomous beings making judgments in concord. It is this which constitutes citizenship.

What the community does is not the incidental, and mechanical, by-product of the discrete activities of individuals, but is consciously and intentionally done. Deliberation is necessary among citizens who, because they are different and autonomous, may genuinely disagree about the answer to the question: 'How are we to live together?' Coordination among autonomous beings who genuinely differ, but also hold each other in mutual respect, is achieved by their public judgment on matters of common concern. Political judgment, thus, is that capacity of autonomous beings exercised by them as members of a community. The principles which are constitutive of the concept of community, therefore, are also those active principles which are constitutive of the way of life – or 'constitution', to use that term in its Graeco-Roman sense[34] – of the community in question.

To summarize so far: any viable sense of community, and any viable concept of citizenship, must take account of the nature of modern individuals. They have been described here as autonomous. They are, at least in principle and in potential, self-determined, in the sense that their wills are not subject to the will of others; their 'selves' are also authentic, in the sense that they are either chosen by them, or, more normally, are ones to which they give rational assent. They fill a variety of social roles – some inherited, some chosen – but they are rarely unable to make a choice when the demands of different roles conflict. The other important characteristic of autonomous individuals is that they are active. They have purpose and will, and are able to give reasons – often in terms of the demands of a role – for their actions. If they are to live in company with other autonomous individuals – and, further, if they are to act as citizens – then it is important that their actions be informed by a sense of responsibility towards their fellow-citizens. They must recognize their mutual dependence. This has been identified as the spirit of 'concord', or that form of friendship which Aristotle thought appropriate between citizens. Finally, in acting, citizens use their judgment in deliberating on matters of common concern. The judgments that are crucial here, and which underlie all others, are those which provide the community of which they are members with its identity.

Implications for political practice

Citizenship in these terms is difficult to achieve in the modern world: potential citizens lack the resources for engaging in the practice of citizenship; they lack the opportunities; and they lack the appropriate attitudes of mind – in other words motivation.

Resources can be seen as enabling or empowering individuals to be active agents in this world. For activity of any kind, including that involved in the practice of citizenship, people need certain resources. Some of these have to do with what liberal individualism identifies as civil, political and legal rights. Others have to do with economic and social resources. Without health, education and a reasonable living income, for instance, individuals do not have the capacity to be effective agents in the world, and the possibilities of a practice of citizenship are thus foreclosed in advance. Such rights and resources have to be secured for citizens, for citizenship is an egalitarian practice.

Merely to empower individuals in this way, though necessary, is not, of course, sufficient for the practice of citizenship. The institutional setting has to be appropriate. There have to be arenas where potentially everyone can take part, where everyone can do something. In the modern state, this means the decentralization of political tasks and functions. Not everything that needs doing to make life possible in the modern world can be decentralized, but much more can be than is usually thought possible or is usually permitted – just as much less can be done at the level of the nation-state than used to be possible. What is to be sought is the creation and widening of opportunities for responsible self-government by citizens. It is not necessary that such self-government be conceived in any narrow political sense, where by 'political' is meant 'that which has an effect on everyone within a community, and which is open to change by collective action on the part of members'. Self-government can refer to any public tasks and activities that a community wishes to engage in. Local initiatives can thus respond and cater to particular 'publics' that are narrower in scope and coverage than the entire community.

Yet even empowerment and opportunity together are not sufficient for the practice of citizenship. What is further required is that a particular attitude of mind be encouraged, an attitude which not only prompts individuals to recognize what their duties are as citizens, but which motivates them to perform them as well. The problem to be overcome is that of the 'free-rider'. The variety and diversity which give vitality to the political community cannot be carried so far that certain individuals, whether from inclination or eccentricity, may renege on their duties as citizens, for this is destructive of 'concord'. The solution is education. Here, civic republicanism has a much broader conception than liberal individualism. Citizens are learners all their lives, and education in the sense of the building of the appropriate character for willing engagement in the practice of citizenship never ceases. This will be the major theme of Part III. For the moment we must turn to the civic-republican tradition itself.

The emphasis in discussing this tradition will be on its concept of citizenship. It will be argued, eventually, that if the tradition yields a viable concept of citizenship, and the conditions for the practice of citizenship can be met, then the issue of community will resolve itself. Again, this argument comes in Part III.

Part II

Citizenship and community in the civic-republican tradition

Chapter three

Machiavelli: citizenship and glory

In the *Discourses*, Machiavelli singled out the founders of republics or kingdoms as second only 'of all men that are praised' to the inspirers of religions.[1] They are to be praised because what they create is glorious. Machiavelli had in mind a particular mode of human living-together which can be encapsulated in the concept of citizenship. He was writing about the creation and maintenance of political communities. The glory of the prince as innovator was to impose form on material he had disturbed by his intervention in human affairs: in other words, to create order out of chaos. The double glory of the prince, however, was to create such an order whose survival would no longer require his integrative powers but which, on the contrary, would be sustained by the engaged energies of its entire citizen body:

> If princes are superior to populaces in drawing-up laws, codes of civic life, statutes and new institutions, the populace is so superior in sustaining what has been instituted, that it indubitably adds to the glory of those who have instituted them.
>
> (*D*, I, lviii)

Machiavelli was well aware that the task before the new prince was a difficult one, for he inhabited a world of contingency, of uncertainty and unpredictability, the domain of fortune: the new prince required extraordinary *virtù*. Machiavelli was also aware that men had seldom lived in the political communities he described and praised. They were rare creations, but they had existed once.

The ideal of civic *virtù*

Machiavelli's ideal political community was the Roman republic. The 'constitution'[2] of the Roman republic, however, was not founded by the kind of great prophet and legislator – Lycurgus, for instance – to whom Machiavelli attributed the founding of Sparta. On the con-

31

trary, the constitution of Rome came about almost by accident. It acquired its laws 'by chance and at different times as occasion arose'. True, Romulus was the founding figure, but it was Numa who provided Rome with its religion, and the mixed constitution of the one, the few and the many was the product of generations of strife between patricians and plebians: 'chance effected what had not been provided by a lawgiver' (*D*, I, ii).

In the *Discourses*, Machiavelli held up the Roman republic to contemporary Italians as an example of practices to be followed, for in the republic Rome achieved security and glory for itself, and liberty for its citizens. Rome is Machiavelli's ideal of a political community of citizens imbued with civic *virtù*. 'At its best' – the phrase is Hanna Pitkin's[3] – Machiavelli's political thought presents a community whose members have mutual respect for each other, and whose judgments on matters of public concern are delivered autonomously (that is, freely), and with due consideration for the *patria*, in whose welfare and prosperity they share. Machiavelli's best understanding of politics is reminiscent of Aristotle, especially the teleological idea that man is by nature a political animal. This does not mean that man is always and everywhere found in the *polis*, but rather that politics is a peculiarly human activity, and in its practice men have the possibility of realizing their full potential as human beings.

Machiavelli's preoccupation is with the civic way of life. Within the bounds of necessity – that is, of the culture, law and history of which they are the products – men's free, autonomous actions have the capacity to make a difference. After all, as he remarked in *The Prince*, 'I believe that it is probably true that fortune is the arbiter of half the things we do, leaving the other half or so to be controlled by ourselves.'[4] Men develop their humanness not in communion with an extra-terrestrial God, or as discrete individuals, but, on the contrary, only in the company of others. Such sociability as they do achieve takes care and effort: it is not automatic. It depends upon men's capacity for judgment, and their capacity for distinguishing right from wrong, which is not simply a matter of following rules, but rather one of linking justice and right in an indeterminate, or non-rule-governed, way to what is humanly possible. In this way, the citizen continually enacts and renews the civic way of life. Machiavelli is an activist, and hence an optimist. He saw his task as one of arousing his contemporaries to action, but action always within the limits of both circumstance and human power. The summons was to *virtù* and glory in the cause of community welfare and political liberty: the summons was a challenge to men to be men, to take responsibility for their shared concerns.

In deliberation and political conflict, citizens are reminded of their stake in the community, and recognize their interdependence and shared membership. What is involved here is a redefinition of the self: an enlarged awareness of how individuality and community are connected in the self. What characterizes membership in a community is mutuality – a recognition that the civic way of life, political life, is predicated not on relationships of domination and servility, but on a relationship among peers or equals. Citizens must share something to become and remain a community, but there is room for much difference, and even conflict. The mutuality which community life requires is respect for the distinctness and autonomy of others which characterizes that relationship of friendship among citizens which Aristotle called 'concord'.

This is, so Pitkin tells us, Machiavelli at his best. It was ideals such as these that he sought to arouse his contemporaries to emulate, and there is plenty of evidence – both in *The Prince* and in the *Discourses* – to sustain Machiavelli's endorsement of them. We might turn, for instance, to what he writes about the tenacity with which a free people protects its independence. In Chapter V of *The Prince*, he draws attention to the task of the new prince in imposing his own rule upon a people accustomed to liberty. The easiest course, but the one with least prospect of success, is to rule such a city 'through its own citizens'. But history shows for Machiavelli, that:

> whoever becomes the master of a city accustomed to freedom, and does not destroy it, may expect to be destroyed himself; because, when there is a rebellion, such a city justifies itself by calling on the name of liberty and its ancient institutions, never forgotten despite the passing of time and the benefit received from the new ruler. Whatever the conqueror's actions or foresight, they will forget neither the name nor those institutions; and at the first opportunity they will at once have recourse to them, ... the memory of their ancient liberty does not and cannot let them rest.
>
> (*P*, 48–9)

This theme is repeated in Book II of the *Discourses*. In ancient times Italy abounded in free peoples, and Rome had great difficulty conquering them because of 'the love which in those times many people had for liberty':

> so obstinately did they defend it that only by outstanding virtue could they ever have been subjugated. For numerous instances show to what danger they exposed themselves in order to maintain or recover it, and what vendettas they kept up against those who had taken it away.
>
> (*D*, II, ii)

It is Machiavelli's argument that a free people is much more likely to prosper and increase in dominion than one kept in servitude. This was so both in Athens, once it was liberated from the tyranny of Pisistratus, and, of course, in Rome:

> The reason is easy to understand; for it is not the well-being of individuals that makes cities great, but the well-being of the community; and it is beyond question that it is only in republics that the common good is looked to properly in that all that promotes it is carried out; and, however much this or that private person may be the loser on this account, there are so many who benefit thereby that the common good can be realized in spite of those few who suffer in consequence.

In a free regime, men are ready to marry and have children because they know that their well-being and patrimony are not under threat, and further that if their children possess *virtù*, they have a chance of becoming rulers. It is security which enables a people to prosper, and which a republic alone can ensure, for with security comes trust and such confidence in the future that men, industrious in their own concerns, 'look both to their own advantage and to that of the public' (*D*, II, ii).

When Machiavelli is writing about 'freedom' and 'independence' one must beware of reading back into him connotations which those terms have only acquired in post-Machiavellian individualist thinking. Freedom meant self-government, or not being subject to alien power. In this sense, a princedom could be as free as a republic, and not all republics were like Rome, where undoubtedly some 'liberties', in a proto-modern sense, were enjoyed by its citizens. But, as we shall see below, such liberties were enjoyed not as rights, but because they were necessary for the purposes which the Roman republic set itself.

Civic *virtù* in a corrupt and uncertain world

Machiavelli's picture of an autonomous citizenry, imbued with civic *virtù* and thus attentive to civic glory and greatness, is an ideal picture. But it is not an idyll – it had once existed, in Rome, so it could be a realistic ideal. Machiavelli knew full well, however, that it did not exist in the Italy of his day. The *Discourses* abound with references to the pusillanimity, servility and short-sightedness of his contemporaries, as well as their arrogance, their vanity and their gullibility. It is not so much that Machiavelli is ambivalent about human nature. It is rather that the way men act, the values they possess and the models they put before themselves to emulate, are crucially dependent on the circumstances and environment in which they live.

These circumstances can sometimes be changed by men, by the extra-ordinary actions of men of great wisdom and *virtù*. In so changing the arena in which ordinary men live and act, their very actions take on a new quality, inspired by new values and models. Civic *virtù* is not natural to man, and man will not display it unless he is kneaded and manipulated, unless he is inspired or shamed, terrorized or coerced.

Machiavelli's pessimism about human nature can be brought out by considering, first, what he has to say about religion. It is well-known that Machiavelli preferred a pagan religion to a Christian one, at least to the kind of Christian religion represented by the Church of his day. A pagan religion would emphasize those qualities in man which would be of service to the state, rather than instruct them to foster those qualities which would prepare them for the after-life. Early in Book II of the *Discourses*, Machiavelli asks why the 'peoples of old were more fond of liberty than they are today'? He finds his answer in 'the same cause that makes men less bold than they used to be'. And this cause is their education, which reflects dif-ferences in religion:

> Our religion has glorified humble and comtemplative men, rather than men of action. It has assigned as man's highest good humility, abnegation and contempt for mundane things, whereas the other [the religion of Rome, that is] identified it with magnanimity, bod-ily strength, and everything else that conduces to make men very bold. And, if our religion demands that in you there be strength, what it asks for is strength to suffer rather than strength to do bold things.

With such a religion as the basis of education, it is not surprising to Machiavelli 'that we see in the world fewer republics than there used to be of old, and that, consequently, in peoples we do not find the same love of liberty as there then was' (*D*, II, ii).

What Machiavelli is more than intimating here is that without an underpinning of religion, civic *virtù* cannot be expected to flourish. The values which sustain a republic do not spontaneously arise with-in the minds and hearts of the members of a community. Hence Machiavelli's insistence elsewhere on the important role of the prophet or legislator in providing a people with its constitution (again, 'constitution' as way of life). Left to themselves, a people will be disorderly and corrupt, or must be expected to be, and in no sense a community. 'In constituting and legislating for a commonwealth,' he writes,

> it must needs be taken for granted that all men are wicked and that they will always give vent to the malignity that is in their minds

when opportunity offers.... Men never do good unless necessity drives them to it; but when they are too free to choose and can do just as they please, confusion and disorder become everywhere rampant.

(*D*, I, iii)

Such an analysis would later be amply endorsed by Hobbes, and it is in this light that Machiavelli reflects on the wisdom of the Roman senate in choosing Numa Pompilius as Romulus's successor:

Numa, finding the people ferocious and desiring to reduce them to civic obedience by means of the arts of peace, turned to religion as the instrument necessary above all others for the maintenance of a civilized state, and so constituted it that there was never for so many centuries so great a fear of God as there was in this republic.

It was this fear of God among Romans which 'helped in the control of armies, in encouraging the plebs, in producing good men, and in shaming the bad' (*D*, I, xi). As he puts it in *The Art of War*,

the ancients used to call in the aid of religion and, with many imposing ceremonies and great solemnity, make their soldiers take a very strict oath to pay due obedience to military discipline. In addition, they used all other methods to inspire them with a fear of the gods, so that if they violated their oaths, they might have not only the asperity of human laws but the vengeance of heaven to dread.[5]

Religion is only one, if the most important, of the institutional supports of republican life. Elsewhere, Machiavelli writes of good examples set, from time to time, by great men in reminding a people of its constitution, and of good laws and institutions, as well as of good armies. Unless republics are kept 'up to the mark' (*D*, III, i), they are prone to degeneration from within. Ultimate degeneration cannot be prevented – taking the organic metaphor seriously, Machiavelli writes: 'It is impossible to constitute a republic that shall last for ever, since there are a thousand unpredictable ways in which its downfall may be brought about' (*D*, III, xvii). Nevertheless, this ultimate fate can be delayed: republican life can be prolonged beyond its 'normal' term, as it were. All those forces contributing to internal decay – the growth of inequality, the turning-aside from public life to private concerns, the promotion of private interest through divisive faction, the cultivation of a life of ease and indolence – all these can be confronted and counteracted if one acts in time to take precautions. In his discussion of fortune in Chapter XXV of *The Prince*, where he compares fortune 'to one of those violent rivers which,

when they are enraged, flood the plains, tear down trees and build-
ings, wash soil from one place to deposit it in another', Machiavelli
argues that it does not follow:

> that when they are flowing quietly one cannot take precautions,
> constructing dykes and embankments so that when the river is in
> flood they would keep to one channel or their impetus be less wild
> and dangerous.

(*P*, 130)

Religion, as we have noted, is one of these dykes or embankments; it
is one of the crucial supports of civic *virtù*. It is also, however, prone
to perversion from its pristine state. It is in these terms that Machiavelli writes of the need that all institutions have for renewal or
rebirth, for return to their original principles. Though external
events, or forces – such as war – may sometimes bring a people to its
senses, as it were, it is better that its own institutions provide for
renewal, or that the example of great men be available for a people
to follow. States and religions, he writes at the beginning of Book III
of the *Discourses*, 'are better constituted and have a longer life whose
institutions make frequent renovations possible'. All institutions
have some good in them,

> but since in the process of time this goodness is corrupted, such a
> body must of necessity die unless something happens which brings
> it up to the mark.... Such a return to their original principles in re-
> publics is sometimes due to the simple virtue of one man alone,
> independently of any laws spurring you to action. For of such ef-
> fect is a good reputation and good example that men seek to
> imitate it, and the bad are ashamed to lead lives which go contrary
> to it.

(*D*, III, i)

Such good examples need to occur at least every ten years, or corruption will set in, and much of Book II of the *Discourses* is devoted to
those leaders, men of *virtù*, who provided Romans with examples to
emulate. Nothing is more necessary to a religion or a republic than
their example (*D*, III, i). But, of course, fortune is not so reliable as
to provide that such men appear when the times call for them. If, indeed, they did so appear in a republic, and 'by their example give
fresh life to its laws', restoring 'their former vigour, such a republic
would last for ever' (*D*, III, xxii). Machiavelli knows, however, that
such thinking is wishful. Rome was fortunate in its early history to
have a succession of leaders after Romulus who displayed the same
virtue as he had, thus preventing the city becoming 'effeminate' and
falling 'a prey to its neighbours' (*D*, I, xix).

But a republic cannot ensure such a steady supply of great men, and must therefore so design its laws and institutions that the otherwise destructive tendencies of its citizens are channelled into forms of action which sustain republican life, which keep a people 'rich in virtue' (*D*, I, ii) as an adjunct to the models of behaviour provided by religion. Rome's laws and institutions placed that city under such 'strict discipline ... that, in consequence, neither its fertile situation, the convenience afforded by the sea, its frequent victories, nor the greatness of its empire, were for many centuries able to corrupt it' (*D*, I, i). After reviewing the Aristotelian/Polybian classification of types of government, Machiavelli claims that they are all unsatisfactory – the three good ones of Principality, Aristocracy and Democracy, 'because their life is so short', and the three bad ones of Tyranny, Oligarchy and Anarchy, 'because of their inherent malignity'. Prudent legislators, therefore,

> aware of their defects, refrained from adopting as such any one of these forms, and chose instead one that shared in them all, since they thought such a government would be stronger and more stable, for if in one and the same state there was principality, aristocracy and democracy each would keep watch over the other.
>
> (*D*, I, ii)

This is what Lycurgus did and it was what Rome, not being so fortunate as Sparta, achieved over the generations as a result of strife between different parts of the republic. Thus civil conflict and commotion were not only necessary to produce the mixed constitution of the one, the few and the many, they were also necessary to prevent the republic from lapsing into one of the bad forms of government, in which one interest dominated at the expense of all others. Private interest and ambition were thus channelled in ways acceptable to the maintenance of republican life. To the extent that citizens also took their religion seriously – and followed, for whatever reason, the example of great men of *virtù* when these presented themselves – then it became possible also to speak of a citizen body possessing civic *virtù*. Machiavelli was much concerned with external conduct. But the terms in which he praises civic virtue are such that external conduct should emanate from an inner conviction within the citizen, whatever the degree to which the citizen himself is repsonsible for that conviction. It needs noting that Machiavelli reserves most praise for those great men of *virtù* whose actions for the public good do result directly from an inner conviction that they are the right thing to do. Most men, however, are more mortal, or are weaker than this, and require both support and direction.

It is the level and nature of the support and direction which seem to be required, that lead to some serious questioning of the autonomy of the resulting civic *virtù*. For it begins to look as though a people is either coerced and manipulated into the practice of civic *virtù*, or it is bribed into orderly conduct and love of *patria* by being given some means for institutional expression of its private interests. What cannot be relied on, it seems, is the good faith of citizens. Where a genuine practice of civic *virtù* does bloom and flourish, it is a delicate plant and subject both to internal decay and to the inclemencies of its environment. No civic life will endure for long unless it bears some relation to man's nature and needs, but it is still a highly unnatural form of life. It is not self-sustaining, and it needs support from religion, from great men, from good laws and institutions. With such support, not only do relationships among members become characterized by a high degree of concord, but it also becomes possible to trust the political judgment of citizens.

The autonomy that Machiavelli extols, however, is that of the republic itself. At this point, it is appropriate to refer to Hanna Pitkin's assessment of Machiavelli's central concept of *virtù*. Even if one discounts the question about the autonomy of citizens, there is, for Pitkin, a crucial flaw in this concept of *virtù*, and that is its very masculinity. It is not so much that women were excluded from citizenship – here Machiavelli was simply of his time, and to expect him to have accorded an equal position to women is anachronistic. It is rather that Machiavelli's image of what it is to be adult and human, and a citizen, is a masculine image. Machiavelli is aware that political life is fragile: it is not always achieved, and where it is, it is continuously threatened. The threatening forces are feminine, nowhere more so than in his conception of fortune, the goddess who controls fully half of man's destiny, but whose favours can be won by the *virtuoso* man, the truly manly man. Machiavelli's conception of citizenship is thus based on man's need both to dominate and to fear dependence upon feminine forces. As such, it is, for Pitkin, an impoverished conception, for it confuses humanity with masculinity. She writes:

> the equation of humanness with masculinity is distorting not just in terms of an anxious and defensive understanding of masculinity, but in terms of any understanding of masculinity. Men who deny the humanity of women are bound to misunderstand their own.[6]

Machiavelli's thinking thus represents only a partial overcoming and growing out of childhood. It is, however, the very masculinity of the concept of *virtù* which Machiavelli requires for the autonomy of the republic.

The military dimension of civic life

Here belongs all Machiavelli's thinking about the need for good armies. Indeed, this is his paramount consideration when writing about the republic. Early in Book I of the *Discourses*, he discusses whether the kind of public strife between the senate and plebs that characterized the Roman republic can be avoided. Is such strife a good or a bad thing?

> To which I answer that every city should provide ways and means whereby the ambitions of the populace may find an outlet, especially a city which proposes to avail itself of the populace in important undertakings.
>
> (*D*, I, iv)

Thus the crucial question was whether Rome needed her populace for 'important undertakings'. And the answer to this depended on whether a republic should follow the example of Venice or Sparta, and restrict itself to maintaining its fastness by neither employing its plebs in war, nor admitting foreigners. Machiavelli says that Rome both admitted foreigners and armed its plebs, and he suggests that she could not have done otherwise:

> Since ... all human affairs are ever in a state of flux and cannot stand still, either there will be improvement or decline, and necessity will lead you to do many things which reason does not recommend. Hence if a commonwealth be constituted with a view to its maintaining the *status quo*, but not with a view to expansion, and by necessity it be led to expand, its basic principles will be subverted and it will soon be faced with ruin. So, too, should heaven, on the other hand, be so kind that it has no need to go to war, it will then come about that idleness will either render it effeminate or give rise to factions; and these two things, either in conjunction or separately, will bring about its downfall.
>
> (*D*, I, vi)

The security of the republic, therefore, and the possibility of civic *virtù*, depend upon a policy of expansion. This involved a preference for a more popular government. This choice is linked to Machiavelli's concern with the republic's ability to control its external environment. All cities have enemies and live in the domain of fortune. Defensiveness may expose one to greater danger than bold attempts to seize the initiative and expand. Rome chose empire, and therefore had to arm her people. One consequence of this was that Rome had to suffer the strife caused by their demands for more power, and make concessions to those demands. There is thus an intrinsic connection between military expansion, arming the plebs, and popular government. This reciprocal and mutually reinforcing connection is explored by Machiavelli in *The Art of War*. The civil and the military conditions are 'necessarily connected and interrelated ... the best ordinances in the world will be despised and trampled under foot when they are not supported, as they ought to be, by a military power' (*AW*, 4). Military *virtù* was an essential ingredient of Rome's greatness. Thus Machiavelli draws attention to the view 'that the republic of Rome was so tumultuous and so full of confusion that, had not good fortune and military virtue counterbalanced these defects, its condition would have been worse than that of any other republic'. True, he continues, good fortune and military organization contributed to Rome's empire, 'but it seems to me that this view fails to take account of the fact that where military organization is good there must needs be good order' (*D*, I, iv).

The connection between the military and civil conditions goes further than this. Unless the republic makes expansion and war its main object, then one of two consequences may be expected: either the ambitions and aggressiveness of citizens will be limited to the domestic stage, with the result that factions will arise to bring about the downfall of the city;[7] or an effeminate idleness would creep over the city such that when danger did arise, a republic would find it impossible to protect itself. The republic, thus, should follow the advice which Machiavelli put forward in Chapter XIV of *The Prince*:

> A prince ... must have no other object or thought, nor acquire skill in anything, except war, its organization, and its discipline ... we find that princes who have thought more of their pleasures than of arms have lost their states. The first way to lose your state is to neglect the art of war; the first way to win a state is to be skilled in the art of war.

Such a concern for the art of war should, of course, extend into peacetime in 'military exercises' (*P*, 87–8); the republic should attend 'with the utmost care to military training' (*D*, II, xix). Without such training, citizens will grow 'so lazy and degenerate that they will not imitate anything that is good'. It is the absence of any provision for peacetime military exercises that marks one of the serious contrasts between the Romans and contemporary Italians: 'This is the real reason why many states, especially in this country, have become so weak and contemptible' (*AW*, 60).

The business of military expansion, of war and conquest, must on no account, Machiavelli argues, be entrusted to mercenaries or auxiliaries. Mercenary troops are no use 'for they have no cause to stand firm when attacked', and the small pay they get is not sufficient to elicit that loyalty which would 'make them so much your friends that they should want to die for you' (*D*, I, xliii). Auxiliary troops, 'those that a prince or a republic sends to help you under commanders appointed and paid by that prince or republic, ... are the most hurtful, for over them the prince or the republic who accepts their aid, has no authority at all' (*D*, II, xx). A republic must have its own citizen militia:

> The security of all states is based on good military discipline, and ... where it does not exist, there can neither be good laws nor anything else that is good ... the soldiery cannot be good unless they are in training, and ... it is impossible to train them unless they are your own subjects. For, since no soldiery is always at war, nor yet can be, it is important to train it in time of peace; but this training is impossible on account of the cost except in the case of your own subjects.
>
> (*D*, III, xxxi)

And:

> If an army is to win the day it is essential to give it confidence so as to make it feel sure that it must win, whatever happens. The conditions on which such confidence depends are that the troops should be well armed, well disciplined and well acquainted with each other. Nor can there be this confidence or this discipline unless among soldiers who are natives of the same country and have lived together.
>
> (*D*, III, xxxiii)

In *The Art of War*, Machiavelli raises the issue of whether it is dangerous for a republic's citizens to be armed. Might one not expect 'much confusion and disorder, and frequent tumults' (*AW*, 40)? He thinks not. On the contrary, a citizen militia is the surest safeguard against all disturbances, if it is properly organized:

> By establishing a good and well-ordered militia, divisions are extinguished, peace restored, and some people who were unarmed and dispirited, but united, continue in union and become warlike and courageous; others who were brave and had arms in their hands, but were previously given to faction and discord, become united and turn against the enemies of their country those arms and that courage which they used to exert against each other.
>
> (*AW*, 41)

A 'good and well-ordered militia' thus both forms a pacific and spiritless people into a courageous force, and impels a warlike and factious people to direct their energies on to the enemy outside. Such a force requires tight discipline, and courageous and uncorrupted command. 'For men who are well disciplined will always be as cautious of violating the laws when they have arms in their hands as when they have not; and so they will continue, if they are not corrupted by their commanders' (*AW*, 40). The citizen becomes the warrior, and it may be, as J.G.A. Pocock suggests, 'through military discipline that one learns to be a citizen and to display civic virtue'.[8] Thus is citizenship militarized. Pocock again: 'The republic can be morally and civilly virtuous in itself only if it is the lion and the fox, man and beast, in its relations with other peoples.'[9] The justice of the republic is limited to itself. Towards others it could display only military *virtù*; but only to the extent that it could do this, could it maintain civic *virtù* internally. Force and fraud thus underpin the morality of civic life. As Machiavelli remarks right at the end of the *Discourses*:

> For when the safety of one's country wholly depends on the decision to be taken, no attention should be paid either to justice or injustice, to kindness or cruelty, or to its being praiseworthy or ignominious. On the contrary, every other consideration being set aside, that alternative should be wholeheartedly adopted which will save the life and preserve the freedom of one's country.
>
> (*D*, III, xli)

This is what is meant by securing the autonomy of the republic: there is no higher good that the citizen can aim for and, as the citizen-soldier, he shows that civic religion and military discipline have had their required effect if he sacrifices his life to that end. Military discipline serves alongside civic religion as a powerful and indispensable support of the civic *virtù* necessary to sustain republican life. This brings further into question the autonomy and capacity for political judgment of the citizens who are supposed to practice civic *virtù*.

In a corrupt world, such as Machiavelli certainly believed he lived in, one must be prepared not only to defend one's country against the predatoriness of one's neighbours, but to adopt predatoriness as a defensive posture. This is the realm of necessity, and Machiavelli's preference for Rome over Sparta and Venice was partly based on Rome's recognition of this necessity. If Machiavelli had left his argument there, then one might do no more than regret what necessity imposed. Machiavelli chose Rome also, however, from his belief that Rome's conquest of an empire was a glorious undertaking, exhibiting all the characteristics of the *virtuoso* man: courage, boldness, vigour, fortitude, discipline and strength. The price, in terms of the perversion of a genuine political community, seems too high. But such a comment provokes the question as to whether there was any plausible alternative, not just for the Roman republic (here, there may well not have been), but more importantly for Machiavelli's contemporary Italy.

Control of papal politics was crucial in the early sixteenth century. Yet no Italian city-state was strong enough to impose its will on the rest of Italy to secure that control for itself in the context of a united Italy, or strong enough to resist the powerful, hereditary monarchies of France and Spain from regarding the Italian peninsula as a legitimate extension of their own terrain. It was, in Machiavelli's view, the Church which was responsible for Italy's plight:

> The Church ... has neither been able to occupy the whole of Italy, nor has it allowed anyone else to occupy it. Consequently, it has been the cause why Italy has never come under one head, but has been under many princes and *signori*, by whom such disunion and such weakness has been brought about, that it has now become the prey, not only of barbarian potentates, but of anyone who attacks it. For which our Italians have to thank the Church, and nobody else.
>
> (*D*, I, xii)

Machiavelli certainly hoped that an Italian of great *virtù* would appear to lift Italy out of its weak torpor, as the dedicatory letter and final chapter of *The Prince* make clear. He also believed that his contemporaries could learn much from the ancients, if only they would go back and look as he urged them to in the Preface to Book I of the *Discourses*. What more natural than to return to one's own ancients? At least language and terrain were the same or similar, and their example represented a shared history – enough, surely, to recover a common identity and upon which build a political community? It was surely not beyond the capacity of contemporary Italians to follow the example of the ancients: 'I am of the opinion, from what I have both seen and read, that it would not be impossible to revive the discipline of our ancestors and, in some measure, to retrieve our lost *virtù*' (*AW*, 5). In response to a query as to what of ancient practice might be imitated, Machiavelli suggests: 'To honor and reward *virtù*; not to scorn poverty; to value good order and discipline in their armies; to oblige citizens to love one another, to decline faction, and to prefer the good of the public to any private interest' (*AW*, 12). A united Italy, however, would not be achieved without war to overcome the pride and vanity of the separate city-states. It would be necessary, also, to fight to drive the French and Spaniards out of Italy, and secure the integrity of Italian territory. Machiavelli marshals powerful arguments, supporting his view (cited at the beginning of this chapter) that princes are required to impose order and unity on territories, and that republics are necessary to defend the order and unity that has been achieved. Machiavelli's Italy, thus, needed both *The Prince* and the *Discourses*.

Machiavelli does, briefly, consider other models of civic life, principally the German towns. The goodness of contemporary German towns was due to two things. First, 'the towns have but little intercourse with their neighbours, ... since they are content with the goods, live on the food, and are clothed with the wool which their own land provides'. They have no occasion for interference with the French, the Spanish, or the Italians, 'nations which, taken together, are the source of world-wide corruption'. Second, they 'do not permit any of their citizens to live after the fashion of the gentry. On the contrary, they maintain their perfect equality' (*D*, I, lv). Ambition both within the city walls and without is lacking. 'Were conditions in Germany other than these, they would have to seek expansion and disrupt their present tranquillity.' Elsewhere, and particularly in Italy, Machiavelli remarks that conditions are not like this. Other states, thus, 'must needs expand either by means of confederation or in the way the Romans did. To adopt any other policy is to seek not life but death and ruin' (*D*, II, xix). The German towns thus do not provide the Italian city-states with an example, and Machiavelli is thrust back, not unwillingly, upon Rome.

Machiavelli chose the Roman republic as the model for his contemporaries because it seemed to him to be the only one appropriate to the achievement of an autonomous life for a renovated and united Italy. He was acutely aware, however, that there was a limit to the humanly possible, given that fortune controlled fully half of men's lives. It was arrogance to expect human creations to be eternal. Further, he recognized that Rome's pursuit of empire in the search for security was ultimately destructive of the republic itself. This was a cruel dilemma. What Rome did here was to swallow up many previously-independent republics. Yet it was the very multiplicity of such republics that had guaranteed an abundance of men of *virtù*:

> Thus, when the Roman Empire had swallowed up all the Kingdoms and republics in Europe and Africa, and most of those in Asia, *virtù* met with no countenance anywhere but in Rome; so that men of *virtù* began to grow more scarce in Europe, as well as in Asia, until at last there were hardly any to be found. Just as all *virtù* was extinguished, except among the Romans, so when they become corrupt, the whole world was similarly corrupted.
>
> (*AW*, 78–9)

Rome's downfall brought with it the downfall of the world.

One of the strengths of the Roman republic after the overthrow of kings was that, though the title of 'king' was expelled, royal power was retained for emergencies (*D*, I, ii) and, more importantly, for the business of conquest. The office of dictator was limited in time and 'for the purpose of dealing solely with such matters as had led to the appointment'. The dictator received his authority from the senate and people, and 'could do nothing to diminish the constitutional position of the government':

> Of Rome's various institutions this is the one that deserves to be considered and ranked among those to which the greatness of Rome's vast empire was due. For without such an institution cities will with difficulty find a way out of abnormal situations. For the institutions normally used by republics are slow in functioning.... Where there is question of remedying a situation which will not brook delay ... republics ought to have among their institutions some device akin to this.
>
> (*D*, I, xxxiv)

It was through royal powers, in the form of military commands, that Rome gained its empire. It was the prolongation of military commands, however, as that empire grew, that 'made Rome a servile state'. Few of Rome's military commanders were 'as wise and good as Lucius Quintius', who refused to have his command prolonged for fear of the bad example it would set. Two inconveniences resulted from such prolongations:

> First, but a small number of men acquired experience as military commanders, and in consequence but few acquired a reputation for it. Secondly, when a citizen had been for long in command of an army, he won the army over and made it his partisan: so that it came in time to forget the senate and to recognize its commander as its head.... Had the Romans not prolonged offices and military commands, they would not have attained such great power in so short a time, and, had they been slower in making conquests, they would also have been slower to arrive at servitude.
>
> (*D*, III, xxiv)

The precipitant of Rome's 'servitude' was dispute over the Agrarian Law. As Machiavelli tells us, in a clear instance of 'law' and civic conflict being destructive rather than integrative forces, the plebs – once they had secured their position with the creation of the tribunes – began to quarrel with the nobles about the distribution of property. 'This grew into a disease, which led to the dispute about the Agrarian Law and in the end caused the destruction of the republic.' The law provided, first, that no citizen should possess above so many acres of land; and, second, that all lands taken from the enemy should be divided among the Roman people. Both these provisions gave offence to the nobility: they were to be deprived of their 'over plus', and denied the opportunity to enrich themselves. The Agrarian Law lay dormant until the time of the Gracchi, 'and, when they raised it again, it spelt the complete destruction of Rome's liberty'. The issue came to a head in the clash between Caesar and Pompey, both now military commanders almost by profession and, thus, with their retinue of 'partisans', the leaders of 'factions' (*parti*): 'They came to blows, and Caesar got the best of it, and so became Rome's first tyrant. After which that city never again recovered its liberties.' Thus did enmity between senate and populace lead, not to the maintenance of freedom, but to servitude. It took three hundred years for the Agrarian Law to have this effect, and Machiavelli consoled himself with the reflection that 'it would, perchance, have led to servitude much sooner, had not the plebs by means of this law and by other demands, prompted by their appetites, always kept the ambition of the nobles in check' (*D*, I, xxxvii).

The servitude to which a combination of the Agrarian Law and the prolongation of military commands led did not entail the immediate downfall of Rome itself: Rome maintained its autonomy for some time. What was lost was that active citizenry which, in Machiavelli's view, could have been expected to sustain Rome's autonomy even longer. It was this loss that Machiavelli lamented, and he blamed Caesar for not using the occasion of his victory over Pompey to arrest a decline in republican forms before that decline became irreversible.

Machiavelli thus recognized the cost to Rome of empire. The republic would have lasted longer if it had not been so intent on dominating its world. But it would then, of course, have opened itself more to the contingent domain of fortune, and, as he noted, it could not have prevented its ultimate arrival at 'servitude'. Both Sparta and Venice, after all, though their republics lasted longer, eventually succumbed (*D*, I, vi).

Conclusion

By holding up the example of the Roman republic for his contemporaries to emulate, Machiavelli has told us much about what is involved in the civic *virtù* that is necessary to establish and maintain the autonomy of the republic. He has also presented us with the model of an autonomous citizen who pursues a life of civic *virtù* as an expression of his authentic self, even though he has to be inspired or shamed, disciplined and sometimes terrorized into such a life. No doubt some individuals exist at some times and in some places in whom the practice of civic *virtù* is one that is engaged in voluntarily and after due reflection, and the greatest of these, of course, act to inspire a people. But such an attachment to civic *virtù* is not to be expected from the mass of a citizen body.

Now if Machiavelli had set out to provide us with the conditions under which an unforced commitment to civic virtue could, with few exceptions, be expected of an entire citizenry, such a conclusion would be inconvenient, at the very least, for his project would have failed. Machiavelli's implicit question, however, is whether such a project is a realistic one in the first place. Without some kind of education and tutoring, any form of social living together is precarious. The practice of citizenship, of civic *virtù*, is not a natural one; it is one that has to be both learned and sustained. With a pessimistic rather than an optimistic view of human nature, Machiavelli is doing no more than examine the kinds of institutions and influences necessary for the norms of civic *virtù* to be in the forefront of men's minds. This is an issue which will arise again in the discussion of Rousseau's analysis of citizenship. The human self, as a sovereign, choosing self, is anyway a product of its history and environment. It has to be shaped into socially acceptable forms of living. Here Machiavelli simply considers the possibility of systematically doing this, rather than relying on random influences somehow resulting in the desired product. If the purpose of this shaping is the creation of a people for whom civic *virtù* is a customary practice, and one to which they give their rational assent, then it is difficult to see how autonomy might be diminished. The fact that the values by which human beings live have been fashioned for them does not mean that those values are not genuinely held, or that they are not a genuine expression of their authentic selves. If it did, then one would simply never find an authentic self, let alone a genuine citizen. There is a difference between giving an account – from the position of an observer or inquirer, for instance – of how some values come to be held, and acknowledging, as the participant in a practice, that these are the values that one does in fact hold, and that one is justified in holding them.

Machiavelli was writing about what had to be done in a corrupt society and with corruptible men, and he shows us that this is not impossible, even though it may be improbable. It had, after all, been done before. In excluding all women from citizenship, and all but a minority, though a large minority, of male taxpayers,[10] he was no democrat. Still, the numbers were large, and in this respect, and without any change in human nature ('men being taken as they are', to appropriate Rousseau's phrase), Machiavelli nevertheless does show us an active citizenry, exhibiting sufficient 'concord' to sustain the mixed, republican, constitution of Rome for four centuries. But the effort to prevent private interest and ambition from subverting the republic is not self-generated. The political judgment of neither senate nor plebs is to be trusted on its own, that is, without support. Each needs to be checked by the other, or to be disciplined by religion and military codes, and this is so because the practice of civic *virtù* is not natural to man. Further, it only becomes 'second nature', so to speak, to a few: those for whom attentiveness to civic good is the overriding consideration in all judgments. For the rest, the overwhelming majority, civic good competes with private interests, and matters have to be continually arranged to tilt the balance in favour of civic good. It is not that citizens do not possess authentic selves, independent wills and capacities for judgment: it is rather that they do not necessarily possess these attributes as 'citizens'. Civic *virtù* is not authentic to them: that is why their political judgment cannot be trusted unless it is disciplined. Again, it is not so much that citizens may not know what their civic duty is and acknowledge that they ought to perform it, but that unless civic duty is made to coincide with, or to prevail over, private interest and ambition, then mere acknowledgment of an obligation to perform one's duty cannot be relied upon for the performance itself.

In sum, there appear to be three means whereby the behaviour of citizens is brought into conformity with civic ends. First, there is an almost 'invisible hand' type of mechanism ensuring that the pursuit of private interest and ambition leads to public good. Thus the institutionalized strife and conflict between senate and plebs is held, by Machiavelli, to have been both creative of Roman liberties and their guarantor. Second, there is the example of men of great *virtù*, who will either inspire citizens to emulate them, or at least shame them into not engaging in activity contrary to public good. Finally, there is the discipline of religion and military codes to inculcate a love of *patria* and attentiveness to civic ends in peace and war. This is the civic *virtù* required for the harnessing of popular power for public ends – in particular, of course, for that end of establishing and maintaining the autonomy of Rome. Without attempting to establish any priority, we may say that Machiavelli was trying to render two aims consistent with each other: the autonomy of the republic, and the practice of civic *virtù*. The connection between them can be stated in one of two ways: either expansionism and republican autonomy require the practice of civic *virtù*; or the practice of civic *virtù* makes republican autonomy a realistic goal. It is surely better, and it does more justice to Machiavelli's political thought, to say that these goals are mutually reinforcing, and that they are achievable in and through the political community, which is the republic. It is the twin achievement of these goals, after all, that constitutes the 'double glory' of the prince.

Chapter four

Rousseau: freedom, virtue and happiness

The nature of the problem

Much of Machiavelli's discussion of republican government proceeds by way of contrast: the contrast between contemporary Italian political life and the way of life of the Roman republic. Rousseau's political writings also have the character of a dialogue between the present and the past. In Rousseau's case, however, there are two 'pasts' to be confronted: the 'state of nature', and the ancient republics of Rome and Sparta. Machiavelli and Rousseau approach these pasts differently. In Machiavelli the past is sieved, almost seized, for examples of political conduct which, if only his contemporaries would follow them, could restore Italy to that glory and greatness it had enjoyed in ancient times. The past was, no doubt, not recoverable, but it was replicable: human nature and circumstances were not that different. Rousseau did not think this. For him, history was an irreversible process: man and circumstances had changed so much over time that few lessons could be learned. If the contrast between present and past had poignancy for Machiavelli, for Rousseau it was more than touched by despair. Each of them judged their contemporary societies corrupt, and those of the ancients virtuous. But Rousseau did not, and could not, judge the state of nature virtuous. The state of nature was a condition in which man lived an isolated existence. The possibility of morality, and therefore of virtuous conduct, only arises when men begin to associate with each other. The only moral character of the state of nature, tenuous at most, was that men did not do each other harm. What man enjoyed in that state was happiness and independence. If then, by contrast with the ancients, modern man lacked virtue, by contrast with the state of nature he lacked happiness and independence. Modern man's condition was one of corruption, misery and enslavement.

It was not, however, possible to return to the state of nature, and, for Rousseau, developments in the psychology of man made the transplant of the ancient republic into a mid-eighteenth-century

Europe an unthinkable venture. What had contributed to the virtue of the ancient republic was the complete absorption of man into its way of life. Man was not conscious of possessing a will to give expression to a private interest and individuality at odds with the republic. It was precisely such a will, Rousseau argued, that modern man did possess. If virtue, happiness and independence were ever again to describe man's condition, then it would have to be on different terms from those which had obtained in the past, for the problem had changed; another set of actors was on stage, and they were playing different roles. How could virtue, happiness and independence become possible for modern men, 'men as they are'?[1]

Rousseau first put forward his views on modern corruption in the *Discourse on the Arts and Sciences* (1750). It was only some time after this, and partly in response to the reception given to the *Discourse* on its publication,[2] that he began to realize that it was not the arts and sciences in themselves that had corrupted men's morals. Something more profound, more fundamental, had been really at work. That 'something' was society itself, and its institutions, its political institutions in particular. As he put it some years later in the *Confessions*, but echoing thoughts he had expressed earlier in the *Discourse on Political Economy*: 'I had seen that everything depended radically on politics, and that, from whatever point of view one looked at the question, no people would ever be anything but what the nature of its government made it be.'[3] For Rousseau, however, it was more than simply a matter of laying the blame for man's ills on his institutions. Not only were such institutions inescapable, they were the only means whereby man could redeem himself. Virtue, happiness and independence could thus only acquire a meaning for man within the context of society and its institutions.

In *Emile*, Rousseau drew attention to two kinds of dependence: 'dependence on things, which is the work of nature; and dependence on man, which is the work of society'.[4] In the state of nature, man is dependent on things, on the facts of his physical environment. This is something he can 'bear patiently',[5] and it does not infringe his liberty: he is not, because he pursues an isolated existence, dependent on man. His 'will', thus, is free. It is, however, precisely dependence on men which characterizes modern man, and which accounts for his depravity. Relationships of dependence between men – whether based on riches, power or esteem – are relationships of inequality, and involve being subject to other people's wills. The obvious case is the relationship between master and slave. The master is dependent as well, however, because he requires slaves – or, in the eighteenth century, servants – to be a master at all. It is not just that he requires his servants to recognize him as a master: he also requires other people to recognize him as such. The servant too, in his turn, is not just subject to his master's will: in taking on the values of his master, he aspires to be taken for that which he is not. Men live in the opinions and judgments which others make of them, and come to define themselves in this way. Their identity is determined for them by other people.[6] This, for Rousseau, is the utter abrogation of will, degrading and depraving because it denies what it is that makes a human being man: namely, his will.[7] Thus one question for Rousseau was to find some form of social arrangements in which men were no longer dependent on each other. His answer was to make every man dependent on law.

The other characteristic of man in the state of nature was his happiness. Happiness consists in the balance between a man's desires, or his will, and his powers. Again it is in *Emile* that Rousseau tells us what he means: 'A conscious being whose powers were equal to his desires would be perfectly happy.'[8] Natural man, because he does not – indeed, cannot – compare himself with other men, has no stimulus to increase his desires beyond his power to satisfy them. He is thus happy or, as Rousseau puts it in the *Discourse on the Origins of Inequality*, he does not know misery.[9] It is not so with modern man, who, because he compares his present condition so unfavourably both with that of other people and with what he aspires to be, has desires which far outstrip his ability to satisfy them. Hence his wretchedness. 'True happiness', Rousseau writes in *Emile*, 'consists in decreasing the difference between our desires and our powers, in establishing a perfect equilibrium between the power and the will.'[10] This involves an effort of self-mastery, and it is in self-mastery that the springs of virtue lie.

The discrepancy between man's desires and his powers is one aspect of the contradictory nature of man's condition in society. It is not just that man has desires as a social being, and that these desires are beyond his reach, it is also that man has become a moral being – he has acquired a conscience. The conflict within man, in his soul, is between what his interest propels him toward, and what his duty requires of him. The conflict is not the familiar one between man's passions or feelings and his reason, for conscience is the most profound feeling that man can have. Living according to it is the highest form of life that a man can aspire to. Now it is quite possible, and Rousseau tells us in *Emile* how possible it is, for man in modern, corrupt, society to balance his desires and his powers, and to live a virtuous life of sorts in stoic resignation to the ills of the world. Emile is told, after he has spent some time travelling the world to find a society that he would like to live in, that he has a duty to live in that society which nurtured him, and to respond to the call of civic duty when it is made. But he is also assured that this duty will not be very onerous – he will not often be called upon. He and Sophie can retire to a tranquil and undisturbed life in the country, harming no-one and living simply.[11] This, indeed, may be the only choice that is open to modern men. Rousseau wanted, however, to show his contemporaries how they could live together, if only they would choose to do so. The highest form of virtuous life could be lived only in the city, in the republic. This was the life of man as citizen, in which he had the prospect of being fully master of himself.

Man cannot escape the society of other men, but he can achieve self-mastery. Self-mastery involves both releasing himself from dependence on other men, and settling the inner conflict between his interest and his duty by making his duty his interest. In this way man will become integrated within himself; he will be a whole being, not as natural man but as social man. He will also no longer feel that alienation from society that the conditions of dependence and enslavement presently create for him. He will be both free and virtuous, and thus have the prospect of happiness – the prospect only, for freedom and virtue are only necessary conditions, not sufficient ones for happiness. In terms, therefore, of the double contrast noted at the beginning of this chapter – the contrast which measures the present against both the state of nature and the ancient world – Rousseau's intention is to provide us with the same answer to two questions: under what conditions can man be both happy and free? And under what conditions can he live a life of virtue? Freedom is necessary for both happiness and virtue; Rousseau also wants to demonstrate that virtue is necessary for happiness.

Civil and moral liberty

Rousseau gives us an early intimation of his answer to these questions in the Dedication to the Republic of Geneva with which he prefaced the 1754 edition of the *Discourse on the Origins of Inequality*, where he enumerates the characteristics of the society in which he would have chosen to be born. It would be a society 'of which the dimensions were limited by the extent of human faculties, that is to say, by the possibility of being well governed'; one in which all individuals were well-known to each other, such that 'love of country [was] a love for fellow citizens rather than a love for the land'. There would be an identity of interest between sovereign and people, 'so that all the movements of the civil machine always tended to promote the common happiness': a 'wisely tempered democratic government', then, where no-one in the state is above the law. 'For, whatever might be the formal constitution of a government, if there is one man who is not subject to the law, all the others will necessarily be at his discretion.' It would be a peaceful and happy republic, 'which had endured only such hostile attacks as might serve to bring forth and fortify the courage and patriotism of its inhabitants, a commonwealth whose citizens, being long accustomed to a wise independence, were not only free, but fit to be free': one which neither loved conquest itself, nor was such as to provoke conquest by others, but rather receive their protection.

The right of legislation would be vested in all citizens, 'for who could know better than they what laws would most suit their living together in the same society?' No citizen, however, should 'be at liberty to introduce new laws according to his fancy'; this right 'should be vested uniquely in the magistrates' to prevent 'self-interested and ill-conceived projects and all ... hazardous innovations'. Citizens would be content with sanctioning laws, 'making decisions in assemblies on proposals from the leaders on the most important public business', and electing 'year by year the most capable and the most upright of their fellow citizens to administer justice and govern the state'. It would be a republic, in short, 'where the virtue of the magistrates gave such manifest evidence of the wisdom of the people that each did the other a reciprocal honour'. If, Rousseau concludes, providence had added further things,

> a charming location, a temperate climate, a fertile countryside, and the most delectable appearance of any place under the sun, I would have wished to complete my fortune by enjoying all these advantages in the bosom of that happy country, to living peacefully in sweet society with my fellow citizens, and, taking my example from them, exhibiting towards them humanity, friendship, and all the virtues, and leaving after me the honourable memory of a good man and an upright, virtuous patriot.[12]

This is an idyllic picture of Geneva, as the Dedication implies, and it begs almost every question which he was later to address in the *Social Contract*. While it is clear, from the above, that a genuine community is being described – in terms of the sentiments of friendship and patriotism which bond the people into a citizen body – it is less clear how far the political judgment of the citizens is to be trusted, in that they are deprived of the initiative in legislation. The question of how free and independent they are, how far they enjoy autonomy, how far they are responsible for their political life, is yet to be resolved.

Rousseau's *Social Contract* was published in 1762. He had, however, not neglected political issues since the *Discourse on the Origins of Inequality*. In his *Discourse on Political Economy*, published in 1755 as part of Volume V of the *Encyclopedia* edited by his friend Diderot,

Rousseau introduced much of the political vocabulary which was to become peculiarly associated with him. In 1758 his *Letter to d'Alembert on the Theatre* appeared, in which, among other things, he stressed the importance to the well-being of the social and political life of a country of its morals and manners (its *mœurs*),[13] and of public opinion. It is in the *Social Contract*, however, with its subtitle 'The Principles of Political Right', that his political thinking is presented in its systematic maturity.

As the subtitle indicates, Rousseau intends to concern himself with principles of political life rather than with programmes for political reform, and a large part of the argument is conducted at a highly abstract and analytical level. Here, Rousseau attempts to reconcile freedom with authority, right with interest, justice with utility, by requiring each man to subordinate, within himself, his particular self and will to his common self and the general will. His inquiry is into the legitimacy of political arrangements. There is another level of argument, however, which stems from Rousseau taking seriously the remark with which he opens Book I of the *Social Contract*: 'My purpose is to consider if, in political society, there can be any legitimate and sure principle of government, *taking men as they are and laws as they might be*' (*SC*, I, Preface, emphasis added). In the abstract argument of Book I and the first part of Book II of the *Social Contract*, Rousseau clarifies the principles of a legitimate political regime, which is a political community. It is when we come to the second level of argument that Rousseau, like Machiavelli, puts the project of political community in jeopardy, by enumerating the conditions which would have to be met. Further, autonomy and judgment are put at risk by the roles which Rousseau assigns to the Legislator, and to civil religion, and by the degenerative tendencies of government itself; and friendship is rendered fragile by the incorrigibility of the particular self and will.

In the state of nature, there was physical inequality between men, but there were none of those 'moral or political' inequalities[14] which gave rise to the relationships of dependence characteristic of men in contemporary society, in which men are enslaved because they are subject to the wills of others. While nothing can be done about physical inequality, something can be done to mitigate its social effects by significantly reducing, if not eliminating, moral or political inequality. This is achieved by making everyone dependent on law, and on nothing else. Everything thus hinges on what 'law' is, how it is determined, and by whom. Its legitimate foundation must also be defined: what are the grounds upon which it can be said that men have an obligation to obey it? Rousseau has to show that in substituting dependence on law for dependence on men, men are not exchanging one form of subservience for another. He has to show that, in their dependence on law, men are entering a higher realm of freedom.

There are different kinds of law – civil and criminal law, for instance – but more fundamental than such law is what one may call 'constitutional' law: those rules that determine what kind of polity it is that men are to live in. The first stage of Rousseau's inquiry is into the kind of person or body of persons which can legitimately determine this constitutional law so that those subject to it have an obligation to obey it. He rejects the argument that legitimate political society is formed and sustained after the manner of the family. Though the family is a 'natural' society – indeed, for Rousseau, the only natural one – its natural bonds last only until the children are of an age to take responsibility for their own lives. If the family survives thereafter, it is only by agreement or convention. Any attempt by the father to extend his paternal authority in time is an unwarranted infringement of the free will of his children (*SC*, I, ii). Rousseau then considers whether the strongest has any 'right' to impose a form of political society on a body of people, such that an obligation is created on their part to obey. His argument is that if a body of people is responding only to the force of the strongest, 'there is no need to invoke a duty to obey, and if force ceases to compel obedience, there is no longer any obligation'. It is, for Rousseau, meaningless to talk of the 'right' of the strongest, for, 'as soon as man can disobey with impunity, his disobedience becomes legitimate' (*SC*, I, iii).

Rousseau thus comes to the conclusion that 'since no man has any natural authority over his fellows, and since force alone bestows no right, all legitimate authority among men must be based on covenants' (*SC*, I, iv). What this means is that the only way in which men can be said to have any obligation is by taking it on themselves, and for political authority the consent of everyone is required. But men are not permitted to consent to any form of political arrangements. In particular, they may not engage in a 'pact of submission', for this would be to enslave themselves and to deny that they are men. As Rousseau puts it:

> To renounce freedom is to renounce one's humanity, one's rights as a man and equally one's duties. There is no possible *quid pro quo* for one who renounces everything; indeed such renunciation is contrary to man's very nature; for if you take away all freedom of the will, you strip a man's actions of all moral significance.
>
> (*SC*, I, iv)

The only legitimate form of political arrangements, therefore, are those in which everyone is involved in establishing, where everyone consents, and in which political authority is retained by those who establish them. Only if this latter condition is met, do men remain free. There is a distinction, however, between the pact whereby a multitude constitutes itself 'a people', where unanimity is required, and the decision this newly constituted people comes to as to the form of its government, a decision which is reached by majority voting. Without the prior unanimity, there could be no 'obligation on the minority to accept the decision of the majority.... The law of majority-voting itself rests on a covenant, and implies that there has been on at least one occasion unanimity.' Such unanimity is required in the founding pact, otherwise the people would be a mere 'aggregation ... for they would neither have a common good nor be a body politic' (*SC*, I, v). What Rousseau means here is that there could be no motive for a multitude to constitute itself a people unless it recognized some common interest or good. Its unanimity consists in its recognition of this common good, by which it defines itself as its specific body politic rather than any other.

Men engage in the social pact to preserve both their lives and their liberty. In the *Discourse on the Origins of Inequality*, Rousseau had put forward his hypothetical history of the human species from the original state of nature to the corrupt conditions of modernity. Man's development, a result both of his ability to 'perfect' himself and his ever closer contact with his fellow human beings, led to physical inequality being supplemented by moral or political inequality, whose first manifestation was the institution of property. Some men – being stronger, cleverer, more industrious or more ruthless than others – gained material advantage at the expense of their less fortunate fellows. Such advantage as they obtained, however, was precarious, as it did not have the protection of legitimacy, and the state of nature approached that which Hobbes had described in *Leviathan*. It was in these circumstances, Rousseau tells us, that the 'false', or 'bungled', social contract was drawn up, in which the rich agreed to curb their predatoriness if the poor put a rein upon their ambition. Thus was inequality given the protection of law and legitimized. But man as a species had made the wrong choice. As the state of nature develops, with men in closer and closer contact with each other, it does indeed become precarious. It is not, however, primarily property which is threatened, but liberty. In the *Social Contract*, Rousseau is concerned to show his contemporaries the choice which man as a species did not make, could have made, and ought to have made, to preserve both his life and his liberty.

At this stage, Chapter VI of Book I of the *Social Contract*, Rousseau has reached the core of his political teaching. The fundamental problem, he writes, to which the social contract is the solution is:

How to find a form of association which will defend the person and goods of each member with the collective force of all, and under which each individual, while uniting himself with the others, obeys no one but himself, and remains as free as before.

(*SC*, I, vi)

It is clear that Rousseau intends as much to secure each person's liberty as he does to protect their property. In fact, as he later remarks, the social pact changes mere possession into property: 'it changes usurpation into valid right and mere enjoyment into legal ownership' (*SC*, I, ix). Man remains 'as free as before', but not free in the same way. There is a difference between the independence of the state of nature, natural liberty, and the freedom which man comes to enjoy in the civil condition. Rousseau defines what this difference is two chapters later, and, as we shall see, the difference is greatly to man's advantage.

The terms of the contract which men engage in are 'reducible to a single one, namely the total alienation by each associate of himself and all his rights to the whole community'. It is only by such total alienation that moral and political equality is established. It is now no longer possible for some men to be the dependents of others; in particular, it is no longer possible for political authority to be exercised by some to the detriment of others. For the alienation of 'all rights' includes the transfer of all goods and possessions. Thus the economic basis of moral and political inequality is swept away. Moreover, in these conditions, no-one has any motive to restore such inequality. Since, as Rousseau continues, 'the conditions are the same for all, and precisely because they are the same for all, it is in no one's interest to make the conditions onerous for others', for this would be simply to make them onerous for himself. It is necessary, also, that all rights be alienated unconditionally. For man to be able to reclaim any rights would leave the established community with only a precarious authority, 'and in this way the state of nature would be kept in being, and the association inevitably become either tyrannical or void' (*SC*, I, vi).

The total alienation of man and his rights is not a pact of submission by which man renounces his liberty, for the alienation takes place not to other men, but to the community, of which, of course, he is as integral a part as any other. 'Each man gives himself to all' and, in so doing 'gives himself to no one'. He acquires the same rights, as a member of the community, over others, as others do over him by that same fact. He thus 'recovers the equivalent of everything he loses, and in the bargain he acquires more power to preserve what he has', for it is now the community which is charged with protecting his life and ensuring his liberty: he is not, precariously, on his own any more. If then, Rousseau concludes,

> we eliminate from the social pact everything that is not essential to it, we find it comes to this: 'Each one of us puts into the community his person and all his powers under the supreme direction of the general will; and as a body, we incorporate every member as an indivisible part of the whole.'
>
> (*SC*, I, vi)

This is the first mention of the 'general will' in the *Social Contract* and it requires some explanation: on the face of it, it seems that submission is involved after all. Rousseau had introduced the concept in his *Discourse on Political Economy*. In the act of association, the social pact, it is a political community that is created. Rousseau calls this community an 'artificial and collective body', a 'public person', 'the *body politic*' and, by the act of association, the body politic 'acquires its unity, its common *ego*, its life and its will' (*SC*, I, vi). As he writes in the *Discourse on Political Economy*, the body politic is 'a corporate being possessed of a will; and this general will ... tends always to the preservation and welfare of the whole and of every part'.[15] Just as the will of each individual human being tends towards the preservation and welfare of its being, so, too, does the will of this artificial person which is the body politic tend in the same direction. What Rousseau now has to do is show that the general will of the body politic is nothing but the will of each individual member of the association, conceived in a particular and appropriate way. This he does by developing his conception of 'sovereignty'.

The body politic has two roles: an active role, and a passive one :

> In its passive role it is called the *state*, when it plays an active role it is the *sovereign*.... Those who are associated in it take collectively the name of *a people*, and call themselves individually *citizens*, in so far as they share in the sovereign power, and *subjects*, in so far as they put themselves under the laws of the state.
>
> (*SC*, I, vi)

Until Rousseau, the term 'sovereign' had denoted both a ruler or monarch in whom political authority resided, and a relationship of domination and subordination between ruler and ruled. What Rousseau does is to locate sovereignty in the people, which he must do if the people are to remain 'as free as before', thereby annihilating the dominance and subordination entailed in the relationship between ruler and ruled. For ruler and ruled are now the same people conceived in different ways. In making the contract, each person 'finds himself doubly committed, first, as a member of the sovereign in relation to individuals, and second as a member of the state in relation to the sovereign' (*SC*, I, vii). It is almost a matter of each citizen making a contract with himself, but not quite; as Robert Derathé points out: 'Each contracts, in fact, with a whole or a collectivity of which he will become part, but which, at the moment of the pact, has yet only a virtual existence.'[16]

The position so far is that each member of the association, or body politic, is at the same time 'under the supreme direction of the general will', and a 'member of the sovereign'. The purpose of the general will is, as we have seen, to secure the preservation and welfare of the body politic; the purpose of the sovereign is to declare what the general will is – as Rousseau puts it at the beginning of Book II: 'sovereignty, being nothing other than the exercise of the general will' (*SC*, II, i). Since 'the sovereign is formed entirely of the individuals who compose it, it has not, nor could it have, any interest contrary to theirs' (*SC*, I, vii). What this means that when the body politic acts truly as sovereign – when, that is, it gives expression to the general will – its interest and the interests of its members will coincide: it cannot harm or injure them. What this further means is that the general will is a will that each person has as a member of the sovereign body. The general will is what gives expression to that common interest upon the basis of which the social pact was established in the first place. Just as the common interest is the interest of each associate, so, too, the general will is the will of each associate. For each associate, therefore, to place himself 'under the supreme direction of the general will' is nothing other than for him to be directed by his own will. In this way, each associate remains 'as free as before'.

Man is a different creature in civil society than he was in the state of nature. As a social, and now moral being, his conscience compels him 'to act on other principles [than] ... physical impulse [or] ... desire' (*SC*, I, viii). This is not something that takes place automatically and without, at times, some struggle: 'For every individual as a man may have a private will contrary to, or different from, the general will that he has as a citizen. His private interest may speak with a very different voice from that of the public interest' (*SC*, I, vii). The moral quality which his actions now have is the result of his choice, his free will. Natural liberty has been exchanged for civil liberty, and so that we may be clear about what has been lost and what gained in the social contract, Rousseau remarks that 'we must clearly distinguish between *natural* liberty, which has no limit but the physical power of the individual concerned, and *civil* liberty, which is limited by the general will'. More than this is at issue, however, for what civil society makes possible is moral freedom. It is through the exercise of moral freedom that man indicates he has mastered himself; man is, thereby, made fully whole and integrated within himself.

Natural man was, and could be no other than, a creature of impulse. Social man can, and must be, more than this; for him 'to be governed by appetite alone is slavery' (*SC*, I, viii). To be fully a man and enjoy the highest freedom that he can is to obey only those laws which he prescribes to himself: in the one case, this is his conscience, which integrates him as a man; in the other case, it is the laws which he determines as part of the sovereign body to give expression to the general will, and which integrate him into society.

In these arrangements justice is made to conform with interest, for in deliberating as a member of the sovereign body on the common interest of each associate, 'who does not take that word "each" to pertain to himself and in voting for all think of himself?' It is only the moral or political equality of rights which ensures that each associate, in considering his own interest as citizen, will – at the same time, and by that act – be considering the interest of his fellow-associates. The notion of justice which is thus produced derives 'from the predilection which each man has for himself and hence from human nature as such'. Such considerations also prove 'that the general will, to be truly what it is, must be general in its purpose as well as in its nature; that it should spring from all and apply to all'. It must be general in its purpose because its object is that interest which each associate has in common with every other associate – that is what makes it general; it must be general in its nature because unless it is freely willed by each and every associate, it cannot give rise to any obligation – this, then, is what makes it legitimate. 'Hence by the nature of the compact, every act of sovereignty, that is, every authentic act of the general will, binds or favours all the citizens equally' (*SC*, II, iv).

The body politic has now been provided with life; it must still be set in motion. It has not yet been given a constitution. This is the function of law and legislation. It is clear at this stage to Rousseau that the characteristics of law are the same as those of the general will. Just as the general will is the expression of sovereignty, so, too is law the expression of the general will. When the people as a whole, as citizens, make rules for the people as a whole, as subjects, they are dealing only with themselves: 'Here the matter concerning which a rule is made is as general as the will which makes it. And *this* is the kind of act which I call a law.' The general will applies equally to all and comes from all; so does law. It is in this manner that man 'can be both free and subject to laws', for the laws do no more than register what each man wills. It has been noted that there are different kinds of law. The only law that Rousseau is concerned with in the *Social Contract* is that law which determines the nature of the political order: its constitution. What has been established so far is that ultimate political authority – that is, sovereignty – lies with the entire citizenry considered as an 'artificial and collective person', giving expression to its common interest in the general will, which itself is declared in acts of legislation, in law:

> Any state which is ruled by law I call a 'republic', whatever the form of its constitution; for then, and then alone, does the public interest govern and then alone is the 'public thing' – the *res publica* – a reality. All legitimate government is 'republican'.
>
> (*SC*, II, vi)

At this point in his argument, it can be said with confidence that Rousseau has shown that his citizens are free and autonomous. It is their collective will that establishes the laws they are to live under, and by this fact they obey only what they have themselves willed. They thus remain free and autonomous. Further, in the very act of deliberating upon the common interest which ends in the establishment of laws, they are exercising their political judgment as citizens. Beyond saying, however, that human action is now moralized by the fact that men act as citizens – and that they are citizens only by virtue of that common interest which prompted them to engage in the social pact in the first place – Rousseau has said no more about the bonds which unite citizens other than that they lie in the commitment which each of them made in the social pact. In other words, the commitments are only the quasi-legal ones of contract – 'quasi-legal', of course, because it is only after the contract that there is law. For Rousseau, the bonds have to be much stronger than this. Now, however, a more urgent and fundamental question absorbs his attention.

The formation of a people

The question is: granted that no civil society is legitimate unless the entire citizenry as a body decides what its constitution is to be, how can this come about?

> Is it to be by common agreement, by a sudden inspiration? Has the body politic an organ to declare its will? Who is to give it the foresight necessary to formulate enactments and proclaim them in advance, and how is it to announce them in the hour of need? How can a blind multitude, which often does not know what it wants, because it seldom knows what is good for it, undertake by itself an enterprise as vast and difficult as a system of legislation?

It is here that the phrase which had opened the *Social Contract*, 'taking men as they are', begins to have a sustained influence on Rousseau's considerations. Like Machiavelli, Rousseau is very much aware of the limits of unaided human achievement. He knows what men can do, because he knows what they have done in the past in Rome and Sparta. But neither the Romans nor the Spartans formed their political orders unaided. In the case of the Spartans it was Lycurgus who provided them with their constitution; in Rome it was Numa who played the crucial role. It is beyond the wit and reason of ordinary man, everyman, to perceive what it is that needs to be done to establish a political order for a people, which is as yet no more than a 'blind multitude'. Thus it is not, as it is for Machiavelli, human perversity which impedes the creation of a republican political order, it is an insufficiently developed human judgment: 'By themselves the people always will what is good, but by themselves they do not always discern it. The general will is always rightful, but the judgement which guides it is not always enlightened.' Enlightenment has to be brought from outside to enable the people to see the good that it desires. The people need guidance: 'Hence the necessity of a lawgiver' (*SC*, II, vi).

It is the function of the lawgiver to transform a multitude into a people and to provide this people with an appropriate constitution. In the process, however, nothing must detract from the ultimate responsibility of the people to choose their own form of life. The lawgiver must not encroach on the proper domain of sovereignty. He cannot impose his proposals on a people. This makes Rousseau's lawgiver very different from Machiavelli's legislator/prophet, and he is indeed, 'in every respect, an extraordinary man in the state' (*SC*, II, vii). It is not so much his extraordinary character – his superior intelligence, his ability to understand men's passions but not be subject to them – that is of concern here, as the nature of the task he has to perform, and how he performs it. Nothing less is involved than the transformation of man, in accordance with those aspects of his nature appropriate for a social being. His constitution must be 'altered' – the first version of the *Social Contract*, the so-called Geneva Manuscript, had 'mutilated'[17] – in order that it may be fortified. Each man must be stripped of the physical and independent existence which he enjoyed in the state of nature, and given 'a moral and communal existence'. His independent, natural powers must be removed in favour of 'powers which are external to him, and which he cannot use without the help of others'. As his natural powers are extinguished or annihilated, and his acquired powers fortified, so much 'the stronger and more perfect is the social institution' (*SC*, II, vii).

But the lawgiver has no legislative right; he has no authoritative position in a constitution which is yet to be. Neither can he use force, for this would illegitimately override the sovereignty of the people, and could not anyway give rise to an obligation on their part. Furthermore, a 'blind multitude' does not possess the judgment and intelligence to be persuaded by the force of rational argument. There is thus the distinct problem of how the lawgiver is to do his work:

> For a newly formed people to understand the wise principles of politics and to follow the basic rules of statecraft, the effect would have to become the cause; the social spirit which must be the product of social institutions would have to preside over the setting up of those institutions; men would have to have already become before the advent of law that which they become as a result of law.

Denied the use of force and argument, the lawgiver must find his authority elsewhere: he must call upon the Gods. This, after all, as Rousseau says, was what the ancient lawgivers did. He must, however, be able – by his wisdom, by his 'great soul' – to convince people that it is the immortals who have put words into his mouth, rather than the other way round. Only if he can do this will a people be prepared to believe that the God who created nature and man also created the nation, and thus 'obey freely and bear with docility the yoke of public welfare' (*SC*, II, vii).

The role of the lawgiver obviously raises questions about the autonomy and judgment of the people subject to his sleight of hand. Rousseau's whole point, however, is that until something like the work of the lawgiver is done, no people will possess the autonomy and judgment required to sustain civil society in a manner consistent with that moral existence which it is possible for man to achieve, and which is the only life in which man can recapture anything like the unity of being, and the independence, which characterized his existence in the state of nature. It does not follow from the fact that people may be able to recognize the need for some kind of order that they will choose one particular kind of order, unless they are given some compelling reason. In invoking divine inspiration, the lawgiver gives them that compelling reason. When he has done his work and his prescriptions have coalesced into the traditions, habits and morals – the *mœurs* – of a people, then that people can be left, with guarded confidence, to govern itself. A revealed, and mysterious, religion is necessary at the start to give a people a sense of identity as this people and not any other. Over generations, such a religion will be supplemented by the ingrained *mœurs* of an established community. The art of the lawgiver is so to devise his prescriptions that they can ultimately take this form. Every established people and community may be said to have its *mœurs*, but not every one – indeed none so far as Rousseau could see in the mid-eighteenth century – had those *mœurs* which were conducive to a proper civic mode of living. If Rousseau can be said to call in question the autonomy and judgment of a people by the role he gives to the lawgiver, it is for the purpose of establishing a citizen body able and willing to exercise its autonomous judgment in ways consistent with civic life.

The art of the lawgiver is to match a constitution to the circumstances in which a people finds itself. His task is never an easy one, but certain conditions can make his project more likely to succeed. Just as with men, whose education is best given them when they are young, so, too, with peoples: the best time for them to become the object of a lawgiver's attention is in their youth, before 'customs are established and prejudices rooted', for these are difficult to eradicate. Alternatively, a people might be receptive to a lawgiver if it has undergone a period of violence and revolution in which existing customs and prejudices have been dislodged from their authoritative position. Such periods, however, are exceptional; they cannot be relied upon to occur conveniently. It is also the case that the lawgiver's task cannot be performed when a people is in its infancy. A certain maturity is required so that it can recognize the value of customs and prejudices, but these latter should not be so old as to be unshakeable: 'For nations, as for men, there is a time of youth, or, if you prefer, of maturity, which they must reach before they are made subject to law' (*SC*, II, viii). It is not easy to recognize when a people reaches this time, but the lawgiver's work will be abortive if he attempts it too soon.

A second consideration governing the deliberations of the lawgiver concerns the size of the state. Social unity is the important objective. The less homogenous the state, the less likely there is to be any recognizable common interest for the general will to express. The larger the state, the greater the heterogeneity of its people, and therefore the less chance of social unity. So, the state should not be so large that it cannot be 'well-governed'. A state small in numbers is required, for 'the more the social bond is stretched, the slacker it becomes'. A large state not only makes 'the government less vigorous and swift in enforcing respect for the law', but 'the people has less feeling for governors whom it never sees, for a fatherland that seems as vast as the world, and for fellow-citizens who are mostly strangers' (*SC*, II, ix). Rousseau does not say what numbers he considers appropriate though, in his discussion of Roman political institutions in Book IV, he is prepared to contemplate a citizen assembly of 200,000 men (*SC*, IV, iii). Size is also a matter of territory. The relevant consideration here is that a state should be large enough to maintain itself. Self-sufficiency is the objective. Too great and too frequent contact with other states not only carries with it the danger or war, which is always disruptive of civic life, but also threatens to dilute the integrity and social homogeneity of the state. It is best for states to live in quiet indifference to each other. So a balance needs to be struck, such that 'there be land enough to feed the inhabitants and as many inhabitants as the land can feed'. Precisely how this objective of self-sufficiency is to be achieved will depend upon 'the distinctive features of the land' (*SC*, II, x), and the kind of economy most appropriate to them (*SC*, II, xi). While Rousseau does not here express a marked preference for an agricultural, rural economy over an industrial, commercial and urban one, in his later discussion of Rome he remarks that the vigour and strength of the early Roman republic lay in the countryside, in rural life. It was from the country that Rome's most 'illustrious men' came, those who preserved its morals and contributed to the growth of its empire (*SC*, IV, iv). Whatever the economy, however, it is one in which there should be rough economic equality, so 'that no citizen shall be rich enough to buy another, and none so poor as to be forced to sell himself'. If 'coherence in the state' is what is required, Rousseau adds in a footnote, then extremes of wealth should be brought 'as close together as possible', for extremes beget both tyrants and lovers of tyranny (*SC*, II, xi). Equality is an instrumental good; without it, liberty in the state is not possible.

The task before the lawgiver is a difficult one, not just because success depends so much on the foregoing conditions being met, but because however favourable the circumstances and perfect his creation, the prospects for sustained and genuine civic life are thin and precarious. For there are ineradicable degenerative tendencies – both in the body politic and in man himself – whose effects cannot ultimately be stilled, only temporarily staunched. These tendencies have to do with the particular self and will. If, as Rousseau says at the beginning of Book II, it was the existence of common interests among people that made the social pact possible, it was the conflict between private interests that made the pact necessary (*SC*, II, i). Though man may become a citizen in civil society, his particular self is not thereby annihilated. Nor is his particular will, and it is of the nature of the particular will to be partial to whomsoever it belongs. It is also of the nature of the general will to be partial to that body whose will it is, namely the body politic. It thus follows that the general will of the body politic has constantly to do battle with the particular wills of the associate members of that body. To the extent that the general will prevails, then the body politic remains healthy and is sustained. The moment particular wills begin to prevail, then the body politic is in danger: it begins to atrophy and die. It is not impossible, Rousseau says, 'for a private will to coincide with the general will on some point or other', but 'it is impossible for such a coincidence to be regular and enduring', and any guarantee of such harmony is 'inconceivable' (*SC*, II, i). A particular or private will can reside in individuals, and it can reside in institutions of lesser scope than the body politic. It is clear that, for Rousseau, the greatest danger to the general will of the body politic comes from the direction of such partial institutions, for he thought that the particular wills of individuals would somehow cancel each other out (*SC*, II, iii). Hence he argued for the total suppression of partial associations or, if this was not possible, for their multiplication, on the basis that their subsequent more equal status would put them into a similar position to the particular wills of individuals. There is one partial association, however, which is indispensable to the body politic, and this is government itself.

It will be recalled that all that has as yet been created is a body politic, with a sovereign body whose task it is to declare laws in accordance with the general will. These laws, just like the general will of which they are the expression, are – and can only be – general in scope. There is need of a body to administer them, and this body is government. Government is required to apply law to particular cases. This the sovereign body cannot do because it is restricted to matters of general scope. Thus the sovereign body can decide – indeed, it is its first task to decide – what form government should take, but it cannot decide which particular person should occupy office in that government. In the first instance what happens is that the sovereign constitutes itself as a democratic government (*SC*, II, xvii). This it can do because no particular persons are being chosen. Now it might be thought that the best solution would be for the government, itself, to be democratic – composed, that is, of the entire citizen body – so that 'sovereign' and 'government' would be the same people, under different denominations. Quite apart from the number of conditions that would have to be met for such a government, there is contained in such a solution a great danger: that the citizen body in becoming, as government, involved in matters of particular concern, would lose sight of those general perspectives which are its proper concern as sovereign. In other words, democratic government is likely to be subversive of democratic sovereignty (*SC*, III, iv). All this points to the great distinction which Rousseau made between sovereignty and government. The latter was to be no more than servant or minister of the former (*SC*, III, xviii).

The distinction was between legislative power, which belongs to the sovereign, and executive power, which is the province of government. Government is, therefore, 'an intermediary body established between the subject and the sovereign for their mutual communication' (*SC*, III, i). Its sphere of competence is to execute the laws and to maintain civil and political freedom, including the maintenance of internal order and 'the acts of declaring war and making peace'. What is of less concern than the range of its activities – eighteenth-century government, while it might have been oppressive, was not extensive

Citizenship and community

by later standards – is the problem of keeping government in its proper place. For if one takes the occupants of governmental office – the magistrates, or the 'prince' as Rousseau sometimes calls them collectively – they contain within them three distinct wills: a will which belongs to them as individuals; one which pertains to their corporate capacity as magistrates; and finally, the general will which they have as citizens. In the matter of government, it is the latter which should prevail, but: 'In the order of nature, on the contrary, these different wills become the more active as they are the more concentrated' (*SC*, III, ii). In relation to the general will, the corporate will of magistrates is just as much a private or particular will as that which they have as individuals. Since every will tends to the preservation and welfare of the body whose will it is, the tendency of government is always potentially destructive of the general will, and therefore of sovereignty and the body politic itself. 'This is the inherent and inescapable defect which, from the birth of the political body, tends relentlessly to destroy it, just as old age and death destroy the body of a man' (*SC*, III, x).

While no human creation can be expected to last for ever, it is possible for men to forestall these degenerative tendencies, and prolong the life of the body politic by wisely adopted measures. The purport of these measures is for the sovereign to keep as tight a rein upon government as it can. Thus while the first purpose of the sovereign body, or assembly of citizens, is to provide the body politic with a government, this does not exhaust its duties (*SC*, III, xiii). It must meet regularly, at times fixed in advance which cannot be altered: 'The moment the people is lawfully assembled as a sovereign body all jurisdiction of the government ceases; the executive power is suspended.' This suspension is to remind the prince, or government, that it is subject to a 'real superior' (*SC*, III, xiv). These periodic assemblies have as their only purpose 'the maintenance of the social treaty', and they have always before them two motions:

The first: 'Does it please the sovereign to maintain the present form of government?'

The second: 'Does it please the people to leave the administration to those at present charged with it?'

(*SC*, III, xviii)

The assembly asks the first question as sovereign, and the second – since it is concerned with particular people occupying office – as a reconstituted democratic government. In this way, one might hope that government could be prevented from usurping sovereign authority.

The efficacy of these assemblies in keeping government in check depends on the assiduity with which each associate member of the sovereign body performs his duty. This is not something that can be relied upon for within the person of each associate resides, as has already been noted, an incorrigible and ineradicable particular will. To the extent that citizens ignore or forget their public duties, then the way is left open for government to encroach ever more on that legislative power which does not rightfully belong to it:

> As soon as public service ceases to be the main concern of the citizen and they come to prefer to serve the state with their purse rather than their person, the state is already close to ruin. Are troops needed to march to war? They pay mercenaries and stay at home. Is it time to go to an assembly? They pay deputies and stay at home. Thanks to laziness and money, they end up with soldiers to enslave the country and deputies to sell it.
>
> (*SC*, III, xv)

It is here that a people's morals and manners – its *mœurs* – come into their full significance. Rousseau does not say much about a people's *mœurs* in the *Social Contract*, for as he notes (*SC*, IV, vii) he has already discussed the issue at length before, namely in his *Letter to d'Alembert on the Theatre*. The purpose of *mœurs* is to strengthen national character, to give pride to the performance of civic duty, to instill a genuine and warm patriotism, and above all to reinforce the voice of conscience – not to make conscience heard, for once it has begun to form part of man's waking life it is never still,[18] but to make man want to follow it.

The education of a people

In the final chapter of Book II of the *Social Contract*, Rousseau draws attention to different kinds of law: political, civil and criminal. But there is a fourth, 'the most important of all ... upon which the success of all other laws depends'. It is this law,

> inscribed neither on marble nor brass, but in the hearts of citizens, ... which forms the true constitution of the state, ... which sustains a nation in the spirit of its institution and imperceptibly substitutes the force of habit for the force of authority. I refer to morals [*mœurs*], customs and, above all, opinion.
>
> (*SC*, II, xii)

He returns to the subject towards the end of Book IV, where his concern is with what governments may do to foster appropriate *mœurs*. While a people's *mœurs* exist within a context of legislation, it is not through law that a government will most effectively influence *mœurs*, but through acting on public opinion: 'Among all the peoples of the world, it is not nature but opinion which governs their choice of pleasures. Reform the opinions of men, and their morals will be purified of themselves' (*SC*, IV, vii).

Everything that Rousseau recommends in this respect has the object of reminding men that they are citizens, and may be seen as part of an extensive and continuing process of education and re-education. The periodic popular assemblies have a function to perform here, for they are as much occasions for maintaining a check upon governments as they are for the reaffirmation and renewal of the social contract itself. Their frequency and regularity are necessary for both purposes. Aside from the assemblies, Rousseau's recommendations are four: a system of education in the conventional sense; public entertainments or '*spectacles*'; public censorship; and civil religion.

Rousseau had nothing to say about education in the *Social Contract*. He had, of course, published *Emile* in the same year, 1762, but, as he makes clear right at the beginning of Book I, there is a difference between private and public education. The one is appropriate to man as man, the other to man as citizen: they cannot be combined. One must choose to train either the man or the citizen, and it is the private education of man that is Rousseau's concern in *Emile*.[19] Emile is not being educated to take his place in the civil society of the *Social Contract*, and he is only required to perform any civic duties when he is called upon, which is seldom.[20]

The training of future generations into citizenship is, none the less, a crucial task for the republic. It was an issue which Rousseau addressed in both the *Discourse on Political Economy* (1755), and the *Considerations on the Government of Poland*, which he wrote in 1771. In both, a system of public education is held to be the most important way of inculcating the habits of citizenship. In the *Discourse*, such education is to begin at birth: 'Since it is at the instant of birth that we partake of the rights of citizens, that instant ought to be the beginning of the exercise of our duty.' The task is too crucial to be left to the discretion of fathers, though they can resume as citizens the role of teacher, which they relinquish as fathers. It is to take place under the aegis of the state, 'under regulations prescribed by the government, and under magistrates established by the sovereign':

> If children are brought up in common in the bosom of equality; if they are imbued with the laws of the state and the precepts of the general will; if they are taught to respect these above all things; if they are surrounded by examples and objects which constantly remind them of the tender mother who nourishes them, of the love

she bears them, of the inestimable benefits they receive from her, and of the return they owe her, we cannot doubt that they will learn to cherish one another mutually as brothers, to will nothing contrary to the will of society.[21]

It does not detract from the importance of education that, in the *Social Contract*, Rousseau was by implication less than sanguine that the results would be so irreversibly beneficial. No amount of education could eradicate the partiality of the individual, particular will. In the *Considerations*, he writes similarly that public adoration must begin at birth, and that it be preferably communal rather than private. His thoughts are couched in terms of the need to instill the virtue of patriotism:

> Every true republican takes in with his mother's milk the love of his fatherland [*patrie*] .... This love forms all his existence; he sees nothing but his fatherland, he lives only for it; as soon as he is alone, he is nothing; as soon as he no longer has a fatherland, he is no longer, and if he is not dead, he is worse.[22]

Rousseau also insists, no doubt bearing in mind what he had written in *Emile*,[23] that a proper public education is a negative one: 'Prevent vices from being born, and you will have done enough for virtue.' The object of public education is not just to give citizens robust constitutions, 'but to accustom them in good time to the rules, to equality, to fraternity, to competitions, to live in the sight of their fellow-citizens and to desire public approbation'.[24] The contrast between life as the citizen of a republican fatherland and a life outside such a framework is presented in such stark terms as to leave no feeling, intelligent man in any doubt as to where his choice should lie. But though men may make the choice that Rousseau thinks they ought, as men, to make, there is the consistent theme in the *Social Contract* that they need to be reminded of the choice they have made.

The idea of reinforcing habits of citizenship by having men live under the open gaze of their fellows is carried through into what Rousseau has to say about '*spectacles*', or public entertainments. Again, it is to a source other than the *Social Contract* that we have to turn for his thoughts here, to the *Letter to d'Alembert*. In his article on Geneva for the *Encyclopedia*, d'Alembert had proposed that Geneva, whose Calvinist elders had adopted a strictness of posture in the matter of what amusements were appropriate for its inhabitants, introduce the theatre as a harmless form of public entertainment. In his *Letter*, Rousseau objected: he is fulsome in his praise of the theatre of ancient Greece which 'presented on all sides only combats, victories, prizes, objects capable of inspiring the Greeks with an ardent emulation and of warming their hearts with sentiments of honor and glory'.[25] Such inspiration, however, was not to be expected from the eighteenth-century theatre. Both the tragedy and the comedy of this theatre could not but have harmful effects on the *mœurs* of any people exposed to them, and especially on a simple, hardworking, and virtuous people like the Genevans. The most likely effect of tragedy would be

> to reduce all the duties of man to some pressing and sterile emotions that have no consequence, to make us applaud our courage in praising that of others, our humanity in pitying the ills that we could have cured.[26]

Comedy would be even worse, for in caricaturing both vices and virtues it renders both only ridiculous, and makes neither the first hateful, nor the second an object of emulation. Further, the concern with young lovers in the theatre means that the old are always given detestable and incongruous roles, thus denigrating their wisdom, authority and experience; duty and virtue are too often sacrificed to love.[27] Finally, the eighteenth-century theatre would encourage a 'taste for luxury, adornment, and dissipation',[28] at odds with the *mœurs* of a simple and frugal people.

But there are other *spectacles* which could be sponsored or encouraged by governments to produce the same effect that the theatre had in ancient Greece: public festivals and games, 'in the open air, under the sky':

> Plant a stake crowned with flowers in the middle of a square; gather the people together there, and you will have a festival. Do better yet; let the spectators become an entertainment to themselves; make them actors themselves; do it so that each sees and loves himself in the others so that all will be better united.[29]

For a healthy republic, it was important to instill 'public fraternity' and 'concord' among citizens,[30] and this could only be done by an open appeal to opinion through the heart. Unity within the nation was as important as unity in the human soul. Such unity, in both respects, could also be sustained by the office of public censor.

Rousseau insists that it is no part of the task of the public censor to *decide* what public opinion ought to be: should he decide in ways contrary to public opinion then his decisions are 'void and without effect'. He has rather to declare public opinion, to act as its 'spokesman'. It thus follows, for Rousseau, that the utility of the office of public censor lies 'in preserving morals, but never in restoring morals'. His advice is to establish such an office when laws are still in full vigour, 'for as soon as the vigour is lost, everything is hopeless; nothing legitimate has any force once the laws have force no longer'. The role of the public censor is preventative in character, sustaining *mœurs* 'by preventing opinions from being corrupted' (*SC*, IV, vii). Everything that Rousseau says about this rather limited role of the censor – limited, that is, in comparison with similar Roman and Spartan offices to which he refers – follows from his view that the health of a republic depends on the inner conviction in citizens of the worth of appropriate *mœurs*. More than outward behaviour is at issue; the heart must be involved. Thus force is out of place, and the censor can only be effective when he reflects opinion back on to those who hold it.

Finally, Rousseau turns to civil religion. Rousseau's approach towards religion was very similar to that of Machiavelli. He noted that in pagan times, the times of Ancient Greece and Rome, there was no distinction in the state 'between its Gods and its laws ... the provinces of the Gods were determined, so to speak, by the frontiers of nations'. The change came with Jesus, with the separation of the theological from the political realm. Thereafter, men had two masters, and such conflict of jurisdiction 'made any kind of good policy impossible in Christian states'. Only Hobbes had seen clearly the need for unity between Church and state for a well-ordered realm (*SC*, IV, viii).

There are three kinds of religion: the religion of man, that of the citizen, and that of the priest. Catholic Christianity was a form of the latter, and, in giving man 'two legislative orders', it demonstrated how bad it was by dividing their loyalties: 'Everything that destroys social unity is worthless; and all institutions that set man at odds with himself are worthless.' There is nothing that can be said for Catholic Christianity. The religion of man, 'inward devotion to the supreme God' – the Christianity, not of today, but of the Gospel – was even 'more contrary to the social spirit', for 'far from attracting the hearts of citizens to the state, this religion detaches them from it as from all other things of the world'. It was a religion more appropriate to tyranny than any other political form, for the servitude and submission it preached made true Christians into willing 'slaves'. Christianity, then, in either of its forms, was not a candidate for a civil religion (*SC*, IV, viii).

Only a religion limited to the nation, to which 'everything outside is infidel, alien, barbarous', and extending 'the rights and duties of men only so far as it extends its altars', could serve the purpose of generating and sustaining political loyalty – patriotism. Joining divine worship to the love of the law, such a religion would make 'the fatherland the object of the citizens' adoration' and teach them 'that the service of the state is the service of a tutelary God'. It has the danger, however, that it can make a people intolerant of other deities, and prompt them to 'believe they are doing a holy deed in killing those who do not accept their Gods'. Such a warlike posture would ultimately destroy the security of the republic (*SC*, IV, viii).

Rousseau's prescriptions follow from these considerations. While the dogmas of a civil religion are to be few and simple, and concerned only with the social behaviour of citizens to each other, Rousseau insists that unless the heart is involved the religion will not have its desired effect. The dogmas are 'sentiments of sociability, without which it is impossible to be either a good citizen or a loyal subject':

> The existence of an omnipotent, intelligent, benevolent divinity that foresees and provides; the life to come; the happiness of the just; the punishment of sinners; the sanctity of the social contract and the law.

These are what Rousseau calls the 'positive dogmas' of a civil religion; in giving divine authority to the social contract, civil religion is reinforcing the similar sanction which was given to it originally by the lawgiver. There is one 'negative' dogma: no intolerance, for intolerance is inimical to peace. Since there can no longer be any such thing as an exclusive, national religion, 'all religions which themselves tolerate others must be tolerated, provided only that their dogmas contain nothing contrary to the duties of the citizen'. These dogmas can be insisted upon by the sovereign. Non-belief invites banishment as an anti-social being and, more severely, death is proper for one who has professed belief in the dogmas but who behaves in ways inconsistent with them (*SC*, IV, viii).

In his proposals on public education, public entertainment, the office of censor and civil religion, Rousseau was attempting to devise institutional forms and practices which would minimize the tendencies of both the body politic to disintegrate from within, and man to forget that his happiness and interest depended upon his performing his duty as citizen. The degenerative tendencies of government are to be checked by a vigilant citizen body – a body formed for vigilance by public education and kept vigilant by a civil religion, by public entertainments encouraged by government itself, and by the public censor. It is a precarious balance that is struck between these twin destructive forces, and there can, in the end, be no institutional guarantees that they will not triumph. The body politic is, from birth, doomed to die. 'We can succeed', Rousseau wrote – in terms very reminiscent of Machiavelli – 'only if we avoid attempting the impossible and flattering ourselves that we can give to the work of man a durability that does not belong to human things' (*SC*, III, xi).

Conclusion

Rousseau's principal concern was with man's happiness. Natural man, in the original state of nature, was happy – first, because there was equilibrium between his desires and his powers and, second, because he was free. As an isolated being, he was not dependent on the will of any other men. Rousseau's problem was, thus, with the conditions for modern, social man's happiness. He needed to be freed both from his dependence on the wills of others, and from subservience to physical impulse. It was more than a matter of achieving equilibrium between his desires and his powers; it was rather that, as a social being, his desires required civilizing or moralizing. Social life was a higher form of life than natural life, but it was a more difficult life to lead satisfactorily. The prospect of happiness was there, but it could not be guaranteed. And there was no turning back; the state of nature was lost for ever. Social life was what man was stuck with.

As a social being, man only has this prospect of happiness if he regards himself primarily as a citizen and acts as one. As citizen, he is the equal of his fellows; as a body, they collectively determine the laws they are going to live under and acknowledge an obligation to obey. In this way they free themselves from their dependence on each other's wills, and overcome their enslavement to mere physical impulse. They achieve both civil and moral liberty and, in the process, render themselves once more whole, but this time as morally autonomous beings. The bonds that unite them are no longer, as they are in contemporary society, those of dependence: they are those of love, fraternity and patriotism. While Rousseau often writes about these bonds in xenophobic terms – there is one standard for citizens, and another for the rest of humanity; foreigners are at best to be mistrusted and tolerated – he does not use patriotism as a justification for war and conquest. Despite his youthful enthusiasm for military parades, he has a genuine horror of war and, in any case, believes that too close a contact with foreigners is disruptive of the republic.

At this point we can accept that what Rousseau is writing about is a genuine political community. Its citizens are autonomous beings, who make judgments about their form of life in a spirit of concord. But the weak point in this community, as Rousseau recognizes, is the faculty of judgment. If citizens are left to themselves to make their judgments, then the result is unlikely to be supportive of civic or community life, for their judgment cannot be relied upon. This is partly because men are beings of limited intelligence, and partly because of the indestructible nature of their particular wills. Thus, even in the most perfectly created civil society, citizens have no initiative in proposing legislative measures, but only the responsibility of

pronouncing on proposals put to them, as sovereign, by the government. And of course, in its beginnings, a people is too 'blind' to
recognize what kind of constitution it needs. The lawgiver, denied
the use of force and rational argument, must invest his proposals
with divine authority in order to make them acceptable. In this way
the lawgiver forms a people, but not with any prospect of per-
manence unless other means are instituted to support the habits of
citizenship, so that the judgments citizens make will be in accord with
a genuine form of civic life. If their faculty of judgment is, thus, weak,
the questions which ultimately arise are how autonomous they are as
citizens, and how genuine is the sentiment of concord that they feel
for each other.

It is certainly with individual happiness that Rousseau is concerned, but this is the happiness of the individual as a purely social
being, and not, as in much of liberal-individualist thinking, as a being
who is somehow independent of society. Rousseau's project is the
creation of social man. Citizenship is not a natural form of life –
though it is, for Rousseau, in accordance with what man's nature can
become – nor is it one which man would spontaneously choose. It is,
thus, something that has to be prepared for, and something which,
thereafter, has to be sustained. It was Rousseau's position that men
are a product of the society in which they live, and in particular of its
political institutions. This position is, perhaps, less exceptional today
than it was when he was writing. The issue, therefore, was between
either letting the formative influences work upon man in a hap-
hazard manner, or becoming more systematic about man's education
and his introduction into social life. The most likely result of the former choice was the prolongation of man's current misery, for it was
not to be expected that the holders of political power would seek to
bring about changes which, though they might result in human happiness, would, in the end, undermine their power. At least the second
choice, if ever it should be in prospect, held out the hope of happiness and, Rousseau thought, it was what men would give their
rational assent to if only they were given the option. The choice is,
thus, not between an autonomous form of life as a result of random
influences and a systematically conditioned form of life – all forms of
life are conditioned, and men are inescapably social beings. In this
context, autonomy means the ability to give rational assent. Though
man was, for Rousseau, a being of limited intelligence, he did possess
this much rationality. Just as much as he was, therefore, in this respect autonomous, we can also accept that his 'sentiments of
sociability' are genuine, even though they have to be supported by
various forms of public entertainment and a civil religion. For man
to do his duty, to follow his conscience, always involves inner

struggle. Without such a struggle, man would not be human; he would be a saint, or a god.

Chapter five

Hegel: rational freedom in the ethical community

Hegel writes about the state as a form of community. He is concerned with a form of human freedom – based on will, commitment and action – that can be only realized in such a state. There is, however, a notable difference between *The Philosophy of History*, a work which considers historically the abstract arguments of the earlier *The Phenomenology of Spirit*, and his major work on political thought, *The Philosophy of Right*. In *The Philosophy of History*, a conception of freedom is put forward as the goal of history which is only reached when *all* humankind has achieved such freedom and practises it: the thrust is democratic. In *The Philosophy of Right*, on the other hand, where Hegel considers the political arrangements for the realization of human freedom in the context of the modern world, one is left wondering about the scope for citizen action within the state: it appears extremely narrow. The difficulty, thus, is one of locating Hegel in that civic-republican tradition in which it is relatively easy to place both Machiavelli and Rousseau. The difficulty may be stated in the following terms: for Machiavelli and Rousseau, the effort required from citizens was both a cognitive and a conative one – that is, the effort was one which required citizens to come to knowledge and understanding of their conditions, and to will and act as citizens accordingly. For Hegel, on the other hand, the conative aspect – the aspect of will – is eroded between *The Philosophy of History* and *The Philosophy of Right*, and the cognitive aspect correspondingly heightened. Citizens were required less to act in the political world – should one still, then, call them 'citizens'? – than to come to an understanding of the necessary nature of the historical process which culminated, for the present, in the state. 'Freedom' was to be based on that integration into the community which comes from such understanding. This is rather different from that freedom, based upon will and action in the political arena, which Hegel himself had seemed to prefigure in *The Philosophy of History*, and which is so prominent a feature of citizenship in the political thought of

Machiavelli and Rousseau.

Despite these difficulties, we must nevertheless pay attention to Hegel's thought: first, because of what he does say in *The Philosophy of History* and second, because he does write about human freedom and community in the context of the large modern state. He thus has things to say which either were not or could not be said by Machiavelli or Rousseau, and which are highly pertinent to any modern consideration of the republican tradition. His thought was not a simple rehearsal of their themes, though he looked back to both, as he did to ancient Greece. He was concerned with how history had moved on irreversibly from earlier times, and with what, in conditions of modernity, human freedom could possibly mean. If he does seem to depart from the idea of citizenship integral to the republican tradition, it was not from want of trying to incorporate in his political thinking that freedom upon which, alone, the practice of citizenship depended.

History as the progress of spirit

Like Rousseau, Hegel believes that human history is an intelligible process which is irreversible. Unlike Rousseau, he did not start from the state of nature but from an idealized picture of the ethical polity of fifth-century Greece. He did share with Rousseau, however, and in a similar way, a preoccupation with human freedom, which he conceived in terms of will. Man was free if his will was free, and his will could only be free if his personal goals were in inextricable harmony with the public ends of the polity. Hegel thought that man had experienced such harmony at one stage in the ancient Greek *polis*. Man had then lived an ethical life with no inner conflicts in his heart or soul, and had thus felt completely at home in the life of the *polis*. It made no demands upon him that he was not ready to meet, even to the extent of sacrificing his life for it. He did not think of public institutions as somehow external to him. They were not extensions of his self and will, so much as intrusions and percolations by which he identified himself not as this or that particular individual, but as Athenian.

We will return to Hegel's account of Greek life. The important point to note at this stage is that Hegel knew that man's present condition could not be described as a state of harmony: it could more appropriately be described as an experience of alienation or estrangement. There was nothing that integrated him into the political world: he was excluded from it, being at most and at best a bearer of individual rights against the state. He would find some solace for this exclusion in religion, but this could not solve the problem of his worldly estrangement, for Christianity postulated a goal for him which he could not reach on this earth. Because of his separation, therefore, from both the secular and the spiritual worlds, man experienced a profound sense of disharmony. Hegel's problem, thus, was to provide an account of those conditions in which modern man might find a form of harmonious life, in which he could be free. To what extent was the harmony of the Greek *polis*, the perfect integration of man into his world, now realizable? Hegel gave his answer to this question in terms of the unity within man of the 'particular' and the 'universal', which he described as 'ethical life'. We must therefore examine what Hegel meant by such concepts.

We have said that, for Hegel, history is an intelligible process, but it is also a rational process[1] because it has a goal or final consummation: human freedom. Human freedom is that harmony which is achieved when the particular goals of individuals are at one with the universal ends of the state. This is not altogether dissimilar from the vision of harmony which Rousseau presented in the first part of the *Social Contract*, though Rousseau, of course, did not postulate this vision as a goal of history; for him it was a yardstick against which to measure man's achievement. Again, for Rousseau, the 'universal' ends were given by a sovereign people reflecting conscientiously on their common interests, and expressing the product of these reflections as the general will. The ends are not so given for Hegel. The universal ends of the state are given by 'Spirit', but they only have force in human history – and Spirit itself only has force in human history – when both ends and Spirit are willed, consciously or unconsciously, by particular individuals. So the course of human history is one in which the universality of Spirit gradually realizes itself in the activity of man, and also one in which man moves from unconscious to conscious willing of the ends which Spirit prescribes. When Spirit is thus fully realized, or particularized, in the consciousness of man, and when man has fully incorporated the universality of Spirit, then is the goal of human history reached. Man is then, and only then, truly free, in the sense of self-consciously living harmoniously both within himself and with his world. This is the world of the ethical community: the state. All the above requires substantial explanation if we are not to conclude, with Marx, that Hegel's political thought is an exercise in 'mystification'.[2]

It is Hegel's claim that history has a goal or purpose, and that this purpose is provided by, or encapsulated in – or that it simply *is* – 'Spirit'. Spirit is Hegel's analogue for God, in the sense that it supplies the underlying rationale for man's existence; but Spirit is not God, or at least not the Christian God. For, whereas at least one of the characteristics of the Christian God is omnipotence, Spirit is powerless unless it finds a place in the activity of man, that is, in 'the need, the instinct, the inclination, and passion of man' (*RH*, 28). Throughout history, though, man is the thoroughly unconscious agent of Spirit. It is only when history is approaching the achievement or consummation of the purpose provided for it by Spirit that man becomes conscious of Spirit. Only then is man fully aware of the rationality of history. The historical process may thus be interpreted as one in which man gradually approaches knowledge of Spirit, which is self-knowledge – that is, knowledge of himself as incorporating within himself the universality of the ends of history. The purpose *provided by* Spirit is to give rationality to the historical process: the purpose *of* Spirit is to have this rationality realized in the activity of man. Thus, from a different perspective, the historical process is one in which Spirit gradually realizes itself in man's consciousness. When this happens, the universality of Spirit is allied with the particularity of man in a unity which represents both Spirit's and man's full self-consciousness. In self-consciousness two things coincide: 'first, *that* I know and secondly, *what* I know' (*RH*, 23). In self-consciousness, thus, both Spirit and man know themselves, and since they only come to this gradually, the process is one of becoming, of making actual the potential which is within both man and Spirit.

The goal or purpose of history, therefore, is something which is present at history's beginnings as potentiality: 'the first traces of Spirit virtually contain the whole of history' (*RH*, 23). At the beginning, man does not know the purpose of history, nor does he know during the course of history that in acting as he does he is bringing about the realization of this purpose. There is thus both necessity and freedom in history: necessity in its purpose, freedom in the activity of man. Here 'necessity' refers to 'the immanent development of Spirit, existing in and for itself'; and 'freedom' to 'the interests contained in man's conscious volitions' (*RH*, 31–2). The culmination of history is the overcoming in unity of this opposition between freedom and necessity. This is the higher form of self-conscious freedom. Thus in coming to self-consciousness man is not just gaining knowledge of Spirit, but is recognizing the necessity of its immanent purpose. It is in his recognition of, and his reconciliation to, the necessity of this purpose that man's self-knowledge, his self-consciousness, his true freedom consist. He is free only when 'knowing, believing, and willing the universal'. Here his own particular, or subjective, will has found its union with the rational, or universal, will. This union takes place in 'the moral whole' which is 'the *State*' (*RH*, 49). It is necessary, in other words, for the state to exist in order that Spirit can fulfil its purpose, and man enjoy a harmonious, self-consciously ethical – and, therefore, free – life. It is in the state that the opposition between necessity and freedom is overcome. Man does not exist in order that the state be; he is not the means, and the state the end. Just as Spirit can only realize its purpose through the activity of man, so, too, the state, as 'moral whole', is nothing without man's active will: 'the state is not the abstract confronting the citizens; they are part of it, like members of an organic body, where no member is end and none is means' (*RH*, 52). Nevertheless, the state, like Spirit, does have some kind of ontological priority in the sense that it defines both who and what man is:

> All the value man has, all spiritual reality, he has only through the state. For his spiritual reality is the knowing presence to him of his own essence, of rationality, of its objective, immediate actuality present in and for him. Only thus is he truly a consciousness, only thus does he partake in morality, in the legal and moral life of the state.
>
> (*RH*, 52–3)

This ontological priority of the state is not, however, also a moral priority. It is simply that it is in relation to the state that everything else finds its proper place, for the state represents the union between the particular and the universal:

> The State, thus, is the foundation and center of the other concrete aspects of national life, of art, law, morality, religion, science. All spiritual activity, then, has the aim of becoming conscious of this union, that is, of its freedom .... The universal which appears and becomes known in the state, the form into which is cast all reality, constitutes what is generally called the *culture* of a nation. The definite content, however, which receives the form of universality and is contained in the concrete reality of the State, is the *spirit of the people*.
>
> (*RH*, 63)

We have yet to inquire into the nature of this state, into the kind of harmony, or union of particular and universal in ethical life, which is both the precondition and the practice of human freedom. For this, we must return to Hegel's discussion of the Greek *polis*.

What the Greek *polis* possessed, and what Hegel thought the modern state in its necessary potential possessed as well, was unity and harmony: 'ethical life'. But they possessed this attribute in different ways. The difference centred on the fact that the Greek experienced his unity with the *polis*, and lived his ethical life, automatically and without thinking about it. In other words, he lived in unreflective identity with the *polis* and its ethical order, its customs, laws and religion. As Hegel put it in *The Philosophy of Right*: 'The subject is thus directly linked to the ethical order by a relation which is more like an identity than even the relation of faith or trust'.[3] He added the remark: 'For example, it is one thing to be a pagan, a different thing to believe in a pagan religion' (*PR*, 147R).

Everything about Greek life – its art, its language, its theatre, its games and festivals, its customs and traditions, its religion, its laws and political forms – served to integrate every Greek into an immediate (that is, an unmediated or unreflective) unity and harmony:

> Of the Greeks in the first and genuine form of their freedom, we may assert, that they had no conscience; the habit of living for their country without further analysis or reflection, was the principle dominant among them. The consideration of the State in the abstract – which to our understanding is the essential point – was alien to them. Their grand object was their country in its living and real aspect; *this actual* Athens, this Sparta, these Temples, these Altars, this form of social life, this union of fellow-citizens, these manners and customs. To the Greek his country was a necessary of life, without which existence was impossible.[4]

What the Greek lacked was a consciousness of his own individuality and 'subjective' freedom. His life was one of 'objective' freedom: he lived a free life, indeed, but without knowing it, he lived in 'unconscious unity' with the *polis* (*PH*, 107). 'Subjective' freedom – that is, freedom based upon reflection and insight into his condition and upon will as expressive of his individuality – was, by contrast, precisely what modern man did possess (*PH*, 104). What the Greek, thus, experienced instinctively, modern man had to achieve self-consciously after due reflection. The unity and harmony of the ethical life of modern man in the potentiality of the modern state was, thus, to be a mediated one – mediated, that is, by his own conscience and consciousness, and by a variety of institutional forms foreign to the Greek *polis*. This had to be, because the modern world was not the Greek world. Nevertheless, it was because ethical life had once been experienced that it was possible to conceive of it again being achieved, albeit under different circumstances and in a different form. What had to be taken account of were the ways in which man and the world had changed over time: in other words, what had to be considered was the progress of Spirit itself.

The world of the Greek *polis* was not static, and two developments occurred which shattered its integrated and unmediated harmony. The first was when people started to question the basis of the Greek ethical order, a development in which, for Hegel, Socrates is the critical figure. The second was the absorption of the Greek world into the Roman which, by vastly increasing the size of the political unit, cut man off from any integral part in political life. The effect of these twin occurrences was to usher in the era of the 'unhappy Consciousness',[5] which could then only find a meaning for life not just outside the *polis*, but beyond this world, in the Christian after-life.

The principle of Greek corruption lies, Hegel tells us is *The Philosophy of History*, in '*subjectivity obtaining emancipation for itself*', and subjectivity obtains this emancipation in 'Thought'. The 'concrete vitality' of the Greeks was their 'Customary Morality – a life for Religion, for the State, without further reflection, and without analysis leading to abstract definitions'. Thought betokens the questioning and investigation of everything: laws, customs, traditions, political forms – even religion – now require justification. Reasons have to be given as to why this *polis*, with its ethical order, should be supported. Thought, 'as a result of its investigations ... forms for itself an idea of an improved state of society, and demands that this ideal should take the place of things as they are'. It was the Sophists who were involved in the 'self-emancipation of Thought', in making man 'the measure of all things'. And it was in Socrates that 'the principle of subjectivity – of the absolute inherent independence of Thought – attained free expression' (*PH*, 267–9). Hegel's assessment of the destructiveness of Socrates is worth quoting at some length:

> The Greeks had a *customary* morality; but Socrates undertook to teach them what moral virtues, duties, etc., were. The moral man is not he who merely wills and does that which is right – not the merely innocent man – but he who has the consciousness of what he is doing. Socrates – in assigning to insight, to conviction, the determination of man's actions – posited the Individual as capable of a final moral decision, in contraposition to Country and to Customary Morality, and thus made himself an Oracle, in the Greek sense .... The principle of Socrates manifests a revolutionary aspect towards the Athenian State; for the peculiarity of this State was, that Customary Morality was the form in which its existence was moulded, viz – an inseparable connection of Thought with actual life. When Socrates wishes to induce his friends to reflection, the discourse has always a negative tone; he brings them to the consciousness that they do not know what the Right is (*PH*, 269–70).

The Athenians recognized what Socrates was doing, and had done. He was undermining the foundations of Greek ethical order. They condemned him to die. Once such questioning had begun, however, there was no prospect of returning to the *status quo ante*. For what was involved was an irreversible development of the individual in the direction of self-consciousness. Man now knows himself to be the 'measure' of his political arrangements and ethical commitments. If he makes reference to the gods or to his country, then these are considerations among others, and not necessarily overriding. Moreover, for Hegel, and despite the sometimes regretful tone of his comments – he writes, for instance, of 'that beautiful and moral necessity of united life in the Polis' (*PH*, 295) – such a development was necessary, because it was in accordance with Spirit. It was necessary, in other words, for the progress of Spirit that the Greek *polis* be superseded, despite the beauty of its creation – in *The Philosophy of History* Hegel called it 'The Political Work of Art' (*PH*, 250).

As if Socratic questioning were not enough to set man apart from his ethical order, the absorption of the Greek world into the much larger Roman one forever destroyed that close integration into political life which had been characteristic of the Greek citizen in his *polis*. The individual's mind had been set free, but he was now no more than an atomized unit in a large political order in whose determination he did not participate; nor did he necessarily endorse it. What he possessed to reinforce and emphasize his separateness was the legal right to person and property. What thus characterized Roman political order was conflict between these atomized bearers of legal rights; there was lacking any 'substantial national unity' (*PH*, 295). There was some respite, as civil discord was overcome during the time of the Roman republic when it directed its energies outward to the creation of an empire, but as soon as Caesar triumphed, and the achievements of the republic were transformed into personalized power, Rome returned to its true principles. 'The aim of patriotism – that of preserving the State – ceases when the lust of personal dominion becomes the impelling passion. The citizens were alienated from the State, for they found in it no objective satisfaction' (*PH*, 312).

Hegel describes this atomized world of legal relations as one of 'individual subjectivity ... entirely emancipated from control .... The springs of action are none other than desire, lust, passion, fancy – in short, caprice absolutely unfettered' (*PH*, 315). The development of private right 'involved the decay of political life' (*PH*, 317). Man's atomized condition is far from satisfactory to him; it is alien, it does not speak to his soul. The possession of private, legal right does not fulfil his personality. The lack of ethical bonds leaves him 'a divided and discordant being' with a 'longing to transcend this condition of [his] soul' (*PH*, 320–1). In such circumstances Christianity makes its appeal. For Christianity makes the suffering and misery of this world intelligible. Suffering and misery are 'henceforth recognized as [the] instrument necessary for producing the unity of man with God' (*PH*, 324).

According to Christ, 'outward sufferings, as such, are not to be feared or fled from, for they are nothing as compared with that glory' – that is, the glory of the Kingdom of God (*PH*, 327). Christianity, however, does not just remain the refuge for 'the unhappy consciousness'; it becomes a hierarchical Church. To the individual member of the Christian community, the Church becomes 'an authority for the truth and for the relation of each individual to the truth, determining how he should conduct himself so as to act in accordance with the Truth'. The existence of such authority 'shows that human subjectivity in its proper form has not yet developed itself ... the human will is emancipated only abstractly – not in its concrete reality' (*PH*, 332–3). In Christianity man has recognized Spirit, but has located its essence in another world and not in this one; in the Church he has placed a barrier, in the form of a priesthood, to his immediate access to Spirit, and thus lost part of that freedom he acquired with the break-up of the Greek *polis*.

The achievement of the Romano-Christian world is the partial emancipation of the human will, and the recognition that Spirit is a force in human affairs. What remains to be done is to bring these into correspondence and harmony with one another, and this is the task of the Germanic world, by which Hegel broadly means Protestant Northern Europe, and possibly North America (see *PH*, 84–7). In these circumstances, yet fully to come, Reason – as 'Thought determining itself in absolute freedom' (*RH*, 15) – will come into its own. Religion is not to be discarded: on the contrary, it is to be freed from its ecclesiastical hierarchy, and its promise of harmony is to be brought down to earth, if not secularized. The former aim is achieved in the Protestant Reformation, with Luther as the key figure responsible for 'the restoration of Christian freedom' (*PH*, 344),[6] which acts as the spur to the achievement of freedom in the secular realm. The latter aim is to be realized in a rationalized state, a state informed by the true principle of religion. At this stage, just prior to his consideration of the Germanic world, the term 'Religion' appears to stand for both Spirit and Reason, in Hegel's language. He sums up the 'vocation' of the Germanic world as follows:

> Reason in general is the Positive Existence of Spirit, divine as well as human ... Religion as such, is Reason in the soul and heart ... it is a temple in which Truth and Freedom in God are presented to the conceptive faculty: the State, on the other hand, regulated by the self-same Reason, is a temple of Human Freedom concerned with the perception and volition of a reality, whose purport may itself be called divine. Thus Freedom in the State is preserved and established by Religion, since moral rectitude in the State is only the carrying out of that which constitutes the fundamental prin-

ciple of Religion. The process displayed in History is only the manifestation of Religion as Human Reason – the production of the religious principle which dwells in the heart of man, in the form of Secular Freedom. Thus discord between the inner life of the heart and the actual world is removed.

(PH, 335)

Before moving on to discuss the analysis which Hegel presents of the modern state in *The Philosophy of Right*, it is necessary to pause and note what was identified earlier as the clear democratic thrust of his philosophical review of human history. He writes of the freedom which is achieved in the rational state as follows:

Secular life is the positive and definite embodiment of the Spiritual Kingdom – the Kingdom of the *Will* manifesting itself in outward existence ....

The Freedom of the will *per se*, is the principal and substantial basis of all Right – is itself absolute, inherently eternal Right, and the Supreme Right in comparison with other specific Rights; nay, it is even that by which Man becomes Man, and is therefore the fundamental principle of Spirit .... Rationality of Will is none other than the maintaining of one's self in pure Freedom – willing this and this alone – Right purely for the sake of Right. Duty purely for the sake of Duty.

(PH, 442–3)

Such a rational will has a disposition, not just to the customary observance of, or acquiescence in, laws, but to

the cordial recognition of laws and the Constitution as in principle fixed and immutable, and of the supreme obligation of individuals to subject their particular wills to them. There may be various opinions and views respecting laws, constitution and government, but there must be a disposition on the part of the citizen to regard all these opinions as subordinate to the substantial interest of the State, and to insist upon them no further than that interest will allow; moreover nothing must be considered higher and more sacred than good will towards the State.

(PH, 449)

We might almost be back in Rousseau's territory here. The state has a sanctity because it is the guarantor – the only guarantor – of rational freedom: a rational freedom based upon will and, from the appearance of these passages, a freedom available to all men, or at least to all citizens. This I take to be the democratic thrust of Hegel's discussion. However, whereas for Rousseau such a will was rational

– or 'general' to use his term – only if it both genuinely expressed common interest and was expressed as such by each citizen within an appropriate institutional setting, the same cannot be said for Hegel. For him it is Spirit which accounts for the rationality of human will and provides it with its content. What is required for the will of citizens to be rational is recognition of this. There does not seem to be much scope for any deliberative effort on the part of citizens. Whether or not they deliberate, whether or not they have an institutional framework for registering the results of their deliberations, makes no difference to the rationality of their will, for this is independent of them and provided by Spirit. This makes the 'will' that Hegel is writing about a much weaker concept in respect of individuals than Rousseau's 'will', and, as we shall see, allows Hegel to escape the democratic hook. 'Will' may be the basis of the state, but it is not upon will that man's freedom is founded. Man's freedom rests upon his acknowledging rational necessity, acknowledging the rationality of Spirit. It is an effort of cognition that is demanded of him, not an effort of conation. Indeed, in the Preface at the very beginning of *The Philosophy of Right*, Hegel writes that it is not the business of philosophy to prescribe, but only to provide understanding. The purpose of the book 'is to be nothing other than the endeavour to apprehend and portray the State as something inherently rational'. Philosophy cannot consist in 'teaching the State what it ought to be; it can only show how the State, the ethical universe, is to be understood' (*PR*, Preface). The object of philosophy is to 'reconcile' man to the rationality of his world.

We do not need to follow all the dialectical stages of the argument by which Hegel establishes the philosophical foundations of the state, since our concern is not with philosophical justification, but with the extent to which Hegel's view of the state and its structure exemplifies a valid combination or endorsement of the ideas of citizenship and community. It has been noted that, for Hegel, the historical process involves a development from unmediated harmony (Greece), through separation and alienation (the Romano-Christian world until the French Revolution), to the mediated harmony which is found in the modern state. Corresponding to this chronological pattern of change there are, in the modern state, three ontological levels of ethical life: in the family, in the sphere of civil society, and in the realm of the state proper. Both chronologically – as man more nearly approaches the present – and ontologically, as he ascends the levels of ethical life, man becomes progressively more self-consciously free as he incorporates the universality of Spirit in his rational will. It is in *The Philosophy of Right* that Hegel discusses these levels of ethical life, and to which we now, thus, turn.

The family and civil society

The ethical order is that order in which man lives a free, and therefore rational, life to the extent that he self-consciously incorporates into his own will the principles of that order. Now, an ethical order is not any kind of order; it is an order of a particular kind. It is an order whose principles are the universal ends of Spirit. These principles are 'the ethical powers which regulate the life of individuals' (*PR*, 145), and from one perspective they have the appearance of something set over against the individual, since they are authoritative for him. 'On the other hand', Hegel continues,

> they are not something alien to the subject. On the contrary, his spirit bears witness to them as to its own essence, the essence in which he has a feeling of his selfhood, and in which he lives as in his own element which is not distinguished from himself.
>
> (*PR*, 147)

When these ethical powers are substantively embodied in laws and institutions, they impose duties upon the individual: the bond of duty so created, however, is not a restriction upon the individual, for it is on the acknowledgment of duty that 'the individual finds his liberation' from dependence upon natural impulse: 'In duty the individual acquires his substantive freedom' (*PR*, 149). In so living an ethical life, the individual recognizes that 'the end which moves him to act [is] the universal', but more than this, it is within the context of the stability of such a life that he is able to pursue and attain his particular ends (*PR*, 152):

> The right of individuals to be subjectively destined to freedom is fulfilled when they belong to an actual ethical order, because their conviction of their freedom finds its truth in such an objective order, and it is in an ethical order that they are actually in possession of their own essence or their own inner universality.
>
> (*PR*, 153)

As Hegel later concludes, 'in this identity of the universal will with the particular will, right and duty coalesce' (*PR*, 155).

The family is the first 'moment' of ethical life. Its ethical principle is love as a natural and unreflective feeling. Its basis is the marriage bond, which Hegel claims 'is one of the absolute principles on which the ethical life of a community depends' (*PR*, 167R). It has physical extension in the institution of private property (*PR*, 169), but only becomes explicit 'a spiritual unity' with children (*PR*, 173). Children are potential adults, and thus the duty of parents is to prepare their children accordingly, and in this respect education has a twofold task:

one of positively equipping children 'with the foundation of an ethical life'; and the other, of negatively raising them 'out of the instinctive, physical, level on which they are originally, to self-subsistence and freedom of personality'. In this way they are given the 'power to leave the natural unity of the family' (*PR*, 175). At the end of the process of education, thus, the family is ethically dissolved, the sons to become 'heads of new families', the daughters to become 'wives' (*PR*, 177): as the children leave, the family 'disintegrates ... into a plurality of families', and this disintegration marks the transition to the next level of ethical life, which is civil society (*PR*, 181). Looked at historically, this disintegration can be seem as the peaceful expansion of a family into 'a people, i.e. a nation, which thus has a common natural origin' (*PR*, 181R). But after the family, it is civil society which is the next moment of ethical life.

At first sight, it seems rather odd to designate civil society one of the 'moments' of ethical life, for it is the realm in which private interest and particular will have sway. Nevertheless, Hegel wishes to show that the actual attainment of selfish ends gives rise to 'a system of complete interdependence' (*PR*, 183), which thus marks the mediation of particular ends by the universal, even though universality is not present as intention in the mind and will of the 'burghers' of civil society (*PR*, 187). Civil society itself contains three 'moments': 'the System of Needs', by which men through their work come, in the division of labour, to satisfy the needs of all others; 'the Administration of Justice', which is concerned with the protection of freedom and property; and the institutions of 'the Police', or public authority, and 'the Corporation', which 'care for particular interests as a common interest' (*PR*, 188).

In the System of Needs, both the division of labour and the multiplication of needs create and make necessary everywhere 'the dependence of men on one another and their reciprocal relation in the satisfaction of their other needs' (*PR*, 198). This interdependence represents 'the mediation of the particular through the universal, with the result that each man in earning, producing, and enjoying on his own account is *eo ipso* producing and earning for the enjoyment of everyone else' (*PR*, 199). But men are not equal either in skill or resources, and in time such inequalities become systematically 'crystallized' into classes 'to one or other of which individuals are assigned' (*PR*, 200–1). There are three classes: the 'immediate' or agricultural class, the 'reflective' or business class, and the 'universal' class of civil servants (*PR*, 202).

The nature of agricultural production – its seasonality – means that it is a 'mode of subsistence ... which owes comparatively little to reflection and independence of will'. The correct moment for the harvest, for example, is as naturally determined as the fact that cows require milking every day. The ethical life of such a mode is therefore 'immediate, resting on family relationship and trust' (*PR*, 203). The concern of the business class is with the adaptation of raw materials, and this requires 'reflection and intelligence' to anticipate men's needs, and to coordinate the work involved in satisfying them: crafts-manship, manufacture and trade are all involved (*PR*, 204). The universal class of civil servants is preoccupied with 'the universal interests of the community', and, in being paid by the state, 'finds its satisfaction in its work for the universal' (*PR*, 205). Such a division of civil society into classes reflects the rational necessity of the tasks to be performed, but, whereas the classes themselves may be fixed, any particular person's class is not so determined. This depends upon a variety of factors, some of which are within the individual's control (*PR*, 206). Furthermore, and as we shall come to see in discussion of the state proper, the classes become locked into a system of institutional interdependence, particularly in the Assembly of Estates.

The second 'moment' of civil society is the Administration of Justice. Civil society is the realm in which individuals enjoy rights to person and property. It is by claiming such rights that individuals give expression to their personality and particularity. But such rights only become 'determinate' when they have 'the form of being posited as positive law' (*PR*, 213). It is this which the Administration of Justice is designed to secure and advance. For the proper protection of rights and freedom it is necessary that such laws 'be made universally known' (*PR*, 215), and that court procedures be both 'demonstrable' (*PR*, 222) and public, for 'an integral part of justice is the confidence which citizens have in it' (*PR*, 224). At all events, the danger to be guarded against is that knowledge of the law, and of court procedures, becomes 'the property of a class which makes itself an exclusive clique by the use of a terminology like a foreign tongue to those whose rights are at issue' (*PR*, 228). If such circumstances should prevail, then justice is empty. In law, the particularity of individual rights partakes of universality, in the sense that positive law is universal, holding irrespective of persons. A further step towards unity is taken in the third 'moment' of civil society: the Police, or public authority, and the Corporation.

The possibility exists in civil society for securing the livelihood and welfare of every individual, but the possibility is not always realized. The Administration of Justice ensures that the rights necessary for individual pursuit of livelihood and welfare are protected, but there are many other tasks for which some form of public authority is required. Thus, private actions often have unforeseen consequences which escape the agent's control, and which – either potentially or actually – injure others. While there is no hard and fast line to be drawn between what is or is not injurious, suspicious, or to be forbidden, public authority must make some determinations here in accordance with 'custom, the spirit of the rest of the constitution, contemporary conditions, the crisis of the hour, and so forth' (*PR*, 232–4). Further, the interconnectedness of the System of Needs makes many matters of common concern. 'These universal activities and organizations of general utility' – ensuring, for instance, the adequate functioning of the market – 'call for the oversight and care of the public authority' (*PR*, 235). Again, 'the differing interests of producers and consumers may come into collision', and some balance needs to be consciously struck between them – in the matter, for example, of fixing prices, or ensuring that the public is not defrauded (*PR*, 236). Public authority also has the right and duty to superintend and influence education: 'Society's right here is paramount over the arbitrary and contingent preferences of parents' (*PR*, 239). Finally, public authority is required to secure that 'every single person's livelihood and welfare be treated and actualized as a right' (*PR*, 230). While individual extravagance, if it inhibits the ability of families to provide for themselves, is to be frowned upon even if not specifically penalized (*PR*, 240), factors grounded in circumstances beyond their control may reduce men to poverty. The poor, nevertheless, have the same needs as other members of civil society for subsistence, education, health and even religion. If they cannot secure assistance from either family or charitable organizations, public authority has the duty to step in and take 'the place of the family' (*PR*, 241–2). Hegel may not have had a solution for the problem of poverty, in the sense of thinking that it could at some time be made to disappear, but he did regard it as a responsibility which fell properly within the domain of public authority. The place of the poor in Hegel's overall political arrangements is another question, and will be considered later. The primary purpose of public authority is thus to attend to common interests as these are revealed by the individual pursuit of particular ends within civil society. In this way, a further element of universality is introduced to reinforce that which results from the interdependence revealed in the System of Needs. But it is in the Corporation that ethical life finds its first conscious manifestation in civil society, that the immanence of ethical life first becomes explicit (*PR*, 249).

The agricultural class has immediate universality or ethical life within itself by virtue of the unreflective nature of its mode of subsistence and of its grounding in family relationships of love and trust. The bureaucracy, or civil service, 'is universal in character and so has the universal explicitly as its ground and as the aim of its activity'. So, the Corporation is specially appropriate to the business class

(*PR*, 250). It is an organization of manufacturers and traders. From the point of view of its members, the purpose of the Corporation is universal, though in relation to civil society it is particular: 'Hence a selfish purpose, directed towards its particular self-interest, apprehends and evinces itself at the same time as universal' (*PR*, 251). The Corporation member – manufacturer, businessman, trader, artisan – 'belongs to a whole which is itself an organ of the entire society', and, as a member, 'is actively concerned in promoting the comparatively disinterested end of the whole' (*PR*, 253). Without membership in an authorized Corporation, 'an individual is without rank or dignity' (*PR*, 253R), and, as we shall see, is thereby denied any political role. This is especially important, for Hegel specifically excludes the poor from membership in the Corporation; he is not to be understood as including the 'day labourer', or the 'man who is prepared to undertake casual employment on a single occasion' (*PR*, 252R). To qualify for membership a man must at least have what in nineteenth-century England would have been called 'a trade', and be regularly practising it. It is only as such that he can adequately take part in that aspect of ethical life which civil society permits. The Corporation, thus, is the second – the family was the first – 'ethical root of the State, the one planted in civil society' (*PR*, 255). But the Corporation has an added importance for ethical life, in that modern political conditions do not allow many citizens to have a direct role in the work of the State. It is thus essential 'to provide men – ethical entities – with work of a public character over and above their private interest'. Such work is found in the Corporation (*PR*, 255A).

With the Corporation, Hegel has completed his account of civil society. It was a presupposition of civil society that the individual, who is its member, is first of all a person who is conscious of his subjective freedom – that is, he knows himself as this particular free-willed agent rather than any other. Second, and consequently, he is a person who needs to give expression to the individuality of his personality. This he does in his choice of particular ends, as well as in that extension of himself materially, into private property. In these respects, the individual inhabits civil society, which is precisely that realm of human affairs where particular ends are pursued. Hegel has also sought to show that it is in civil society, as well as in the family, that the roots of the universal ethical life of the state proper are to be found. A level of interdependence is entailed in the System of Needs; there is an element of universality in the Administration of Justice, in that positive law protects the universal rights of individuals to person and property. Police authority attends to common interests revealed in the System of Needs, and the Corporation introduces a specific, though limited, form of ethical life in the common purposes which unite its members. The respective spheres of civil society and the family

> constitute the two moments, still ideal moments, whose true ground is the State, although it is from them that the State springs .... The philosophic proof of the concept of the state is this development of ethical life from its immediate phase through civil society, the phase of division, to the State, which reveals itself as the true ground of these phases.
>
> *(PR,* 256R)

What Hegel means here is that, whereas historically the family and civil society are prior to the state, in the sense that the state grows out of them, the state – as the highest embodiment of ethical life – has ontological priority: insofar as the family and civil society exemplify or contribute to the emergence of ethical life, they have justification for their existence. The family and civil society exist, in other words, precisely so that ethical life shall be eventually realized in the state. Thus the state is their 'true ground'. In the context and terminology of *The Philosophy of History*, the modern state appears as the goal or purpose of Spirit, a goal present throughout human history, though only implicit or immanent. Human history has been such as it is *in order that* it should culminate in the modern state. Thus the state is also the 'true ground' of human history, for in it alone is the rational freedom of ethical life realized.

The state as ethical community

In his discussion of ethical life so far, and of the family and civil society, while there are moments of universality in the unreflective, ethical life of the family – and intimations of universality in various aspects of civil society – there is no true recognition of universality until the determination of the public ends of the polity, of the state. It is to this level of universality that the individual must raise and reconcile himself if he would be truly free. It is when this happens that 'the State is the actuality of the ethical Idea'. At that point,

> the State exists immediately in custom, mediately in individual self-consciousness, knowledge, and activity, while self-consciousness in virtue of its sentiment towards the State finds in the State, as its essence and the end and product of its activity, its substantive freedom.
>
> *(PR,* 257)

Hegel's discussion of the modern state is not intended as an endorsement of any actually existing state. He was critical of both Prussia and

England. In *The Philosophy of History*, he locates future development in the North American continent (*PH*, 82–7), but in *The Philosophy of Right* he is concerned only with the culmination of the historical process in the present; neither philosophy nor history have any business with the future: 'It is just as absurd to fancy that a philosophy can transcend its contemporary world as it is to fancy that an individual can overleap his own age, jump over Rhodes' (*PR*, Preface). What philosophy and history have revealed so far is the form which the modern state must take if it is to be in accordance with the purpose of Spirit. This form of the modern state does in many respects seem oddly conservative in view of the stress so far – and throughout – on human freedom, as if it were the aim of humankind, of all men. But this is not to be explained by interpreting *The Philosophy of Right* as a covert apology for the Prussian state of his day, still less for what the Prussian state was later to become. The explanation is to be found elsewhere, and largely in the very size of the modern state. In this respect, the conclusions of Hegel and Rousseau are, perhaps surprisingly, in close coincidence: both argued that the larger the state, the greater the need, on the one hand, for monarchy and the modification of democratic forms, and, on the other, for pluralism, in its federal or corporatist forms.[7]

'The state is the actuality of concrete freedom' (*PR*, 260), by which Hegel means that it is in the state that the individual, self-consciously and deliberately, appropriates the public ends of the polity as his own. Thus the universal ends, which are now the publicly acknowledged expression of Spirit, are joined specifically and intricately with the particularity of the individual. It is in this unity of the universal and the particular in the mind of the individual that 'concrete freedom' exists, and it is in the state that it is made 'actual'. Spirit has come to full fruition in the individual as a member of the state: the individual, by raising himself to the level of the universality of Spirit, has also come into the full realization of his freedom. From the point of view of the family and civil society, the state is their higher authority; it is, however, 'the end immanent within them', and the strength of the state 'lies in unity of its own universal end and aim with the particular interest of individuals' (*PR*, 261). We have already noted that the roots of the ethical life of the state are found in the family and the Corporation, but these latter are also the 'firm foundation' of the citizen's trust in the state and his sentiment towards it: 'They are the pillars of public freedom since in them particular freedom is realized and rational, and therefore there is *implicitly* present even in them the union of freedom and necessity' (*PR*, 265). Public freedom is the freedom of the state to act, or rather to will, which is the unity of thought and action. Particular freedom is rational insofar as it advances this end, and when it is so identified with public freedom, the 'political sentiment' flourishes. This political sentiment is nothing but 'patriotism pure and simple'; it is in general,

> trust ... or the consciousness that my interest, both substantive and particular, is contained and preserved in another's (i.e. in the state's) interest and end, i.e. in the other's relation to me as an individual. In this way, this very other is immediately not an other in my eyes, and in being conscious of this fact, I am free.
>
> (*PR*, 268)

Patriotism is not something which is only called upon in times of crisis, but is rather that sentiment by which individuals jointly recognize that they are members of the same polity. It is essentially 'the sentiment which, in the relationships of our daily life and under ordinary conditions, habitually recognizes that the community is one's substantive groundwork and end' (*PR*, 268R). Both education and religion have a role in promoting this political sentiment (*PR*, 270).

It is in this way that Hegel shows that the state is different from civil society, and that they must not be confused. If they are confused, then the end of the state is no more than that advanced by previous contract theorists like Hobbes and Locke, namely, 'the security and protection of property and personal freedom'. Here, 'the interest of individuals as such becomes the ultimate end of their association, and it follows that membership of the state is something optional'. But it is precisely Hegel's point to deny that membership of the state is open to the kind of choice involved in a contract (see *PR*, 75, 100), for he has been at some pains to emphasize that it is only as a member of the state 'that the individual himself has objectivity, genuine individuality, and an ethical life' (*PR*, 258). The state is his 'groundwork' as man and citizen.

In this philosophical analysis of the state there is the clear implication that the freedom to be gained therein is something which is available to every man – not to every woman, for the 'natural' difference between the sexes makes the family her proper domain (see *PR*, 166) – and that freedom is the freedom of the rational will. It is this which makes the citizen a participant in ethical life. However, when Hegel comes to discuss the constitution of the state (from *PR*, 272 on), this equality is substantially belied. The institutional means by which individuals register this will are restricted to the few. It is more than that in any large state some form of representation is necessary: large sections of the population are simply denied any political role at all – they are excluded from the polity, do not participate in ethical life, and thus in an important sense do not even possess a rational will. Yet the state is, nevertheless, an 'ethical community'

(*PR*, 150R). We must see how far this claim remains substantiated.

Drawing on Montesquieu, Hegel begins his discussion of the constitution of the state by noting 'the necessity for a division of powers within the state'. This division is not to be interpreted as different powers existing in opposition to each other: each, therefore, acting as a check on the pretensions of the others. The division is rather 'the guarantee of public freedom', because it gives expression to the essential difference between the components of the state, a difference which reflects that very particularity which is to be united, in the state, with the universal (*PR*, 272). Without this difference, grounded in particularity, there would be no unity for the state to achieve and express. The three powers of the state are the Legislature, which is 'the power to determine the universal'; the Executive, which is 'the power to subsume single cases and the spheres of particularity under the universal'; and the Crown, which is 'the power of subjectivity, as the will with the power of ultimate decision'. It is in the Crown that 'the different powers are bound into an individual unity which is thus at once the apex and basis of the whole, i.e. of constitutional monarchy' (*PR*, 273). The state, thus, has its unity expressed in the will of the single person of the constitutional monarch, and the constitutional monarch is both the ontological 'groundwork', or 'basis', of all the other 'moments' of the state, and the immanent goal and content, or 'apex', of 'the whole course of world-history' (*PR*, 273R). What makes up the constitution, or way of life, of the state – its 'mind' or Spirit[8] – is more than just its institutions and its laws, but also 'the manners and consciousness of its citizens' (*PR*, 274). It is the Crown, however, that brings unity to the whole.

It is this unity which is 'the fundamental characteristic of the state as a practical entity' (*PR*, 276), the unity of the universality of its constitution and laws with the particularity of their reference to the lives of its inhabitants (*PR*, 275). This is what Hegel calls 'the sovereignty of the state', which

> depends on the fact that the particular functions and powers of the state are not self-subsistent or firmly founded on their own account or in the particular will of the individual functionaries, but have their roots ultimately in the unity of the state as their single self.
>
> (*PR*, 278)

What Hegel means here is that the various institutions which make up the state have no independent existence or justification: their very meaning as the functions and powers that they are derives from the fact that they are parts or 'moments' of the whole which is the state. Rather than being 'constituent' elements of the state, it is the state that 'constitutes' them – that is, it is the state that makes them what they are. This is the sovereignty of the state within itself, 'at home', and Hegel likens it to the unity of an animal organism. What 'constitutes sovereignty is the same characteristic as that in accordance with which the so-called "parts" of an animal organism are not parts but members, moments in an organic whole, whose isolation and independence spell disease' (*PR*, 278R).

The sovereignty, however, has to be made 'actual' – it has to be realized in practice. It is 'will' that makes sovereignty actual, and will is 'the moment of ultimate decision, as the *self-determination* to which everything else reverts and from which everything else derives the beginning of its actuality' (*PR*, 275). The will that makes sovereignty actual must be that of a determinate, single, individual – that is, a monarch (*PR*, 279). This will is the third 'moment' of that whole which is 'the power of the crown' – the other two moments being the universality of law, and the particularity of their reference to individuals (*PR*, 275). The sovereignty of the state is thus the power of the Crown, which is expressed or made actual by the will of the monarch, as a single individual: 'in virtue of this alone is the state *one*' (*PR*, 279). This will of the monarch is neither arbitrary nor absolute, for it is only legitimate if it is rational – that is, in accordance with Spirit. What we are dealing with here, as Hegel repeatedly stresses, is a *constitutional* monarch, not a despot or a tyrant. Sovereignty belongs to the state, and finds its 'actuality' in the will of the monarch. Hegel specifically rejects the Rousseauist idea of 'the sovereignty of the people', which he regards as a 'confused' and 'wild' notion. Without the unity and wholeness provided by a monarch,

> the people is a formless mass and no longer a state. It lacks every one of those determinate characteristics – sovereignty, government, judges, magistrates, class-divisions, etc., – which are to be found only in a whole which is inwardly organized.

Hegel somewhat misrepresents Rousseau here, for it is only when a people is 'inwardly organized' as a 'personality', in Rousseau's eyes by a lawgiver, that it is proper to speak of the sovereignty of the people. Hegel's claim is that such a 'personality' is adequately expressive of 'an inwardly developed, genuinely organic, totality' only when it is located in 'the person of the monarch'. He is drawing attention, here, to the necessity for political leadership, and his argument is that this requires 'a leader' who is uncontaminated by the contingent and the particular. It is this kind of contamination which Hegel suggests is an inevitable characteristic of leaders in democracies and aristocracies, who emerge 'by chance and in accordance with the particular needs of the hour'. A monarch is not so compromised, first because he is always there – 'The King is dead, long live the King' – but more importantly because he has 'the position of a pinnacle, explicitly distinct from, and raised above, all that is particular and conditional' (*PR*, 279R).

Hegel is writing about the position of the monarch in a 'well-organized' and 'stable' constitution. As we have noted, such a monarch is 'constitutional' and therefore does not act 'capriciously'. In stable circumstances, 'he has often no more to do than sign his name. But this name is important. It is the last word beyond which it is impossible to go.' In the ancient world, when decisions had to be made, men consulted and looked for omens and auguries. In the modern world, 'an "I will" must be pronounced by man himself', that is, by a monarch (*PR*, 279A). Furthermore, the *particular* character of any monarch is not at issue, for, 'in a completely organized state, it is only a question of the culminating point of formal decision'. The monarch 'has only to say "yes" and dot the "i", because the throne should be such that the significant thing in its holder is not his particular make-up'. If it is the case that the private character of the monarch has 'prominence', then

> the state is either not fully developed, or else is badly constructed. In a well-organized monarchy, the objective aspect belongs to law alone, and the monarch's part is merely to set to the law the subjective 'I will'.
>
> (*PR*, 280A)

It is important to differentiate the person of the monarch from the power of the Crown. The power of the Crown contains 'three moments', first, the universality of the constitution of the state and its laws; second, the reference of particular cases to this universality – their subsumption under the universal; and last, a determinate will, that of the monarch, to make the unity of these moments actual (*PR*, 275). The monarch, thus, is part, but not the whole, of the power of the Crown. It is the unity of the three moments which constitutes the power of the Crown, or the sovereignty of the state.

So far, what Hegel has examined is the third of these 'moments', that which is concerned with the unity of the whole, and with the will which makes that unity actual. He has now to consider the other two moments: that which concerns the reference of the particular to the universal - the Executive; and that which determines the nature and character of the universal - the Legislature. Here, perhaps, we move on to more straightforward, though no less contentious, terrain.

Executive power is the task of 'subsuming the particular under the universal', and in this are included all those functions in civil society which have already been discussed under the Administration of Justice, and various aspects of the work of the Police, or public authority (*PR*, 287). In this section, however, Hegel is concerned with 'the maintenance of the state's universal interest'. This task belongs to the universal class of civil servants and involves bringing the particular rights guaranteed to citizens, and exercised by them, in civil society, into conformity with the universality of law (*PR*, 289). Struggle must be expected here:

> Just as civil society is the battlefield where everyone's individual private interest meets everyone else's, so here we have the struggle (a) of private interests against particular matters of common concern and (b) of both of these together against the organization of the state and its higher outlook.

In these struggles, civil servants are assisted by the associations of civil society, in particular by the Corporations. Indeed, Hegel goes so far as to claim that 'the corporation mind ... is now inwardly converted into the mind of the state, since it finds in the state the means of maintaining its particular ends'. Further, it is in the Corporation mind that 'the secret of the patriotism of the citizens' lies, for 'they know that state as their substance, because it is the state that maintains their particular spheres of interest together with the title, authority, and welfare of these' (*PR*, 289R). This is very reminiscent of what Machiavelli claimed for the attachment of citizens to the republic. Their preparedness to fight for the republic, and if necessary die for it, was based on their recognition that it was in the republic that they had their homes, families and livelihoods. In protecting the republic, they were protecting their possibility of enjoying these. In the Corporations, 'the individual finds protection in the exercise of his rights and so links his private interests with the maintenance of the whole' (*PR*, 290A). Hegel has more to say about patriotism in a later section dealing with the relationship between sovereign states (*PR*, 321–9). For the moment, he is concerned with the nature and functions of the universal class of civil servants.

Occupation of office in the civil service is based solely on 'knowledge and proof of ability', and thus is open to anyone who qualifies (*PR*, 291). The tenure of a civil servant is conditional upon his fulfilling the duties of his office:

> What the service of the state really requires is that men shall forego the selfish and capricious satisfaction of their subjective ends; by this sacrifice, they acquire the right to find their satisfaction in, but only in, the dutiful discharge of their public functions.
>
> (*PR*, 294R)

In a 'well-organized' state, this sacrifice is made, but Hegel is alive to the possibility of 'the misuse of power by ministers and their officials' (*PR*, 295), as well as to the fact that the universal ends of the state may 'be hindered by interests common to officials who form a clique against their inferiors on one side and their superiors on the other' (*PR*, 295R). There are safeguards against these dangers. In the first place, the civil service is hierarchically organized, and there are thus various levels of answerability or accountability. Then, too, the authority given to the Corporations is a check upon any 'subjective caprice' on the part of civil servants (*PR*, 295). On certain occasions even the monarch might have to intervene to secure parity of attention to the ends of the state (*PR*, 295R). It is education in ethical conduct, however, which is of more importance in ensuring that 'a dispassionate, upright, and polite demeanour becomes customary' in civil servants. Further, the size of the state removes them from too close an affinity with 'family and other personal ties'. Preoccupied, as civil servants are in a great state, with the 'important questions' that arise therein, 'these subjective interests automatically disappear, and the habit is generated of adopting universal interests, points of view, and activities' (*PR*, 296). Finally, it is from the middle class that the members of the class of civil servants are drawn, and it is in the middle class that 'the consciousness of right and the developed intelligence of the mass of the people is found'. Thus,

> The sovereign working on the middle class at the top, and Corporation-rights working on it at the bottom, are the institutions which effectively prevent it from acquiring the isolated position of an aristocracy and using its education and skill as means to an arbitrary tyranny.
>
> (*PR*, 297)

In a 'well-organized' state, no doubt few of these safeguards would be necessary; given that Hegel's concern *is* with a 'well-organized' state, it is puzzling that he feels he has to draw attention to them. Since he has done, we may well feel, in our turn – and especially after reading what Rousseau has to say about the degenerative tendencies of government – that Hegel is altogether too sanguine about the effectiveness of the measures for ensuring the disinterestedness of the class of civil servants. But Hegel was not Rousseau, and his analysis of the state is more than a standard by which to judge contemporary states; it is, as he has shown in *The Philosophy of History*, the goal and end of history. Contemporary states exhibit numerous imperfections, which can be countered, to some degree, by measures such as he has considered above. Ultimately, however, Hegel is in no doubt that the 'well-organized' state will be actualized. The stage of history that man has currently reached is that in which he 'knows' what form this 'well-organized' state will take.

Hegel finally turns his attention to the Legislature. He comments on its roles or function, and its composition, and in the course of his discussion he considers the kind of services which the state can demand of its citizens, as well as commenting on 'false' notions of the people and of the idea of representation. It is here that we learn what the practice of citizenship involves in Hegel's state, the extent of the participation of citizens in political life, and the degree to which their judgment can be trusted.

Hegel begins by noting that since the Legislature is part of the constitution, and is presupposed by it, the nature of the constitution 'lies absolutely outside the sphere directly determined by' the Legislature. As an historical phenomenon, however, which progressively matures, the constitution is affected by the laws which are determined by the Legislature, and by the growth of the state towards universality (*PR*, 298). The sphere of competence of the Legislature is the renewal and extension of laws, when required, and the domestic affairs of the state. In relation to private individuals, it is concerned with their well-being and happiness, and with the nature of the services which they owe to the state: 'The former comprises laws dealing with all sorts of private rights, the rights of communities, Corporations, and organizations affecting the entire state.' Except for military service, which Hegel considers in a later section, the only thing required of citizens by the state is money (*PR*, 299). We shall return to this. More broadly than these responsibilities, however, the function of the Legislature is to act as a mediating link between the universal ends and interests represented by the Crown and the Executive, and the particularity of civil society, bringing each into close proximity. The operative force in the Legislature is the Estates. These are the classes of civil society, 'given a political significance' (*PR*, 303R). The Estates perform an important mediating function because 'it is through them that the state enters the subjective consciousness of the people and that the people begins to participate in the state' (*PR*, 301A). They stand between the Crown and the Executive, on the one hand, and the distinct associations of civil society on the other. Like the class of civil servants, 'they are a middle term preventing the extreme isolation of the power of the Crown, which otherwise might seem a mere arbitrary tyranny, and also the isolation of the particular interests of persons, societies, and Corporations' (*PR*, 302). The nature of the composition and organization of the Legislature enables it to act in this role.

The Estates are organized into two Assemblies, whose membership is drawn respectively from the two divisions of the 'unofficial class' – that is, from the agricultural class and the business class.

Representatives in each Assembly appear there as members of their classes, and not as the representatives of atomistic individuals (*PR*, 303). Hegel is particularly concerned to argue against prevalent theories of individual representation, and his argument is quite straightforward. In the classes and Corporations of civil society, individuals have already broken away from atomistic particularity into communities; indeed, they have done so as members of families. In both the family and civil society, 'the individual is in evidence only as a member of a group'. It would, Hegel argues, clearly be absurd to break up these communities 'into a mere conglomeration of individuals as soon as they enter the field of politics, i.e. the field of highest concrete universality'. To do this would be to sever the link between civil society and the state, 'to hold civil and political life apart from one another and as it were to hang the latter in the air' (*PR*, 303R; see also *PR*, 308). Members of the two Assemblies, as representatives of their classes, are able to perform a mediating function between the particularity of civil society and the universal ends of the state, and thus contribute to that unity which finds its ultimate expression in the Crown.

The members of the two Assemblies are, however, chosen in different ways. The better-endowed of the agricultural class are particularly suited to political office, because their ethical life is natural, being based on family life and the possession of land (*PR*, 305). What Hegel is saying here is that there is an unmediated contact in their ethical life between the particular and the universal which makes members of this class readily appropriate to take on the role of mediation in the political realm. Furthermore, their suitability is enhanced by the fact that they are dependent, for their capital, neither on the state, nor on 'the uncertainty of business'; and they have no need for favours from either the Executive or 'the mob' (*PR*, 306). The naturalness of their ethical life and the independence of their work – by which Hegel means that they are, as independent landowners, not subject to the uncertainties of relationships of interdependence which characterize the work of the business class – mean that they are justified in being 'summoned and entitled to ... political vocation by birth without the hazards of election' (*PR*, 307).

It is different with the other Assembly. The business class has to be represented by deputies. This necessity partly reflects the very size of the class, but it has more to do with the nature of the class in civil society. Of all the various elements in civil society, the business class is the one most preoccupied with the particular, in satisfying the various demands that arise within the System of Needs. It is thus the class which is most distanced from ethical life, for whom ethical life is most unnatural. As Hegel puts it, it 'comprises the fluctuating element in civil society' (*PR*, 308). It must not, therefore, be supposed that all members of this class are equally capable of participating in 'the business of the state' (*PR*, 308R) in the same way that this was a perfectly acceptable assumption to make about the agricultural class. The deputies of the business class are to be chosen on the basis of 'the strength of confidence felt in them'. More is involved in this choice than the matter of selecting those who have a better understanding of public affairs than the electors; it is also necessary to choose those who 'essentially vindicate the universal interest, not the particular interest of a society or a Corporation in preference to that interest'. Hence, they are not agents or delegates of their electors, but are expected to exercise their independent judgment on public affairs (*PR*, 309). The members of this 'fluctuating and changeable element in civil society', who require to be chosen, are those who exhibit 'the knowledge (of the organization and interests of the state and civil society), the temperament, and the skill "acquired" as a result of the actual transaction of business in managerial or official positions'. Thus, those of this class who are likely to make the most suitable deputies, are the managers of businesses or the officials of Corporations – the people, in other words, who are most aware of the emerging universal elements in civil society (*PR*, 310). Once again, and repeating arguments he has made earlier (see *PR*, 303R), the deputies are 'the deputies of the various Corporations' – that is, they are chosen on this functional basis of their membership of a Corporation, and not upon the basis of an atomistic individualism (*PR*, 311). The deputies here, thus, face two ways, and this is the nature of their mediating role. They represent the particular interests of the Corporations to the universal ends of the state, and they introduce the latter into the deliberations of the former. While the primary role of mediation between the Crown and civil society might belong to the first Assembly of the agricultural class, this does not mean that the business class is of no importance in this respect. What it does mean, however, is that it is rational that there be two Assemblies, for each Estate discharges its functions in different ways (*PR*, 312).

What the Estates do jointly, 'in their pooled political knowledge, deliberations, and decisions', is to bring 'the moment of formal freedom ... into its right in respect of those members of civil society who are without any share in the executive'. This is a task of political education, for those who have no direct part in political life, and it is performed by the publicity which is given to the debates of the Estates (*PR*, 314). It is through the dissemination of this knowledge of public business that

public opinion first reaches thoughts that are true and attains insight into the situation and concept of the state and its affairs, and so first acquires ability to estimate these more rationally. By this means also, it becomes acquainted with and learns to respect the work, abilities, virtue, and dexterity of ministers and officials.

(*PR*, 315)

An untutored public opinion is positively harmful, since in such opinion

we have to do with the consciousness of an insight and conviction peculiarly one's own, [and] the more peculiarly one's own an opinion may be the worse its content is, because the bad is that which is wholly private and personal in its content.

(*PR*, 317)

Once public opinion is educated, however, by the publicity given to the debates of the Assemblies, it acquires 'a sound and mature insight into the concerns of the state'. The result is that 'the members of the general public are left with nothing much of importance to say, and above all are deprived of the opinion that what they say is of peculiar importance and efficacy' (*PR*, 319). Once, thus, the 'general public' appreciates the inherent rationality of the state, there is nothing left for it to do except render service to the state when required. This service, however, is not an external burden imposed on individuals, but is accepted as following naturally from the rationality of the entire enterprise.

With this analysis of the legislature and the formation of public opinion, Hegel has completed his discussion of the nature of the internal constitution of the state. He next considers sovereignty as a relation between states, but before we examine his discussion of this, it is perhaps appropriate to make one or two comments on his argument so far, especially in regard to what he has to say about 'the people'.

It has just been noted that very little is demanded of the 'general public' politically beyond an acknowledgment of the rationality of the state. In this acknowledgment the public realizes that its particular ends are bound up with the ends of the state, and only have existence and justification as part of the united whole which is the state as an 'ethical community'. What is demanded, thus, is reconciliation with the rationality, the philosophical necessity, of the state as such a community. In this reconciliation, man both overcomes the division within himself, and is reintegrated – but now as a being conscious of his individuality and freedom – in the life of the community. In this way he partakes of and lives an 'ethical life'. If 'will' is the basis of the state, and Hegel paid tribute to Rousseau for recognizing this (see *PR*, 258R), then it is not the will of the 'general public', for this is not engaged politically in any intelligible sense. It is not an effort or exercise of will which results in reconciliation, but one of cognition. In the early paragraphs of *The Philosophy of Right*, Hegel writes of the 'will' as an attribute or property of individuals, by which they manifest themselves as free. Such freedom is not genuine or rational, however, if it is arbitrary or capricious. The will is only rational, and thus human freedom is only rational, when, through thought and reflection, it incorporates into itself, and *wills*, the universal ends provided for it by Spirit, or mind (see *PR*,21–33). Spirit, after all, is not 'actualized' except through the actions of individuals, even if for most of human history they are not conscious that they are the vehicles of Spirit's self-realization. The point about the modern world is that men now *are* so conscious. They have knowledge of the rationality of Spirit, and of the fact that their wills are rational when in accordance with it. In Hegel's later discussion, however, of the constituent elements of the highest level of politics – that level, in other words, in which ethical life is lived – there is no institutional arena in which the now rational will of individuals can be registered. Once individuals have recognized the rationality of Spirit, and adopted it as the principle of their being, there is nothing left, politically, for their wills to do. What remains to them, of course, is the 'freedom' which they exercise as members of civil society; but this is different from the rational freedom of the ethical community of the state. They may indeed feel themselves to belong to an ethical community, but their political judgment is not called upon. Patriotism, the 'political sentiment', may have been aroused, but this is not expressed in active citizenship. Yet is precisely such a vision of active citizenship which Hegel holds out as the goal of human history in *The Phenomenology of Spirit* and *The Philosophy of History*.

Such comments presuppose that Hegel thought such reconciliation to the rationality of Spirit was a form of knowledge which was genuinely open to all. Early on, in the Preface to *The Phenomenology of Spirit*, he had remarked that such knowledge was not easily attained, and that its attainment could not be rushed: 'Impatience demands what is impossible, namely acquiring end without the means. First the length of the way must be suffered for every moment is necessary.' [9] In *The Philosophy of Right*, he was even more sceptical about popular access to knowledge of the rational will. He draws attention to a common view underlying the summoning of representatives of the people – that either the people, or their representatives, know best what their interest is, and that 'their will for its promotion is undoubtedly the most disinterested'. But, he continues, 'to know what one wills, and still more to know what the absolute will, Reason, wills, is the fruit of profound apprehension and insight, precisely the things which are *not* popular' (*PR*, 301R). The possibility of any individual living an ethical life, however, depends upon his knowledge of the rational will, for only then has he overcome both his alienation from the world and the division within himself. This cognitive effort, thus, appears to be beyond the capacity of most individuals. They do not have the possibility of living and 'willing' that rational freedom which is at the basis of ethical life.

On the one hand, then, for those who are able to make the required cognitive effort, there is little for their rational will to do politically. On the other, the reconciliation which results from such an effort is not available to the many, because they are intellectually deficient. Finally, large sections of the population are anyway excluded from even that level of participation in public affairs which is vouchsafed members of the two Estates: the agricultural and the business classes. They are excluded either because they are not members of either class, or because they are the inferior or more lowly members. Thus, in the case of the agricultural class, it is only the more substantial landowners who have any political role at all, and they acquire this role by birth and inheritance – they are not subject to election, so the lesser gentry and the peasantry are not even involved in choosing them. Their compensation, no doubt, is that they live an ethical life which is natural, but this is far removed from that life of rational freedom which is lived in the state. In relation to the business class, Hegel makes it clear, first, that membership of a Corporation is not open to casual or day labourers (*PR*, 252R), nor indeed to those even more disadvantaged, the poor and destitute. In this connection, in his enumeration of those who are members of the business class, Hegel includes craftsmen, manufacturers and traders. It is not clear from what he says about the nature of manufacture – 'mass production to satisfy single needs, but needs in more universal demand' – whether workers who engage in manufacture are included as well as owners and managers (*PR*, 204). Second, Hegel remarks that 'unless he is a member of an authorized Corporation ... an individual is without rank or dignity' (*PR*, 253R). More importantly, it is only as a member of a Corporation that 'the single person attains his actual and living destiny for universality' (*PR*, 308R). To have any political role, he must be a member of a Corporation (or some other association of civil society, which Hegel does not specify), yet such membership is not open to all in civil society who do not otherwise belong to the agricultural class. Once again, a political role is denied them.

Hegel's ethical community is a political hierarchy. Full, active citizenship is restricted to the better-endowed of the agricultural class, and to the managers of business and the officials of the Corporations. The connection of the remainder with political life is the service which they owe the state. Aside from military service, all that is required from 'citizens' is money: 'As for the services to be exacted, it is only if these are reduced to terms of money, the really existent and universal value of both things and services, that they can be fixed justly' (*PR*, 299). Hegel is concerned to leave the individual with the maximum freedom of his particular will. If the state, therefore, were to demand from individuals the kind of services which the ancient Egyptians exacted for their architectural undertakings, this 'principle of subjective freedom' would be infringed. The demand for money equitably and efficiently universalizes the services required, and leaves the principle of subjective freedom intact (*PR*, 299R).

After his consideration of the internal organization of the state, Hegel discusses the state as sovereign in relation to other states. It is here that the real unity of the state is revealed, for what the state possesses is 'individuality' (*PR*, 321):

> Individuality is awareness of one's existence as a unit in sharp distinction from others. It manifests itself here in the state as a relation to other states, each of which is autonomous *vis-à-vis* the others. This autonomy embodies mind's ['Spirit', in the terminology of *The Philosophy of History*] actual awareness of itself as a unit and hence it is the most fundamental freedom which a people possesses as well as its highest dignity.
>
> (*PR*, 322)

The duty of the individual, the only substantive 'service' which may be exacted from him, is that of maintaining this individuality of the state – that is, its sovereignty and independence. No sacrifice is too great here. The state can call upon the individual's property and life in its defence (*PR*, 324): 'Sacrifice on behalf of the individuality of the state is the substantial tie between the state and all its members and so is a universal duty' (*PR*, 325). It is a legitimate duty to demand of the individual, for it is only in the state that the individual has the possibility of enjoying the rational freedom of ethical life.

Hegel's thoughts about war are somewhat ambivalent. War does not describe a condition in which there is 'right' only on one side. As he pointed out in his earlier writing on 'The German Constitution', war does not decide 'which of the rights alleged by the two parties is the genuine right – since both parties have a genuine right – but which of the two rights is to give way.'[10] Until and unless there should be a 'Praetor to judge between states', who is acceptable to all states, war remains a potential occurrence among them. Even with such a judge, war is always possible, for his acceptability to any one state can never be more than conditional, and therefore contingent (*PR*, 333R). But though war must be recognized as a fact of the life of states, it 'is not to be regarded as an absolute evil', for it can have beneficial effects. Since military service and the willingness to sacrifice property, and even life, are the 'substantial tie' between individuals and the state, and indicate that the individual has appropriated the universal ends of the state as his own, war demonstrates, preserves and enhances the ethical vigour of the state. Prolonged periods of peace remove from individuals this opportunity, and lead to the stagnation and corruption of civil life. The result is that men are no longer willing to make the required sacrifices, such that 'their freedom [dies] from the fear of dying'. Furthermore, history shows that war has often been a very effective means of defusing domestic unrest, and thus of consolidating the internal sovereignty of the state. Groups of individuals, otherwise prone to chafe at aspects of civil life, have been brought to demonstrate their 'political sentiment' – patriotism – by a salutary war (*PR*, 324).

It is not clear from the above whether pretexts for war should be positively sought if the monarch, who has the responsibility for questions of war and peace (*PR*, 329), should judge that the ethical health of the state is in jeopardy. The following passage does not conclusively resolve the issue:

> if the state as such, if its autonomy, is in jeopardy, all its citizens are in duty bound to answer the summons to its defence. If in such circumstances the entire state is under arms and is torn from its domestic life at home to fight abroad, the war of defence turns into a war of conquest.
>
> (*PR*, 326)

There is some indication that between states of equivalent levels of 'civilization', only defensive wars are justified: that 'civilized nations' are justified 'in regarding and treating as barbarians those who lag behind them in institutions which are the essential moments of the state'. The rights and autonomy of barbarians are not the equal of those of civilized nations, and may thus be treated 'as only a formality' (*PR*, 351). Hegel does not go as far as Machiavelli in endorsing an aggressive militarism as a condition for the survival of the state. Nevertheless, since the 'substantial welfare of the state' is the supreme consideration (*PR*, 336–7), the state, as an autonomous 'individual', must make its own decisions about whether circumstances are such as to warrant war, and find the justification for the decision within itself. If Hegel is indeterminate on the question of whether or not war should be actively sought, there can be no doubting his conviction, first, that it is only in military service that the majority of individuals have any 'substantial tie' with the universal ends of the state, and, second, that it is in war rather than in peace that the state demonstrates its ethical vigour. Peace is ultimately debilitating: Hegel's conclusion is not far removed from that of Machiavelli.

Conclusion

Among the various terms that Hegel used to describe the state, one was the 'ethical community', for it is in the state that ethical life is lived in a fully self-conscious way. This is the state as 'the actuality of the ethical idea' (*PR*, 257). It will also be recalled that Hegel wrote of three 'moments' of ethical life: the family, civil society and the state.

Now broadly, an ethical life is one in which the individual is not alienated or estranged from the society in which he lives. Neither is he divided within himself between the various elements of his personality or character. Ethical life is lived by an individual who possesses a fully rounded and integrated personality, and who both belongs in and is at one with the society in question. It is relatively easy to see how such a life can be lived in the family, based, as it is, on love and trust; ethical life is lived here unreflectively. It is not as easy, but it is not thereby problematic, to conceive of a self-conscious ethical life in the state. The individual is integrated into the public life of the state because he has appropriated the universal ends of the state to himself and made them his own. The problem here, as we have noted, is that for most individuals there is nothing for them to do politically. It is thus unclear whether ethical life at this level has any meaning for them, unless they should happen to be called upon to defend the state and they defend it, not simply in order to preserve their property – which would be to view the state as no more than civil society – but as the substantial basis and apex of their whole being.

The difficulty comes with civil society as a 'moment' of ethical life. Civil society is the sphere of life where individuals pursue their own particular ends and purposes, where they engage in various kinds of undertakings to satisfy their needs. Now Hegel argues that, with the division of labour, a pattern of interdependence and integration is built up within civil society as individuals, in going about their own business, reciprocally satisfy each other's needs. This, in part, explains civil society as a moment in ethical life. But the integration that is achieved here does not reflect the conscious intention on the part of the individuals which alone could justify it as ethical: it is a by-product of their pursuit of their own particular ends. It is precisely such particularity that has to be overcome in ethical life.

A further element of civil society, however, is the Corporation. It is in the Corporation – as, for instance, the member of a trade – that the individual raises himself above the level of his own particularity, because he comes to recognize that he shares certain interests with his fellow-members. Hegel claims that in such recognition there is an instance of approach towards the universal. It is difficult to see how this can be so if the Corporation is considered solely with regard to its function within civil society: the fact that the individual shares particular ends with others, and acknowledges this sharing by membership in a Corporation, does not change the character of these ends as particular ends. When the Corporation is viewed in terms of its political role – it is from the Corporation that membership of the second Assembly of Estates is drawn – the members chosen as deputies have the dual function of representing the particular interests of the Corporation to the other elements of the political order, and of representing the universal interest of the state to their own members. That they can face in two directions derives from the whole basis of Hegel's philosophical politics: namely the ultimate unity of the particular and the universal in ethical life. Yet the deputies who are chosen are, as we have seen, those who have a 'better understanding' of public affairs – that is, of the universal – than have their electors (*PR*, 309). People of inferior understanding are asked to choose people of superior understanding – or maybe they are not asked. It is not to be supposed that all the managers of businesses or all the officials of Corporations will act as deputies; it is just that it is only these people who are eligible to serve as deputies. Hegel does not tell us what comprises their electorate: whether it is the whole Corporation membership, or only that part of the membership from which deputies are chosen. If the former, then there seems to be no guarantee that those of 'better understanding' will in fact be chosen – unless it is institutionally stipulated, which it is not; if the latter, then clearly not all Corporation members have a political role, and one can only speculate how far appeals to them by deputies on behalf of the universal will have any effect.

There are other elements in civil society – the welfare agencies of the public authority, for instance, or the whole system of the Administration of Justice – but these again cater to the particular interests either of all members of civil society, or of substantial sections. The fact that interests are shared, however, does not make them universal. What makes interests or ends universal is the rationality imparted to them by Spirit. The upshot of all this is that while civil society may be a 'moment' of ethical life, in that it is a necessary element in the totality which makes up the ethical life of the state, it is not itself a sphere in which ethical life is lived, despite Hegel's claim to the contrary. Yet it is in civil society that most individuals live the totality of their lives. The conclusion must be – and it is one we have already reached by a rather different route – that ethical life is not available to most individuals.

This calls into question the whole claim about the state being an ethical community. It is certainly not a community in which the political judgment of autonomous individuals is to be trusted. Most individuals have no political role at all – they have nothing to deliver a political judgment upon. Their autonomy – or 'subjective freedom', to use Hegel's term – is exercised wholly within civil society, and has no opportunity to be raised to the level of universality except in military service. Yet whether military service genuinely expresses the 'substantial tie' between the individual and the state is also in question. For it to be so genuinely expressive, it must be based on the 'political sentiment', or patriotism. Now patriotism as a political sentiment does not have its basis in an idea that the function of the state is to preserve life and property, but rather in an habitual recognition 'that the community is one's substantive groundwork and end' (*PR*, 268R). In other words, more is required for patriotism to be a genuine political sentiment than self-interest or blind devotion to one's country. It is the nature of this 'more' which is a problem: the kind of recognition that is required is not something that can be reached by those, the majority of individuals, who do not experience the rational freedom of ethical life. So it is not even in military service that individuals are necessarily raised to the level of universality. If individuals are willing to fight for their country, and even sacrifice their lives, then it is either because life in civil society is worth living, or because of some deep-seated, irremovable and ultimately unreflective devotion to one's country. Neither of these, however, is patriotism as a political sentiment, which alone justifies military service as the 'substantial tie' between the individual and the state.

There is, as has been noted, a discrepancy between these implications of the arguments of *The Philosophy of Right* and what Hegel sets forth as the goal of human history in *The Philosophy of History*. In the latter, it will be recalled, Spirit's purpose was to be fully achieved when it was grasped and acknowledged in the self-consciousness of individuals. This recognition of, and commitment to, Spirit's purpose meant that the purpose was not achieved unless it involved all mankind, rather than just *some* individuals. In other words, it was not enough that Hegel himself should recognize and commit himself to Spirit's purpose. The road had to be travelled by all.

If rational freedom consists only in this appropriation by the individual of the universal ends of the state as his own then, in principle, there does not seem to be an impediment (beyond intellectual capacity) to the widespread achievement of rational freedom. There is some plausibility in describing such a state as an ethical community, even though most individuals will have only a minimal role in deliberating upon its public affairs. The modern nation state is a large one and Hegel argued – following Montesquieu, on whom he draws (see *PR*, 273R), and Rousseau – that it could not but be hierarchically organized. There would be some people, for instance, for whom political life would be a profession, and others who would only intermittently take part. Hegel's answer to the problem of scale was that the state be organized on a functional principle, on the basis that it does not make sense, for political purposes, to ignore the communities and associations of civil society. This is the point of his class analysis of civil society, and of his basing membership of the two Assemblies of Estates on the economic divisions of class. The weakness of Hegel's argument here, as we have noted, relates to the numbers of people who seem to be excluded. In Hegel's terms, they are both economically and politically functionless. There is another principle of organization, however, which answers to the problem of scale: namely, federalism. Federalism, as a principle or organization, is not necessarily incompatible with functionalism, and it is worth noting that federalism could have been, for Hegel, a mediating influence in raising the individual to the level of universality, and that more people could thereby have been given a political role – some means, that is, of registering their will.

In his analysis of contemporary society, even more in his depiction of the alienated existence of modern man, Hegel is highly reminiscent of Rousseau. Each of them is also concerned with the conditions that are necessary for man to overcome his alienation. While both stress individual autonomy – for Rousseau, each individual must consent to the general will before it becomes obligatory; for Hegel, each individual's appropriation of the universal ends of the state must be his own – it is Rousseau, and not Hegel, who insists upon individual political judgment. Rousseau therefore has to find, as Hegel does not, an ethical bond between citizens which will ensure that this political judgment will reinforce, rather than undermine, the harmony of the political community. The ethical bond is found by Rousseau in each individual's definition of himself as a citizen. It is true that Hegel also insists upon individual recognition of the state as the 'ground and apex' of his existence, but since Hegel's 'citizen' is not called upon to exercise political judgment, it is unclear what effect non-recognition by the individual here would have on the state. The individual would not enjoy ethical life but, as we have discovered, it does not seem important for Hegel's state that more than a few should have this opportunity. It is clear that for Rousseau, on the other hand, the political community is a nullity if the individual does not define himself as a citizen.

Despite its weaknesses – which stem largely from the hopes of rational freedom aroused by the vision presented in *The Philosophy of History* – Hegel's political thought has great relevance to understanding the idea of a political community in the modern state. First of all, he raises questions about when it is appropriate, and when not, to describe something as an ethical community. There is then his analysis of what it is that constitutes rational freedom. Finally, his adoption of the functional principle for the internal organisation of the state answers, in part, the problems posed by the sheer scale of the modern state.

Chapter six

Tocqueville: citizenship in town and state

'Freedom is, in truth, a sacred thing'[1]

Despite his dismissal of Machiavelli as 'only a superficial man',[2] Tocqueville, like Machiavelli, demonstrated in his life that involvement in public affairs as citizen was the highest form of existence and endeavour open to human beings. Political liberty, understood in these terms, was the cardinal human value. Tocqueville's political career lasted almost as long as Machiavelli's, and it ended with the same abruptness and the same regret that he was no longer required to serve his country. Machiavelli retired to his study to write the masterpieces through which we largely know him today. By the time of his own retirement from politics, however – indeed, before he even entered the Chamber of Deputies in 1838 – Tocqueville was already a famous author on both sides of the Atlantic, for *Democracy in America* had appeared in two parts in 1835 and 1840, and had been rapidly translated into English. Machiavelli's concern had been with how a life of citizenship could be restored in the Italy of his day to match that which had been achieved in the ancient Roman republic. Tocqueville wrote about America out of concern that the opportunities for the practice of citizenship in Europe, and especially France, were being eroded by the democratic tendencies of the age, and because America was the place where these tendencies were most advanced. Just as Machiavelli had hoped that Rome's past would be Italy's future, so too, Tocqueville wondered whether America's present might not be Europe's future.

Tocqueville was convinced that aristocratic politics could no longer be contemplated. They had been overtaken by events, mainly by the French Revolution.[3] Although this thought occasioned him some regret, Tocqueville knew the future lay with democracy. He did not endorse this future wholeheartedly, for it was by no means certain that democracy would prove compatible with a republican form of government. Among the tendencies of democracy was the political enervation of a people such that, even given the opportunity, they did not wish to take on the responsibilities of that citizen life which underlay republican politics. Was a democratic republic both conceivable and likely? It was certainly conceivable and, in his introduction to the *Democracy*, Tocqueville permitted himself to imagine, in a manner very reminiscent of Rousseau's idyllic picture of republican life in the *Discourse on the Origins of Inequality*,

> a society in which all men, regarding the law as their common work, would love it and submit to it without difficulty; the authority of the government would be respected as necessary, not as sacred; the love felt toward the head of the state would not be a passion but a calm and rational feeling. Each man having some rights and being sure of the enjoyment of those rights, there would be established between all classes a manly confidence and a sort of reciprocal courtesy, as far removed from pride as from servility. Understanding its own interests, the people would appreciate that in order to enjoy the benefits of society one must shoulder its obligations. Free association of the citizens could then take the place of the individual authority of the nobles, and the state would be protected both from tyranny and from licence.

Such a polity would be less glorious in its deeds than an aristocracy, but it would also be less wretched. There would be fewer extremes of passion and condition, yet a democratic and republican people could be expected to rise to the occasion:

> Without enthusiasm or the zeal of belief, education and experience would sometimes induce the citizens to make great sacrifices; each man being equally weak would feel a like need for the help of his companions, and knowing that he would not get their support without supplying his, he would easily appreciate that for him private interest was mixed up with public interest. The nation as a body would be less brilliant; less glorious and perhaps less strong, but the majority of citizens would enjoy a more prosperous lot, and the people would be pacific not from despair of anything better but from knowing itself to be well-off.
>
> (*DA*, 12)

So a democratic republic was conceivable. Was it likely? Would modern conditions permit it? Could men do anything to ensure it? These were the questions that Tocqueville addressed in the *Democracy*.

If Tocqueville had a mentor, it was Montesquieu. Montesquieu had held that the sustaining principle of republican government was civic virtue, and that the practice of such virtue was only possible in a small territory, such as the city-states of antiquity. Tocqueville, on the other hand, did not think that much could be learnt from classical antiquity. The old republics had been chaotic and unstable, and they were not democracies in the modern sense. Yet his ideal of political liberty as evinced in the public life of a citizen was unmistakably classical in provenance, if not in inspiration. Modern states were large and increasingly democratic, and one of the questions that Tocqueville took with him to America when he visited the country in 1831–2 was whether civic virtue could be the sustaining principle of a large republic. He did not find the Americans a virtuous people in the classical sense, but they were free. It was not civic virtue that underpinned political liberty and citizen life in the new republic, but what he called 'enlightened self-interest'. This did not 'absolutely disprove' Montesquieu, Tocqueville claimed in a draft for the *Democracy*, for what Montesquieu meant by virtue was 'the moral power that each individual exercises over himself'. If it should happen that man's triumph over temptation resulted from the 'weakness of the temptation', then, though this was not classical virtue, the result was the same as if the temptation had been great, and virtue had been necessary to overcome it. Tocqueville continued:

> In America, it is not virtue which is great, it is temptation which is small, which amounts to the same thing. It is not disinterestedness which is great, it is interest which is well-understood, which again almost amounts to the same thing.[4]

Enlightened self-interest, he wrote in 1831, was 'a sort of refined and intelligent selfishness'. Americans

> [did] not trouble themselves to find out whether public virtue is good, but they do claim to prove that it is useful. If the latter point is true, as I think it is in part, this society can pass as enlightened, but not as virtuous.[5]

Tocqueville had two points of departure: an overriding value (political liberty), and the inevitable tendencies of the age, which he described as democratic. By political liberty, he understood a man of independent mind, conscious of his connection with the interests of the collectivity of which he is part, and willing to take on the responsibilities of attending to those interests. Political liberty was the liberty man exercised as a citizen, and he did so in a political community which was in part identified by his very activity. His own private interests were so intimately tied to the interests of the community as to be more often in coincidence than at variance with them. In taking on the responsibilities of citizenship, man more completely realized his potentialities as a human being. He demonstrated that he was fully a moral agent by his willingness to put his private interests into the balance with everyone else's in order to determine the collective interests of his community. This attachment to his community was not that of a blind and unthinking patriotism, but a patriotism founded in rational reflection upon where his true interests lay. The citizen's exercise of his political liberty was not confined to the narrow political arena, but was elicited whenever common causes arose that needed deliberation and action. It was important that the public bodies of the state did not attempt to cater for all of those interests that brought men together, for this would be to undermine the citizen's possibility of moral agency. Voluntary association was as vital an avenue for the exercise of political liberty as was the choosing of, and participation in, political bodies. The area of the 'public' was wider than that of the 'political,' conventionally conceived, but it was in both that man demonstrated that he was a citizen.

In considering Tocqueville's conception of 'political' man, it is clear that we are dealing with autonomous man, whose actions are expected to make a difference in the world, and whose deliberation and judgment about matters of common concern generate a feeling of attachment to and identification with the fellow members of the community with whom he deliberates and judges. The future of this conception of the practice of citizenship Tocqueville viewed with foreboding, for there were threatening forces in the democratic tendencies of the age which, unchecked, would overwhelm political man and eliminate opportunities for his autonomous action. Tocqueville's analysis of the tension between democracy and political liberty is reminiscent of Machiavelli's analysis of the relationship between fortune and *virtù*. It is not that each pair of terms is perfectly matched with the other; it is rather that for both Machiavelli and Tocqueville it was important that man should act and, in Tocqueville's case, that he act to forestall the operation of those tendencies in democracy that were inimical to political liberty.

The first aspect of Tocqueville's thought to be considered, therefore, is his conception of democracy, and especially those tendencies towards 'individualism' and 'centralization' which he identified as harmful for the practice of citizenship. Then we shall turn to his analysis of American political practice, and how it managed to overcome the dangers inherent in democracy, placing particular emphasis on the diffusion of power to the state and the locality. Finally, Tocqueville's analysis of the peculiarities of the American experience – the underlying conditions which encouraged and sustained political liberty – will be examined: the providential circumstances of American life, in which Tocqueville included nature and geography; its history, especially the political practice of the pre-Revolutionary period; and its *mœurs*, which Tocqueville interpreted in terms very close to those of Rousseau.

This ordering of matters somewhat reverses that of Tocqueville's own presentation. It is in the second part of the *Democracy*, published in 1840, that he considered at a more theoretical level the dangers of democracy unchecked, whereas the first part, published in 1835, deals more with specifically American affairs. This has led some commentators to suggest that the *Democracy* is really two books.[6] Tocqueville's purpose, however, was to use America as a model for saying something about democracy in its likely and general impact on the course of European politics, and it was therefore natural for him to proceed as he did. The present analysis, on the other hand, is focused on the American experience of a working political community, and it thus seems appropriate to present his thinking in the order indicated. There are two considerations which make this a legitimate approach (an approach, that is, that does not distort Tocqueville's thought): first, he published the two parts as parts of the same book, and thus must himself have considered them to form a coherent whole; and second, the first part is not devoid of those theoretical matters which receive more extended treatment in the second part, nor are specifically American themes absent from this second part.

Democracy: centralization and individualism

About two things one may be certain when discussing Tocqueville's conception of democracy: that it has something to do with equality, and that it is irresistible. He began his introduction to the *Democracy* by remarking that nothing struck him with more force during his visit to America than the general 'equality of conditions' of the people (*DA*, 5), which pervaded political *mores* and laws, civil society and government, opinions and customs. America was the most advanced part of the world where this 'great revolution' was taking place. 'The social state of America', he went on,

> is a very strange phenomenon. Men there are nearer equality in wealth and in mental endowments, or, in other words, more nearly equally powerful than in any other country of the world or in any other age of recorded history.

> (*DA*, 66)

The impression he gained from his American travels, observations and conversations was reinforced when he went to England in 1833. Noting the decline of aristocratic power in England – it was but a year since the passage of the Great Reform Act – he commented:

119

The century is primarily democratic. Democracy is like a rising tide; it only recoils to come back with greater force, and soon one sees that for all its fluctuations it is always gaining ground. The immediate future of European society is completely democratic; this can in no way be doubted.

(JEI, 67)

In the *Democracy*, he traced the growth of democracy in France from the eleventh century, and concluded:

The gradual progress of equality is something fated. The main feautres of this progress are the following: it is universal and permanent, it is daily passing beyond human control, and every event and every man helps it along.

(DA, 8)

Democracy represented a great levelling – the disappearance of aristocratic political power, a decline in the authority of a hierarchic church, the division of property, the rise of public opinion and of the power of the majority. The effect of this levelling was to remove all intermediary bodies between individuals on the one hand and society and state on the other, such that the individual stood alone in the face of centralized political power. The destruction of traditional authorities in matters of opinion and belief had the effect of leaving the individual isolated, and reliant only on his own reason for the direction of his life. In tracing the implications of these themes, Tocqueville concluded that the tendency of democracy was to one or other form of tyranny, and to the enervation of the individual will to engage in politics. As he repeatedly made clear, these dangers are at their greatest when a people comes upon democracy without a thorough familiarity with free political practices. America and England were fortunate in this respect; France was not. It is the sudden advent of democracy, the sweeping away of all distinction in a grand egalitarian flourish, that is most inimical to the establishment, restoration or maintenance of political liberty: the practice of political liberty rests upon the existence of intermediary, secondary bodies in which it can be exercised. Such bodies, however, are banished in the egalitarian rush. Democratic peoples 'give a ready welcome to simple general ideas. They are put off by complicated systems and like to picture a great nation in which every citizen resembles one set type and is controlled by one single power.' Next comes the idea of 'uniform legislation', which strikes the citizen 'as the first condition of good government':

As conditions become more equal among people, individuals seem of less and society of greater importance; or rather, every citizen, having grown like the rest, is lost in the crowd, and nothing stands out conspicuously but the great and imposing image of the people itself.

(*DA*, 867–8)

Tocqueville does not argue for the wholesale dismantling of the central organs of power, for a certain amount of centralization of function and power is necessary in any state. He distinguishes between what he called 'governmental' and 'administrative' centralization: 'Certain interests, such as the enactment of general laws and the nation's relations with foreigners, are common to all parts of the nation.' Concentration of these under one directing power is governmental centralization, and Tocqueville could not conceive that a nation could live, still less prosper, without a high degree of this. On the other hand, 'there are other interests of special concern to certain parts of the nation, such, for instance, as local enterprises'. Concentration of these in the same way is administrative centralization. It is this that Tocqueville objects to, for it 'only serves to enervate the peoples that submit to it, because it constantly tends to diminish their civic spirit' (*DA*, 106–7). Tocqueville's fear was that people would actually choose to live under a system, or would be happy to acquiesce in one, which concentrated all political decision-making at the centre: that centralization would be combined with the sovereignty of the people. Towards the end of the second part of the *Democracy*, he noted:

when equality starts developing among a people who have never known or long forgotten what freedom is, ... all powers seem spontaneously to rush to the centre. They accumulate there at an astonishing rate and the state reaches the extreme limits of its power all at once, while private persons *allow themselves* to sink in one moment down to the lowest degree of weakness.

(*DA*, 875, emphasis added)

What leads to a people's acquiescence in this servility is in part the very disappearance of intermediary bodies that is the corollary of centralization itself. It is also, however, the result of the fact that in the age of equality the individual had no authority to turn for confirmation of his beliefs and opinions other than the majority. The individual both submits to the majority and withdraws from public life. Though Tocqueville was fearful of the concentration of majority power in the legislative body, it was its tyranny over thought, opinion and belief that was more pervasive and more insidious in its effects. The moral authority of the majority is founded upon 'the notion that there is more enlightenment and wisdom in a numerous assembly than in a single man .... It is the theory of equality applied to brains'

(*DA*, 305). This moral authority gives the majority 'immense actual power and a power of opinion which is almost as great' (*DA*, 307). This makes tyranny possible.

Men need some authority outside themselves for their opinions. In times of equality, of 'a common level of uniformity', men do not believe

> blindly in any man or any class. But they are readier to trust the mass, and public opinion becomes more and more mistress of the world. Not only is public opinion the only guide left to aid private judgment, but its power is infinitely greater in democracies than elsewhere.

For, against the mass – 'this vast entity' – the citizen 'is overwhelmed by a sense of his insignificance and weakness. The same equality which makes him independent of each separate citizen leaves him isolated and defenceless in the face of the majority.' Such is the 'strange power' of public opinion. It confines 'the activity of private judgment within limits too narrow for the dignity and happiness of mankind' (*DA*, 557–8).

A parallel development to centralization and majority tyranny in egalitarian times was the phenomenon of 'individualism'. Tocqueville was very much concerned to preserve 'individuality', that independence of belief, judgment and action which marked each man's distinction from every other, and upon which was grounded the political liberty of the practice of citizenship. It was this individuality that was threatened by democratic forces. Individuality, however, was different from individualism. Tocqueville introduced his conception of individualism by contrasting it with egoism. Egoism is an old phenomenon; individualism is new, and a product of democracy.

'Egoism' is a passionate and exclusive involvement in and love of self in which everything in the world is thought of and judged with reference to an all-consuming 'I'. It 'springs from a blind instinct', and 'sterilises the seeds of every virtue'. Individualism, on the other hand,

> is a calm and considered feeling which disposes each citizen to isolate himself from the mass of his fellows and withdraw into the circle of family and friends; with this little society founded to his taste, he gladly leaves the greater society to look after itself.

While not in itself a 'depraved feeling', individualism is unhealthy for the practice of citizenship. It arises from 'misguided judgment' and 'inadequate understanding' rather than from 'perversity of heart'. At first, it 'only dams the spring of public virtues, but in the long run it attacks and destroys all the others too and finally merges in egoism' (*DA*, 652). This is because it has its own generative forces. It thrives in conditions of centralization and majority tyranny, but it is also nourished by a 'very dangerous' instinct to which equality of condition gives free rein: 'inordinate love of material pleasure' (*DA*, 569). A great danger comes upon democratic peoples 'when the taste for physical pleasures has grown more rapidly than either education or free institutions', for then men concentrate all attention on getting rich:

> There is no need to drag their rights away from citizens of this type: they themselves voluntarily let them go. They find it a tiresome inconvenience to exercise political rights which distract them from industry .... Such folk think they are following the doctrine of self-interest, but they have a very crude idea thereof, and the better to guard their interests, they neglect the chief of them, that is, to remain their own masters.

Thus is the road opened to an institutionalized tyranny, for, 'when the great mass of citizens does not want to bother about anything but private business, even the smallest party need not give up hope of becoming master of public affairs' (*DA*, 697–8; see also *DA*, 871).

Individualism, thus, represents the abdication of civic responsibility, the withdrawal from public life. Man does have inner resources to resist majority tyranny and, in company with his fellows, to fight against every centralizing tendency, but he chooses not to. His sentiments are focused on his children and his friends:

> As for the rest of his fellow citizens, they are near enough, but he does not notice them. He touches them but feels nothing. He exists in and for himself, and though he may still have a family, one can at least say that he has not got a fatherland.
>
> (*DA*, 898)

He has, in other words, ceased to be a citizen. He may participate to the extent of voting, but he asks for nothing more than to be left alone. This is an attitude of mind that an over-centralizing government is only too ready to encourage. Such a government

> does not break men's will, but softens, bends, and guides it; it seldom enjoins, but often inhibits action; it does not destroy anything, but prevents much being born; it is not at all tyrannical, but it hinders, restrains, enervates, stifles, and stultifies so much that in the end each nation is no more than a flock of timid and hard-working animals with the government as its shepherd.
>
> (*DA*, 899)

Such is Tocqueville's frightening portrait of democratic society. If left to proceed unhindered according to its own inner dynamic, democracy, the equality of condition, leaves the individual on his own. He accepts his opinions and beliefs from the majority and either enthusiastically supports a centralized political power which emasculates him as citizen, or resigns from public life voluntarily in order to pursue material gain. In either case, political liberty is dead and man leads a radically incomplete and stunted life.

This scenario of man's future could lead political man to despair, but this, for Tocqueville, can never be a legitimate response. His own ardent and ineradicable belief in the supreme value of political liberty could not make him conclude that conditions could ever be so irreversibly hopeless that stoic resignation was the only posture to adopt. This was not only false; it was cowardly. 'Providence', he continued in the final paragraphs of the *Democracy*,

> did not make mankind entirely free or completely enslaved. Providence has, in truth, drawn a predestined circle around each man beyond which he cannot pass; but within those vast limits man is strong and free, and so are peoples.
>
> The nations of our day cannot prevent conditions of equality from spreading in their midst. But it depends upon themselves whether equality is to lead to servitude or freedom, knowledge or barbarism, prosperity or wretchedness.
>
> (*DA*, 916)

The knowledge that the consequence of democracy lay in the direction he indicated emphatically did not justify a counsel of despair. On the contrary, it was a summons to action.

In America, Tocqueville found a society in which equality of condition had been carried further than anywhere else, and yet where political life nevertheless remained free. He sought lessons for his age, and especially for France, in his observation and study of the American experience. Though he was always at pains to stress that no political practice is directly transferable from one context to another, this did not mean that nothing could be gleaned from reflection upon the experience of others. It was instructive to learn how one society had overcome dangers that were common to all, but much the most important lesson was that the dangers were not in principle insurmountable. Each society would have to find its own remedy, according to its own special circumstances, but the knowledge that remedies could be found ought to be a wonderful spur to action. Tocqueville learnt much from his visit to America, as he did from his later visits to England in 1833 and 1835, and to Ireland in the latter year, and what he learnt gave him hope for France. What did he learn?

American federalism: the locality and the state

American political life began in the township, and that, for Tocqueville, was where its strength still lay. The township was, therefore, his own natural 'point of departure' (*DA*, 35). The early colonists, left largely to their own devices, rapidly developed practices of self-government. It was not until the American Revolution, however, that it was safe to proclaim 'the dogma of the sovereignty of the people', and when that happened it was from the township that it came. It was on the basis of a movement originating in the towns that the American people 'took possession of the government' (*DA*, 69).

For Tocqueville, the township was a 'natural' form of human grouping – 'so well rooted in nature that whenever men assemble it forms itself' – but it was not a grouping that was well equipped to withstand the predatoriness of larger, manmade, groupings like kingdoms and republics. It was, however, where 'the strength of a free people' resided:

> Local institutions are to liberty what primary schools are to science; they put it within the people's reach; they teach people to appreciate its peaceful enjoyment and accustom them to make use of it. Without local institutions a nation may give itself a free government, but it has not got the spirit of liberty.
>
> (*DA*, 73–4)

It was this 'spirit of liberty' that found expression in the New England township – a grouping of two to three thousand people, 'not too large for all the inhabitants to have roughly the same interests, but ... big enough to be sure of finding the elements of a good administration within itself' (*DA*, 75). It should be noted, as some commentators have done,[7] that Tocqueville was highly selective in the part of America that he chose to take as representative, restricting himself to four eastern states – Massachusetts, New York, Pennsylvania and Virginia – and Ohio, and that he concentrated on Massachusetts. He regarded the south as too tainted with slavery for it to have much to contribute to an elucidation of the tendencies of democracy. This would matter if his primary purpose had been to produce a definitive study of American politics and government, but it was not. His purpose was rather to say something definitive about democracy. Hence his selectivity is justifiable.

The New England township, which he studied in Massachusetts, had two characteristics that Tocqueville thought would always 'keenly excite men's interest': independence and power. Though its authority was bounded, 'within that domain its movements are free'. It thus enjoyed an independence that the size of its population would not ordinarily warrant. Furthermore, it was an arena where power could be exercised:

> The New Englander is attached to his township not so much because he was born there as because he sees the township as a free, strong corporation of which he is part and which is worth the trouble of trying to direct.

> (*DA*, 81)

Within the township itself power is diffused among a multiplicity of municipal offices such that 'the maximum possible number of people have some concern with public affairs' (*DA*, 82) by voting and competing for public office. Attachment to the township – which, for Tocqueville, is the foundation of patriotism in a republic – is born of frequent political participation: 'Thus daily duties performed or rights exercised keep municipal life constantly alive. There is continual gentle political activity which keeps society on the move without turmoil' (*DA*, 83). Because the township is 'strong and independent' the New Englander is prepared to invest 'his ambition and future in it'. Tocqueville continues:

> In the restricted sphere within his scope, [the New Englander] learns to rule society; he gets to know those formalities without which freedom can advance only through revolutions, and becoming imbued with their spirit, develops a taste for order, understands the harmony of power, and in the end accumulates clear, practical ideas about the nature of his duties and the extent of his rights.

> (*DA*, 83–5)

Local political power, which Tocqueville otherwise called 'administrative', lacked in itself any degree of centralization or hierarchy. The different township officials were not dependent on one another, having limited and quite separate spheres of authority 'so that there is no central point on which the radii of administrative power converge' (*DA*, 88–9). 'In general', he concluded, 'the striking feature of American public administration is extraordinary decentralization' (*DA*, 102).

American political life, of course, included more than the township. Beyond, there was the state and the Union itself. It is here that Tocqueville considers the nature of American federalism. Before following his discussion of this, it is pertinent to remark upon another aspect of American public life that he regarded as equal in importance to the township: the voluntary association. In the journal of his visit, he noted in October 1831 that America was a society of joiners. Americans formed associations for many purposes, united by trade, political, literary, temperance or religious interests. 'The power of associations', he remarked, 'has reached its highest degree in America .... It is never by recourse to a higher authority that one seeks success, but by an appeal to individual powers working in concert' (*JA*, 212). In the second part of the *Democracy*, he wrote about associations 'in civil life which have no political object'. In a democracy, where each citizen is 'independent and weak', they would collectively 'find themselves helpless if they did not learn to help each other voluntarily'. Fortunately, Americans had 'carried to the highest perfection the art of pursuing in common the objects of common desires' (*DA*, 662–3). Such voluntary non-political associations 'pave the way for political ones'. Indeed, the two forms of association were virtually reinforcing, for he went on to say that 'the art of political association singularly develops and improves this technique for civil purpose' (*DA*, 671). Political associations, however, did have some kind of primacy 'as great free schools to which all citizens come to be taught the general theory of association' (*DA*, 673).

In general, Tocqueville was inclined to believe that it was better, for the citizen's independence and public spirit, that as many as possible of the matters of common concern arising in a community be tackled by voluntary associations rather through the political structure of the township or the state. This was a point he picked up in two separate conversations in 1831 where the issue was state aid for education. Mr Spencer, then a member of the New York legislature, answered that 'it is generally accepted among us that the State should always *help* and never *do everything*' (*JA*, 32). Mr Tuckerman, a 'very zealous Presbyterian minister', agreed that if this happened, then communities 'become rather indifferent about their schools. But when they are putting their own money into them, they take a great interest in seeing that it is well employed' (*JA*, 220). Tocqueville met with similar considerations on his second visit to England in 1835. In Birmingham, he speculated:

> How one should conceive of society's obligation to its members. Is society obliged, as we think in France, to guarantee the individual and to create his well-being? Or is not its only duty rather to give the individual easy and sure means to guarantee it for himself and to create his own well-being? The first notion; simpler, more general, more *uniform*, more easily grasped by half-enlightened and superficial minds. The second; more complicated, not uniform in its application. Harder to grasp; but the only one that is true, the only one compatible with the existence of political liberty, the only one that can make citizens or even men.
>
> (*JEI*, 95–6)

The superiority of voluntary associations was that, in relying on indi-

Citizenship and community

vidual initiative, they acted as an encouragement to the citizen's civic
spirit and played a crucial role in keeping it alive. In this respect, it
was not good that every matter that arose in the public realm should
be dealt with in the strictly political arena. It was important to multiply the points where citizens could exercise their independence and
autonomous judgment.

In his assessment of American federalism, Tocqueville confronted
the problem of size. It was here that he drew a great deal on the
Federalist Papers. The question was whether a republican form of
government, by which he meant one informed by the principle of political liberty, was compatible with great territorial extent. Everything
that he had learnt from Montesquieu, and could have learnt from
Rousseau as well, told him that republics were only appropriate for
small nations. Alexander Hamilton, however, in *Federalist 9*, had
pounced on this as Montesquieu's last word on the subject. Hamilton, quoting at length, established that Montesquieu thought it quite
'expedient for extending the sphere of popular government' to em-
ploy the device of a 'CONFEDERATE REPUBLIC'.[8] The term is
Montesquieu's, and by it he meant, according to Hamilton, 'an "as-
semblage of societies" or an association of two or more States into
one State'. Hamilton concluded that Montesquieu's thinking 'fully
corresponds, in every rational import of the terms, with the idea of a
Federal Government'. [9] Tocqueville agreed. Small nations generally
had the advantage in terms in internal well-being and had 'at all times
... been the cradle of political liberty'. But small nations were vulner-
able especially in time of war. This, of course, was the great security
of a large nation. Happily, 'the federal system was devised to combine
the various advantages of large and small size for nations' (*DA*, 196–8).

The main advantage of federalism as far as the states were concerned was that 'these little societies' did not have to be preoccupied
'with cares of defence or aggrandisement'. At the level of the state the
same interested and enthusiastic concern as in the township could be
shown over matters still considered to be predominantly 'local' in
character. 'The central government of each state,' Tocqueville continued,

> being close to the governed, is continually informed of the needs
> that arise; every year new plans are put forward and discussed in
> the municipal assemblies or in the state legislature and then pub-
> lished in the press, exciting universal interest and eagerness
> among the citizens.

(*DA*, 199)

What had happened in America was that the 'republican spirit',
having been born in the township, was carried over naturally into the

state assemblies. And it was the federal principle that had allowed it to remain rooted in this context. 'It is an opinion generally current throughout America', Tocqueville claimed, and his journal notes are full of references to such an opinion, 'that the existence and survival of republican forms in the New World depend on the federal system.' The strength of the republican spirit at this level, in the 'mores and habits of liberty', made it an easy matter for it then to be 'applied without any trouble in the nation as a whole. Public spirit in the Union is, in a sense, only a summing up of provincial patriotism' (*DA*, 199). The individual citizen's defence of the union was a matter of 'enlightened self-interest':

> In defending the Union, he is defending the increasing prosperity of his district, the right to direct its affairs, and the hope of pressing through plans for improvements there which should enrich himself – all things which, in the normal run, touch men more than the general interests of the country and national glory.
>
> (*DA*, 200)

The government of the Union itself is no threat to the political liberty of the citizen, for there is so little for it to do: 'Its acts are important but rare' (*DA*, 200). It sets some of the parameters for political action elsewhere in the Union, but its overwhelming preoccupation is with defence and foreign affairs which, Tocqueville believed, created few opportunities for it to seek aggrandizement at the expense of the states. Political passion and the ambition for office, thus, find their natural home in the state and township, but the Union can call upon that passion and ambition when required. Tocqueville felt able to conclude that 'the Union is free and happy like a small nation, glorious and strong like a great one' (*DA*, 200).

This was his judgment in 1835 in the first part of the *Democracy*. It remained his judgment in the second part, which appeared in 1840. The practice of citizenship, he held, soon turns men away from narrow self-interest; they become aware that they are not independent of each other and must seek mutual help. The 'lawgivers of America' thought it right

> to give each part of the land its own political life so that there should be an infinite number of occasions for the citizens to act together and so that every day they should feel that they depended on one another. That was wise conduct.
>
> (*DA*, 658)

It was by citizens being entrusted with the management of local affairs that they developed an interest in the 'public welfare' (*DA*, 659):

The free institutions of the United States and the political rights enjoyed there provide a thousand continual reminders to every citizen that he lives in society. At every moment they bring his mind to this idea, that it is the duty as well as the interest of men to be useful to their fellows .... By dint of working for the good of his fellow citizens, he in the end acquires a habit and taste for serving them.

(*DA*, 660–1)

It is this 'enlightened self-interest', rather than civic virtue in the classical sense attributed by Tocqueville to Montesquieu, that is the mainspring of the political liberty of republican government. It allows a large nation to be both democratic and free. Political liberty depended upon a rational calculation of self-interest which demonstrated that more could be done by voluntary cooperative effort, than could be if every man regarded himself as either self-sufficient, which of course he was not, or indifferent to his fellows, which he could easily become. The practice of virtue thus stemmed from self-interest 'properly understood'. It did not dispose men to make great sacrifices,

but every day it prompts some small ones; by itself it cannot make a man virtuous, but its discipline shapes a lot of orderly, temperate, moderate, careful, and self-controlled citizens. If it does not lead the will directly to virtue, it establishes habits which unconsciously turn it that way.

(*DA*, 679)

It was in this same way that Tocqueville wrote more directly about republican patriotism. He distinguished between an 'instinctive' and a 'well-considered' patriotism. The former was 'a sort of religion' – unreflective, appropriate for a people whose mores were simple and for societies where legitimacy was assured. The latter was a rational patriotism – reflective and 'mingled with personal interest'. It was evoked by men being given an interest in their country's fate, and there was no surer means to secure this than by making them 'take a share in its government. In our day it seems to me that civic spirit is inseparable from the exercise of political rights.' It was in this way that national pride and patriotism arose in the United States (*DA*, 290–2). In the final chapter of part one of the *Democracy*, however, Tocqueville argued that this patriotism was not attached to the Union itself, but to the individual states. 'The Union is a vast body', he claimed, 'and somewhat vague as the object of patriotism.' It is in the state that matters of an immediate and familiar nature to the citizen are dealt with, and it is the state, therefore, which elicits his attachment. The state 'is identified with the soil, with the right of property, the family, memories of the past, activities of the present, and dreams for the future'. Interest, custom and feeling are thus concentrated in the political life of the state, not in that of the Union. This did not alter the character of patriotism, 'which is most often nothing but an extension of individual egoism' (at this stage of the *Democracy*, 'egoism' had yet to acquire its pejorative meaning); it simply changed its object (*DA*, 455–6). And Tocqueville could consistently maintain that, if and when the Union should prove necessary to protect the political life of state and township, then this kind of patriotism could be called upon by the Union.

This description of American political life bears little resemblance to Tocqueville's direful analysis of the tendencies of democracy, and it is anyway an incomplete account of his thinking. It represents America at its best. But Tocqueville was alive to the fact that the tendencies of democracy were at work in America. He could, therefore, only be guardedly optimistic about the future of political liberty there. What Tocqueville feared most for America was the tyranny of the majority.

His comments on the power of the majority in the United States follow on from his general discussion which has already been cited. Part of what it meant to describe America as a democracy was that the majority was sovereign, that the people had the power to do anything, no matter that it might be unjust. It was this unlimited power which was dangerous to liberty and which was his 'greatest complaint against democratic government as organized in the United States'; not its weakness, 'but rather its irresistible strength. What I find most repulsive in America is not the extreme freedom reigning there but the shortage of guarantees against tyranny' (*DA*, 311). An aggrieved citizen had nowhere safe to appeal, for public opinion, legislature, executive power, police and juries all emanated from and reflected the majority. It was not that there actually were frequent acts of tyranny, but that there was 'no guarantee against it' (*DA*, 313). But there was more to the tyranny of the majority than its irresistible institutionalized power. This was its power over thought and opinion.

Tocqueville was scathing. 'I know no country', he noted, 'in which, generally speaking, there is less independence of mind and true freedom of discussion than in America.' People were much freer in Europe, even under absolute governments. But, 'in America the majority has enclosed thought within a formidable fence. A writer is free inside that area, but woe to the man who goes beyond it' (*DA*, 314–5). This was why America had yet to produce any great writers, for, 'literary genius cannot exist without freedom of the spirit, and there is no freedom of spirit in America' (*DA*, 317). Furthermore, the ever-increasing despotism of the majority in America accounted for the ever-diminishing number of 'distinguished men in political life'. The American Revolution had produced these in great numbers, but democratic practices meant that the favour of small men had to be courted. In his journal notes, Tocqueville was contemptuous of the results of universal suffrage. He thought Andrew Jackson a singularly poor choice for President – 'a very mediocre man'. And yet what had prompted the people to choose him? The fact that he won the Battle of New Orleans – 'a very ordinary feat of arms' (*JA*, 158). There was worse to come. He was appalled at 'how low the people's choice can descend' in the election of congressmen. Two years prior to his visit,

> the district of which Memphis is the capital, sent to the House of Representatives of Congress an individual called David Crockett, who had received no education, could read only with difficulty, had no property, no fixed dwelling, but spent his time hunting, selling his game for a living, and spending his whole life in the woods.

> (*JA*, 254)

In the *Democracy* itself, Tocqueville insisted that in making these comments about the majority, he was 'speaking not of the federal government but of the governments of each state, where a despotic majority is in control' (*DA*, 321).

Despite these strictures, Tocqueville still felt able to marvel at the American experience, which – against the odds, it seemed – still allowed a high degree of political liberty to co-exist with democratic forms. He was naturally disposed to enquire why. What were the conditions and circumstances which permitted such a state of affairs?

The peculiarities of the Americans

'The habit of dealing with all matters by discussion,' Senator Gray of Massachusetts told Tocqueville, 'and deciding them all, even the smallest, by means of majorities, that is the hardest habit of all to acquire. But it is only that habit that shapes governments that are truly free' (*JA*, 57). Tocqueville agreed: 'Political liberty,' he noted in his journal, 'is a difficult food to digest' (*JA*, 180), but the Americans had been peculiarly fortunate in this respect. One of the consistent themes running through both Tocqueville's notes and the *Democracy* is the alliance of 'the spirit of liberty' and 'the spirit of religion'. Underlying these were the mores of the people: 'the sum of the moral and intellectual dispositions of men in society' (*DA*, 377). The Americans had a long practice of self-government before they sought political independence, and this had contributed to the great political sense, the 'enlightenment' of the people, to which he repeatedly drew attention in the *Democracy*, and which accounted for the fact of their establishing a federal system of government in the immediate post-Revolutionary years, and understanding it sufficiently to make it work.

America's 'point of departure' was the New England settlement, and New England was settled by Puritans. This fact was of crucial significance, for 'Puritanism was not just a religious doctrine; in many respects it shared the most absolute democratic and republican theories' (*DA*, 40). From the start, therefore, religion and liberty were inextricably linked. The original Mayflower Compact of 1620 established 'a civil body politic', which 'enjoyed more internal freedom and political independence than those of other nations' (*DA*, 44–5). The link between the colonies and England was only of the most tenuous kind, and the colonies continually exercised 'rights of sovereignty; they appointed magistrates, made peace and war, promulgated police regulations, and executed laws as if they were dependent on God alone' (*DA*, 46). The political laws were democratic in the extreme, involving 'the participation of the people in public affairs, the free voting of taxes, the responsibility of government officials, individual freedom, and trial by jury' (*DA*, 50). The contrast with Europe – where political life started at the top and only gradually, if at all, percolated down – could not be more stark: 'Contrariwise, in America one may say that the local community was organized before the county, the county before the state, and the state before the Union.' Each local community enjoyed 'a real active political life which was completely democratic and republican'. There were 'no representative institutions. As at Athens, matters of common concern were dealt with in the marketplace and in the general assembly of the citizens' (*DA*, 51).

Such a long familiarity with free political practices resulted in the American people being 'not only the most enlightened in the world, but, – what I put much higher than that advantage – ... the one whose practical political education is the most advanced' (*JA*, 179). In the aftermath of the Revolution, Americans simply resumed a practice to which they had long been accustomed. This made the American Revolution very different to the French. The French Revolution was like a religious revolution in that it was aimed not just at overturning the French social system, but at 'a regeneration of the whole human race. It created an atmosphere of missionary fervor and, indeed, assumed all the aspects of a religious revival.'[10] Not so the American. The American Revolution was more a restoration than an overturning. It 'was caused by a mature and thoughtful taste for freedom, not by some vague, undefined instinct for independence. No disorderly passions drove it on; on the contrary, it proceeded hand in hand with a love of order and legality' (*DA*, 86). Their enlightenment and their political experience equipped the American people well for an understanding of, and ability to manage, a federal system of government.

A federal system was, Tocqueville thought, inherently complex, for it 'necessarily brings two sovereignties face to face', and however skilful the lawgiver is in balancing the two and keeping them within their respective domains, 'he cannot contrive that they shall be but one or prevent their touching somewhere'. This demands, therefore, that the governed, when they engage in politics 'use the lights of their reason everyday'. Tocqueville was frightened 'to see how much diverse knowledge and discernment [the federal constitution] assumes on the part of the governed' (*DA*, 202). A federal system, therefore, 'is only suited to a people long accustomed to manage its affairs, and one in which even the lowest ranks of society have an appreciation of political science'. Such was the American people, whose 'good sense and practical intelligence' enabled them to 'avoid the innumerable difficulties deriving from their federal Constitution' (*DA*, 203). Democratic government was itself a great educator, extending the mental horizons of a people and making for greater enlightenment and creative activity. In the process, 'it spreads throughout the body social a restless activity, superabundant force, and energy never found elsewhere, which, however little favoured by circumstance, can do wonders' (*DA*, 301–2). There was one institution, in particular, that had this educative effect: the jury system. Tocqueville was convinced that 'the main reason for the practical intelligence and the political good sense of the Americans is their long experience with juries in civil cases' (*DA*, 339). As he commented in his journal,

> The jury introduces a habit of argument and experience of public affairs to a great many people. It teaches a people to become involved in public business and to think of the business of society as being its own. It gives great outward strength to justice, it prevents the magistracy from becoming a body outside the people and gives it immense and almost always useful power in political questions. Established in civil affairs as in criminal ones, it gets such a grip on customs and enters so far into ideas and morals that it becomes impossible to abolish it in criminal cases. Now one cannot conceive a people in which a jury is solidly established which is not a free people.
>
> (*JA*, 296–7)

A jury system was both the mark of a free people, and a continual re-

minder to them that 'they have duties toward society .... By making
men pay attention to things other than their own affairs, they combat
individual selfishness which is like rust in society' (*DA*, 339).

Despite the Americans' history of the practice and habits of political liberty – a practice which they had carried over from colonial
times into independence under a federal system – Tocqueville believed that this on its own could not account for the vitality and
energy, and the forbearance, which he found displayed in American
political life. In the introduction to the *Democracy*, he wrote that
democratic governments neglected religion at their peril, for freedom untempered was anarchic: 'One cannot establish the reign of
liberty without mores, and mores cannot be firmly grounded without
beliefs' (*DA*, 15). 'Mores' is the more inclusive term here, for it refers
not only to religious beliefs, but also to the intellectual and moral habits of a people (*DA*, 377). What creates a society is not laws, but
mores: 'only when certain men consider a great many questions from
the same point of view and have the same opinions on a great many
subjects, and when the same events give rise to like thoughts and im-
pressions is there a society.' So mores refer to similarity of thought
and opinion over a wide range. Thus, Tocqueville noted, America has
a plentiful supply of religious sects, but they 'all look at religion from
the same point of view'. They may differ about the most expedient
form of government, 'but they agree about the general principles that
should rule human societies', having 'the same ideas concerning freedom and equality'. They were all committed to the freedoms
enshrined in the Constitution, and accepted that each individual was
not just the best interpreter of his own interest, but also had 'the faculty to rule himself'. Tocqueville did not necessarily think that such
beliefs were correct, 'but they are American' (*DA*, 463–4). No society
could exist, still less prosper, without ideas in common, for if these
were lacking,

> no common action would be possible, and without common action
> men might exist, but there could be no body social. So for society
> to exist and, even more, for society to prosper, it is essential that
> all the minds of the citizens should always be rallied and held
> together by some leading ideas; and that could never happen un-
> less each of them sometimes came to draw his opinions from the
> same source and was ready to accept some beliefs ready made.
>
> (*DA*, 555)

It is when this happens that one may speak of a society's mores. Acceptance of mores means that each individual to an extent places his
mind in bondage, 'but it is a salutary bondage, which allows him to
make good use of freedom' (*DA*, 556).

While, thus, it is mores that are truly fundamental in shaping the political life of a people, yet it is the taking of a religion seriously that results in mores that are conducive to political liberty. This interdependence of liberty and religion was insisted upon by Tocqueville's many interlocutors in America in 1831 and 1832. Joel Poinsett, for instance, a member of the South Carolina legislature and a former US Minister to Mexico, remarked:

> I think that the state of religion in America is one of the things that most powerfully helps us to maintain our republican institutions. The religious spirit exercises a direct power over political passions, and also an indirect power by sustaining morals.
>
> (*JA*, 114)

Religion moralizes politics. 'By their practice,' Tocqueville claimed, 'Americans show that they feel the urgent necessity to instill morality into democracy by means of religion' (*DA*, 700). Conditions of equality and freedom require religion, for, in the absence of aristocratic authority in politics, there would then be nothing to prevent men being 'soon frightened by the limitless independence with which they are faced'. In fact, Tocqueville doubted 'whether man can support complete religious independence and entire political liberty at the same time'. If men are to be free, they must believe (*DA*, 569). Writing of the Puritanism of the New England colonies, he commented upon the 'marvellous combination' of 'the *spirit of religion* and the *spirit of freedom*'. Puritanism held the colonists 'within the narrowest bounds by fixed religious beliefs', but left them 'free from all political prejudices':

> Thus, in the moral world everything is classified, coordinated, foreseen, and decided in advance. In the world of politics everything is in turmoil, contested and uncertain. In the one case obedience is passive, though voluntary; in the other there is independence, contempt of experience, and jealousy of all authority .... Religion is considered as the guardian of mores, and mores are regarded as the guarantee of the laws and pledge for the maintenance of freedom itself.
>
> (*DA*, 54–5)

From the point of view of society it was important that all citizens 'profess religion', whatever its truth; but it was equally important that the citizen genuinely believe his religion to be true – that is, that it hold hope or fear for the after-life – for only if this were so could religion influence a man's conduct. By directing mores and 'regulating domestic life', religion was a most important political institution, for it prevented citizens from 'imagining' – and forbade them 'to dare' –

action inimical to political liberty. Though it did not interfere directly in the Americans' conduct of their government, Tocqueville
believed that religion should 'be considered as the first of their political institutions: ... it did not give them the taste for liberty, [but] it
singularly facilitates their use thereof' (*DA*, 359–62).

The Americans were a religious people; the very diversity of the
sects spoke of the power of religion. But that power rested, Tocqueville held, on a strict and 'complete separation of church and state'.
Such separation prevented clerics being taunted by worldly, political
concerns. Religion could not 'share the material strength of the rulers without being burdened with some of the animosity roused
against them' (*DA*, 365–7). Such a view had been expressed to Tocqueville by a New England Catholic priest in the summer of 1831:
'the less religion and the clergy are mixed up with civil government,'
Mr Mullon told him, 'the less will they come in to political arguments, and the more will religious ideas gain in power' (*JA*, 33). It was
a view that was powerfully reinforced by a succession of Catholic
priests during Tocqueville's visit to Ireland in the summer of 1835,
after publication of the first part of the *Democracy*. Dr Kinsley, for
instance, Bishop of Kilkenny, held that any link between Church and
state

> would break the union now existing between clergy and people.
> Now the people regard us as their own handiwork, and are at-
> tached to us because of what they give us. If we received money
> from the State they would regard us as officials of the State, and
> when we advised them to respect law and order they would say
> 'That is what they are paid for'.
>
> (*JEI*, 145)

Religious belief was powerful in men's souls precisely because the
churches were not connected in any way to the state. Tocqueville returned to this view in the second part of the *Democracy*: 'it is ever the
duty of lawgivers and of all upright educated men to raise up the souls
of their fellow citizens and turn their attention toward heaven', but
not by attaching the Church to the state. Lawgivers should teach by
example, and always act as if they were themselves believers (*DA*,
702–4). It was religion, thus, that gave tone to mores, which in turn
ensured that Americans used their political institutions wisely, kept
the dangerous tendencies of majority tyranny from having their ener-
vating effect, and maintained a lively and rational patriotism.

But the American people enjoyed a further advantage: their geographical position. In many places Tocqueville commented on the
weakness of the federal government, due to the incompleteness of
government centralization. It was weak first of all in relation to the

governments of the states, for whereas the sovereignty of the states is 'natural', that of the Union 'is a work of art'. In the case of conflict between Union and states, therefore, one 'could not assure the pre-ponderance of the federal power' (*DA*, 205). Further, since for most nations war was an ever-present threat, the weakness of the federal power might find itself dangerously revealed if it were compelled to 'defend itself against other completely centralised nations' (*DA*, 207–8). While geographical position could not insure against the first weakness, it could against the second – or so Tocqueville believed:

> Placed in the middle of a huge continent with limitless room for expansion of human endeavour, the Union is almost as isolated from the world as if it were surrounded on all sides by the ocean .... The great good fortune of the United States is not to have found a federal Constitution enabling them to conduct great wars, but to be so situated that there is nothing for them to fear.
>
> (*DA*, 209)

The Union was safe from external threat for, if it had enemies, they were simply too far away to pose any danger. Tocqueville was at times apprehensive about the possibility of conflict between the states and the Union, but he held that the fact that 'the same level of civilisa-tion' obtained from Maine to Georgia, and from the Missouri to the Atlantic, 'wonderfully smooths the existence of the federal govern-ment'. So it is good laws and common mores that ensure that whatever conflict does arise between state and Union is kept from having damaging effects as a result of this 'inherent defect of federal governments' (*DA*, 206–7).

Conclusion

Tocqueville's own commitment was to a life of politics. He believed that every individual ought to have a similar commitment. The man who lived a free life, within the 'predestined circle' that surrounded all men and all societies, was one who attempted to take control and push human potentialities to the limit. The man who lived a free pol-itical life did this in the company of his fellows, and in doing so celebrated both his own capacities as a human being and the fact that living is a shared venture. The man who lived a wholly private life, for whatever reason – either from voluntary withdrawal or through being denied opportunities to act politically – lived an incomplete life. Though Tocqueville did not make it in this way, the distinction was between 'man' and 'citizen'.

Tocqueville's citizen was an autonomous being – not autonomous in the sense of discarding all received customs and opinion, and acting as a sovereign self, untrammelled by historical accretion, as though each man's life could start the world anew; but autonomous in the sense of recognizing that there were limits to human endeavour – the 'predestined circle' again – but that those limits were often drawn more narrowly than they need be, exercising an independent, but conjoint, judgment on matters of common concern in institutions where the initiative for action came from the citizen himself. Citizens act against a determinate background, but a background which is never so determinate and inflexible that it cannot be a matter for negotiation. Citizens, in other words, are not asked simply and merely to respond to proposals emanating from elsewhere; they are to generate the proposals themselves.

The practice of citizenship, which was what Tocqueville meant by 'political' liberty, reflected a balance between the rights and the duties of the individual. Social life was not based upon contract, with the idea that one could withdraw from its obligations if its terms were not being fulfilled. Social life might exist to serve individual purposes, but it needed a less fragile basis than contract. It was something that man was born into – and which thus incorporated duties and responsibilities associated with its continuity – and was sanctioned by prevalent mores that antedated each man's existence. The individual became a citizen by acknowledging these duties and responsibilities, and while he might always, and legitimately, seek to change their terms, he could never renounce them, or simply not perform them, and still remain a citizen. In Tocqueville's eyes, the man who withdrew from public life was not a citizen. He might enjoy a whole array of 'rights' as an individual, rights guaranteed by the civil law of his country, but to be a citizen was to accept responsibility for the intergenerational continuity of social life and, in that acceptance, to pronounce one's autonomy. Social life is ingrained in mores, and mores did not often permit a practice of citizenship; where they did, as Tocqueville believed they did in America, it was gross dereliction not to engage in the practice. For the way of life of a citizen was a fuller life, more active and energetic, overall more dynamically human than that of the withdrawn individual. In this, Tocqueville was at one with Machiavelli.

For Machiavelli, what informed the practice of citizenship was civic *virtù*; for Tocqueville, however, it was 'enlightened self-interest'. But, as we have seen, the civic *virtù* of Machiavelli's citizen was by no means totally devoid of reference to private interest. The citizen is willing to devote himself, when called upon, to public ends, crucially when the republic is under threat, because he realizes that fulfilment of his private good is conditional upon the survival of a republican way of life, which allows him his political role of citizen. His patriotism is not a blind, instinctive feeling, but the result of a considered reflection upon the natural support which both he and the republic need. Just so with Tocqueville's enlightened self-interest. Tocqueville claimed the Americans were not a virtuous people, but they were enlightened. It was utility that directed them into paths of public virtue, not a belief that public virtue was good in itself. American political life was highly participatory; it gave great scope to political liberty, which the citizens used to control those common concerns which most affected their daily living. Because this was so, the citizen was prepared to sacrifice immediate private interest in order to preserve the whole of which he was a part.

Democratic tendencies, however, threatened political liberty. Either an excessive centralization would deny opportunities for its practice, or the citizen's autonomy and independence of judgment would be undermined by majority tyranny. In relation to centralization, Tocqueville believed the Americans had solved the problem: a federal system, especially one which went further than strict federalism to guarantee the political independence of the local community, gave citizens ample scope for political action. The arena for the practice of citizenship was, however, wider than the narrowly political in Tocqueville's emphasis on voluntary associations, economic, intellectual and moral. The experience of cooperative action in both these spheres was powerfully educative, lifting men's mental and moral horizons above their own particular concerns, enlightening them as to where their true self-interest lay. Here Tocqueville has an obvious affinity with Hegel (in the role the latter assigned to the Corporation in the individual's overall *Bildung*), though, of course, for Tocqueville the associations were not systematically integrated into the structure of the state.

Majority tyranny over political action could be countered by the federal system itself, but Tocqueville was more concerned with its tyranny over thought and opinion. It is here that Tocqueville stressed mores, and in the view of some commentators this is one of the great originalities of his thinking.[11] But as we have seen, Rousseau also emphasized *mœurs* as the fundamental factor governing the political practices of any country. Within mores what was important was religion – not the civil religion of Machiavelli or Rousseau, but conventional Christianity which, though it was weak on the duties of citizenship, could incorporate them without difficulty. It was religious faith, acting as a solid foundation of belief as opposed to the ephemeral whimsy of majority opinion, which put a brake upon any tendencies of political liberty towards anarchy and inconstancy. It was religious faith, furthermore, that moralized relationships between citizens. In the township, the original political unit of the

Americans and still the one where the strength of political liberty was most in evidence, religion created a bond of attachment between citizens that prompted them to seek solutions in common to whatever difficulties befell them. The township was not a community of strangers; it was small enough for everybody to know each other, and if they were not 'friends' in the conventional sense, they could approach their relationships with each other in an Aristotelian spirit of 'concord'. From the loyalty which citizens had to their local communities sprang that larger patriotism which could, when the times demanded, be focused on the state, and even the Union itself. Though Tocqueville dismissed classical antiquity, he stands within the civic-republican tradition that originated there.

Part III

Citizenship and community in the modern world

Chapter seven

The modern relevance of the civic-republican tradition

In this chapter and the next, the modern relevance of the civic-republican tradition will be assessed, and recent contributions to democratic theory will be examined in terms of how far they address issues about the practice of citizenship in a political community. This chapter focuses on civic-republican thinking, whilst the emphasis of the next chapter is on recent democratic theory.

An analysis was offered in Chapter 2 of the connections between citizenship and the political community. This analysis was intended to be consistent with major elements of the civic-republican tradition of western political thought. Examination of the four exemplars of that tradition, presented in Part II, indicates that that analysis is now justified. Chapter 2 finished with an indication of the kind of conditions that need to be met before one can expect that individuals will engage in this practice of citizenship. These conditions are that individuals need resources: they need empowering – in terms of knowledge, skills, information, time and well-being – to become effective agents in the world. They need opportunities – in terms of the decentralization of both political and economic power – in which they can be effective agents, that is, citizens. Finally, they need to be provided with the required motivation to take the practice of citizenship seriously, in terms of performing the duties which they owe to the political community of which they are members. The strength of civic republicanism lies in what it has to say about the practice of citizenship, and about how individuals may be motivated to engage in the practice.

Civic republicanism is communitarian. It stresses not that which differentiates individuals from each other and from the community, but rather what they share with other individuals, and what integrates them into the community. The bonds that tie individuals to one another may be the friendly, concordant ones noted in Rousseau and Tocqueville, the loyalty generated by commitment to a common enterprise that characterized the citizen of the Roman republic that

Machiavelli wrote about, or the deep shared understanding of a way of ethical life that Hegel held out for modern man. There is no doubt, however, that civic-republican thinking has, for its subject matter, different individuals. Individuals are different in personality and character, and in interest. This is a statement of empirical fact, and in most cases – Rousseau being the exception – a welcome fact. For Hegel, it is the very differentiation that makes a higher form of ethical life both necessary and possible in the conscious, or subjective, unity of particular and universal. Differences in talent and skill between individuals led Machiavelli to conclude that republican governments are inherently stronger and more durable than princedoms because, in drawing on these skills, they can be more flexible in dealing with whatever issues and problems arise. In Tocqueville's thought, 'individuality' is something to be praised, because it is that which is most expressive of human freedom, which itself achieves its highest expression in political liberty. For Rousseau, on the other hand, difference and particularity are always potentially degenerative of the civil liberty which is secured in the political community. Yet Rousseau's stress on the autonomy of the individual will is arguably the strongest to be found in civic republicanism; but the individual's autonomy is only evidence of moral agency if his particularity is subordinated to the general will, which is his will as citizen.

Difference has to be overcome, but the quality or characteristic that has to be implanted in individuals – for Machiavelli, 'civic *virtù*'; for Rousseau, 'civil liberty'; for Hegel, 'subjective freedom'; and for Tocqueville, 'enlightened self-interest' – has to appeal to individual difference and interest if it is to take root and grow. Tocqueville had been at pains to distinguish enlightened self-interest from what Montesquieu had called 'civic virtue'. Civic virtue, as Montesquieu used the term, appeared to mean for Tocqueville a devotion to the ends of the community in denial of self. Tocqueville was no doubt correct in concluding that Americans were not virtuous in this sense. Yet what is interesting and significant is that neither Machiavelli's *virtù*, nor Rousseau's civil liberty, nor Hegel's subjective freedom, enjoin such a denial of self. Machiavelli's citizen displays civic *virtù* – that is, a willingness to attend to the ends of the republic and in particular, to defend it – because the republic both guarantees his place in the political order, where he can press his individual interest, and protects his economic livelihood and his family. In practising civil liberty, Rousseau's citizen attends to hard personal interest. It is that part of his interest which he shares with his fellow citizens; it finds its expression in law through the general will, which both comes from all and applies to all equally. Hegel's citizen experiences subjective freedom in the union within his consciousness of the particularity of his ends with the universal ends of the state, given by Spirit. The virtue of citizens in civic republicanism thus nowhere demands the denial of self that Tocqueville seemed to think Montesquieu required. Tocqueville's own assessment of enlightened self-interest draws attention to the fact that in involving himself in the public affairs of the community the citizen recognizes where his true interest lies.

Within civic republicanism, citizens earn their title to the status of citizen by an effort of will when they attend to the duties and responsibilities which are the defining characteristics of the practice of citizenship. These duties relate principally to the defence of the republic, and to the exercise of judgment on common affairs. For Machiavelli, the predominant duty of citizenship was military service. It was this that secured the integrity and autonomy of the republic, and it could be both defensive and aggressive, depending on judgment about how best to deal with perceived threats. It was also the function, though for Machiavelli it was hardly the duty, of citizen participation in political deliberation to lend strength to the republic, and to preserve the political liberty on which that strength depended, by acting as a check on aristocratic pretensions to political power. Republican politics was conflictual, but conflict was to be laid aside when the republic was under threat.

In Rousseau's *Social Contract*, the citizen was to take seriously his duty to participate in the deliberations of the sovereign assembly. He was to participate and use his judgment as citizen, and attend only to that part of his will and interest that was general. Should the citizen not perform his duty here – by, for instance, paying other people to act politically on his behalf, or to fight in his place should the republic be threatened – then not only would the practice of citizenship be at an end, but the republic, too, would be dead. It was only by recognizing that his duty was, in this respect, also his interest, that Rousseau's citizen was properly free. In this effort of self-mastery he achieved the moral liberty of virtuous conduct, and thereby the possibility of happiness. Performance of duty, therefore, not only sustained the republic, but also appealed to the citizen's own truest interest: happiness.

For Hegel's citizens, there is clearly great effort involved – not only in coming to recognize what subjective freedom consists in, but also in acting accordingly within the institutional structure of Hegel's state. In the Corporations, and in the Assembly of Estates, citizens use their political judgment to perform a crucial mediating role between individual particularity and the universality of Spirit as much on behalf of others as they do on their own account. It is plausible to think of this as a duty of citizenship, though this is not how Hegel describes this activity. Beyond this, the duty of citizens – and, it would appear, also of those who are not citizens – is, as with Machiavelli, military service. It is in their willingness to risk life in defence of the state that individuals demonstrate, literally almost conclusively, that they have reached the condition of subjective freedom: the full incorporation within their own particularity of the universality of the ethical life of the state.

It is also evidently one of the duties of citizenship in Tocqueville's analysis of American political life to come to the defence of the Union. It was happily not one of those duties which he thought they would often be called upon to perform, given America's relative isolation. Citizens perform their duties more regularly in the judgment they bring to bear on the public affairs of the townships in which they live. Here they demonstrate their attachment to interests larger than their own private concerns, in political assemblies and in a variety of voluntary associations. If citizens are tempted to withdraw from the public arena, as Tocqueville feared they would be all too ready to do in the pursuit of material gain, then political liberty would be no more.

What characterizes this willingness to attend to public duties in civic republicanism is patriotism: the 'political sentiment', as Hegel described it. Attachment and loyalty are shown to the community in the practice of citizenship; this practice, in turn, also reinforces that very loyalty. It is a 'reflective' patriotism, as Tocqueville termed it, based upon a citizen's reasoning about his true interests. Patriotism undoubtedly appeals to 'interest', but interest in the largest and most generous sense.

Something must be said in this context about the place of war in both Machiavelli's and Hegel's political thinking. Military discipline and the display of military *virtù* are, for Machiavelli, seen as reinforcing patriotism and the practice of citizenship. For Hegel, the willingness to risk life in defence of the state is seen as evidence of subjective freedom, but not as necessary for reaching that condition. It is no doubt true that solidarity is elicited when a community is under threat. The 'political sentiment' must exist, however, even if only in latent form, for it to be called forth; and it is not only war that can generate the solidarity of patriotism, but any usurpation of the autonomy and independence of a community. This applies, thus, as much to the state itself as it does to local political units within a state or to functional communities – Tocqueville's voluntary associations, for instance, or Hegel's Corporations.

These considerations relate to a natural part of civic-republican thought: namely that citizens have opportunities for the performance of their duties. This aspect of civic-republican thought has great point and relevance for any modern discussion of the practice of citizenship. The citizen body in Machiavelli's analysis of the Roman republic was a large minority of the Roman people, which both directly and indirectly (through the tribunate) participated in and contributed to the political deliberations of the republic. It is Rousseau, however, who poses the problem for the modern world: if everyone is to be a citizen in the fullest sense, then the state must be small. This problem of size is tackled directly by Hegel, and even more so by Tocqueville.

Hegel recognizes that the opportunities for most people to participate at the highest level in political life – either in the universal class of civil servants, or in the Assembly of Estates – are limited and that therefore opportunities must be provided for public involvement elsewhere. It is in his analysis of the functional communities of the Corporations as one of the 'ethical roots' of the state that Hegel creates these other opportunities. Here citizens are Janus-faced. In their mediating function, they represent the particularity of the Corporation interest to the state, and the universality of the ends of the state to Corporation members. Marx, of course, thought this an impossible task: it was asking people to be schizophrenic.[1] But Marx did not understand, or did not indicate that he understood, what Hegel meant by mediation.

It is Tocqueville, however, who addresses the problem more fully. Not only does he more than cover, in his discussion of voluntary associations, the ground that Hegel deals with in his analysis of the functions of the Corporation, though in a less philosophically rigorous manner; but in his analysis of American federalism he draws attention to the fact that if 'political liberty' is to mean anything in a large state, then political tasks have to be broken down, and as much as possible has to be decentralized, even if this should mean some overall loss in efficiency. Political liberty is exercised at its fullest in the locality, where it is easiest for the citizen to make the transition from his private interest to his public duty. The locality must have some guaranteed autonomy and independence, otherwise citizens will not feel it worth their while to participate in its deliberations. The American Constitution guaranteed, so it seemed, the political autonomy of the states of the Union, but the township enjoyed its independence only at the discretion of the individual state. What would seem to be required, therefore, for any large state is a division of political responsibility in an entrenched way, such that more inclusive units cannot, at their discretion, usurp the functions and powers of less inclusive ones. Tocqueville pointed the way here, or maybe America did. At all events, it is only in the locality, or in the functional community, that the modern citizen of a large state can have the opportunity for the exercise of political liberty.

Citizenship and community

While the major emphasis in civic-republican thought is on citizenship, it does not neglect the need for political leadership. Republican government is mixed government, not a direct democracy; the one, the few and the many are all involved. This is true even for Rousseau, who is often thought of as the advocate of direct democracy. It is only the sovereign assembly that is truly democratic, and its concerns are solely with determination of the form of government, and with the declaration of law. 'Government', in Rousseau's thought, occupies a subordinate place, and can be either monarchical or aristocratic. So long as it rules according to law, then a republican political form obtains. It would, Rousseau believed, be very unwise for government to be democratic, since government has to do with the application of law to particular circumstances and individuals. The *demos* would, as sovereign, be attending to wholly general matters and, as government, to wholly particular matters. Rousseau thought this would undermine the capacity of citizens to keep the general will uppermost in their minds. For Rousseau, one of the functions of government, and hence of political leadership, was to maintain all those institutions which reinforced the *mœurs* of a people and ensured that citizens would perform their duties.

This is also the function of political leadership in Machiavelli's thought. Kings were abolished when the republic was established, but regal power was retained so that the republic could respond to crises. Such leaders provided citizens with examples of heroic devotion to the cause of the republic which they could hope to emulate. In this, they performed a function analogous to that of a legislator or prophet in constituting a people in the first place. Religious leaders were also seen in political terms as sustaining the healthy patriotism of a people.

Political leadership in Hegel's thought is most evident in the power of the Crown and the universal class of civil servants. It is leadership from these sources which represents to the citizen body the effective unity of will of the state. The monarch may or may not be purely symbolic of this unity – Hegel does at times suggest that the monarch does more than dot the 'i', say 'yes', or 'I will' – but the function of the universal class is specifically to apply the universal ends of the state (its laws, that is), to the particularity of individual interest and circumstance.

By contrast, it is Tocqueville who least emphasizes political leadership. Like the framers of the American Constitution, he did not expect the President to have much to do except symbolize the Union. The ultimate guarantor of political liberty was religious belief. If this failed, Tocqueville believed that no amount of political leadership would compensate in inculcating the mores necessary for

150

the practice of citizenship. Tocqueville aside, political leadership in civic republicanism has the task of dealing with human weakness and ignorance.

It is a consistent theme of civic-republican thought that human beings are weak and shortsighted. Whether from ignorance or an insistent selfishness – Tocqueville's 'egoism' – they either do not always see where their true interest lies, or they are prone to forget it. Both Machiavelli and Rousseau write of the propitious founding and formation of a people by some semi-divine being, a legislator or prophet. A legislator can provide a people with the appropriate character, but he can never so mould a people in this way as to eradicate human weakness.

The practice of citizenship is a fragile one, and it needs support. This is found in the *mœurs* of a people, which are themselves sustained for Machiavelli and Rousseau by a civil religion. This places civic duty and patriotism in an elevated position as the overriding concern of citizens, which they neglect on pain of divine disfavour. Neither Machiavelli nor Rousseau – nor, for that matter, Hegel – thought that Christianity, or rather the Christian Church, could fulfil this role: it had little to say about duties to *patria*. There are differences between the civil religions of Machiavelli and Rousseau. Machiavelli's civil religion is an evocation of the pagan religions of the ancient world, striking fear into citizens and, suitably presented, arousing them to heights of patriotic zeal and enthusiasm; Rousseau's is a form of deism – a simple faith that prompts a citizen body never to forget where duty lies. For both, the function of religion was to sustain the republic.

Tocqueville did not believe that Christianity, though it had in the past neglected the duties a citizen owed his country, was without redeeming features. It could be adapted and give support to the mores of citizens, but only if it did not become a state religion. The more a church was separated from the state, the more likely it was to generate and sustain genuine belief. The function of religion overall, however, remained the same. Indeed, Tocqueville went further than Machiavelli or Rousseau in insisting that without religion, political liberty would degenerate into tyranny: a people indifferent to religion could not remain free.

Religion – for Machiavelli, Rousseau and Tocqueville – has the task of ministering to human weakness; it seeks to strengthen the will to performance of civic duty. Hegel's approach towards religion was different; if anything, it brings knowledge, and thus caters to human ignorance. Hegel's objection to Christianity was that it located ultimate human redemption in a life beyond this world, whereas the historical project of Spirit was to have its fulfilment on this earth.

Hegel's political philosophy may be read as a secularized religion. The philosophical reconciliation to the necessity of the historical process, which the individual achieves in subjective freedom, may be likened to a coming-to-terms with the injunctions of a religious faith. It is not the same as a religious conversion, for rational effort is involved and, despite Pascal's wager,[2] one cannot rationally determine to believe. Further, it is not so much that religion reinforces performance of a duty that the citizen already knows about from other sources: it is rather that the philosophical reconciliation is itself a recognition of what the duties are. From knowledge proceeds performance, in a Socratic manner. It is only through ignorance that citizens do not perform their duty.

The reinforcement which the practice of citizenship requires in civic republicanism extends beyond a civil religion. Machiavelli writes about good laws and good examples of patriotic endeavour; Rousseau writes about public games and festivals much after the ancient pattern. Both are much concerned with the education of the young, but both also know that education does not cease the moment the child reaches physical maturity. Much rests upon the mores of a people – the overall customs, habits and moral codes of a specific form of life. This emphasis is explicit in Rousseau and Tocqueville, but it underlies the thought of Machiavelli and Hegel as well. The systematic means by which mores are inculcated and maintained is, fairly clearly, a species of paternalism, and questions have naturally arisen as to how far this is consistent with the moral autonomy of the individual citizen. In some senses citizens are *in statu pupillari* for the whole of their lives.

It is here that civic republicanism definitively parts company with liberal individualism. One of the central tenets of the liberal-individualist tradition of political thinking is that once children reach and pass the threshold of adulthood, the courtesy is paid of regarding them as fully responsible moral agents. That this is a polite fiction disturbs neither the equanimity nor the confidence of the liberal mind – but it is a fiction none the less. Within the broad frame of liberal-individualist thinking, the young are brought up in a plural atmosphere. The influences on them are many – family, friends, school, and the wider environment of work and entertainment, religion and politics – and they do not all say the same thing. This is thought to be a virtue, for it accustoms the young to make choices, and thus become aware of themselves as moral agents, able and willing to take on the responsibilities of the adult world.

It is this ability, but above all this willingness, that civic republicanism challenges. It is not the difference between individuals that is objectionable, but the length to which this difference is allowed to determine human preferences. It is the toleration that liberal individualism has for abdication from politics that marks its division from civic republicanism. Civic republicanism holds out the possibility of a level of moral agency – a form of human consciousness, being and living – that is simply not catered for in liberal individualism. It is also a consistent theme in civic republicanism that human beings will not choose this level of agency and form of consciousness unless they are educated into it, but that they would choose it if they could know, which they never can, everything in advance. Rousseau, the strongest advocate of individual autonomy, poignantly posed the question in a passage already cited:

> For a newly formed people to understand the wise principles of politics and to follow the basic rules of statecraft, the effect would have to become the cause; the social spirit which must be the product of social institutions would have to preside over the setting up of those institutions; men would have to have already become before the advent of law that which they become as a result of law.[3]

Paternalism is necessarily involved here, but it is a paternalism which has as its object the creation of free and autonomous moral beings.

Crucial in the division between civic republicanism and liberal individualism is a difference as to what freedom means, and what, therefore, autonomy consists of. The most basic conception of freedom in liberal individualism is that, in Hobbes's phrase, it lies in 'the silence of the law'.[4] Individuals are free and act in an unconstrained manner – that is, autonomously – in those areas of life where they are left alone by society and the state, where the 'lets and hindrances of motion' are absent.[5] Civic-republican thinking does not have this same conception of freedom and autonomy. Individuals are free only when their duty and their interest coincide. It is in this coincidence that their moral autonomy consists, and it is a coincidence which does not happen upon individuals randomly, by chance; neither is it the automatic accompaniment of physical maturity. Freedom in this sense, as Tocqueville recognized, involves apprenticeship and, to continue what is not a metaphor, periodic retraining. The *Bildung*, about which Hegel wrote, lasts a lifetime. Human beings not only have to be taught what moral autonomy means as a practice, but, being weak and shortsighted, they also have to be reminded of what it is that they have been taught.

The practice of citizenship, which is what moral autonomy means within civic republicanism, is an unnatural practice for human beings, and Rousseau was correct to say that their 'natural' character has to be 'mutilated' before they will engage in it. This is the cost of the practice of citizenship. It is not surprising that liberal individualists will not pay it: it is an unwelcome entrance fee to social living. Liberal individualists object to having their characters systematically mutilated (as if this did not already take place); civic republicans know that it is worth paying the price. What civic republicans know, just as much as what liberal individualists know, is that they live full and free lives as morally autonomous agents. They both use the same words, but they could be – indeed they are – speaking different languages: central concepts are untranslatable.

These considerations would seem to point to the conclusion that the practice of citizenship contained within civic republicanism is inappropriate for the modern world – not because opportunities are lacking for citizens to engage in the practice, for these can always be created; nor because individuals do not possess the resources to be effective and therefore autonomous agents, for these can always be provided. The lesson from the civic-republican tradition is that it is the will to engage in the practice that is crucial. Now within civic republicanism this will was to be generated and sustained by religion, and it may be that in the modern world the civic-republican project does require a civic faith. This creates difficulties. It is not so much that a civic faith could not be devised, a national priesthood ordained, and temples consecrated for proclamation of the faith – the twentieth century is littered with attempts to do as much. It is rather that such civic faiths, when they are devised with intent and consciously propagated, are not effective in encouraging a rational commitment to a practice of citizenship; what is developed is not Hegel's 'political sentiment', but Tocqueville's 'blind' and 'unreflective' patriotism.

This suggests that one must build on whatever religion is available, and that a different social institution must be brought into focus: education. Precisely what can be demanded of an educational system, and how far its efforts can and must be supplemented in adult life, are more properly considered when recent democratic theory has been examined. Two questions are addressed to this literature: (1) to what extent are the duties of the practice of citizenship considered? And (2) to what extent is attention paid to the need to generate the will to engage in the practice of citizenship?

Chapter eight

Citizenship in modern democratic theory

Many of the recent 'communitarian critics of liberalism',[1] or democratic theorists as they will be called – Michael Walzer, Benjamin Barber, Philip Green, Jane Mansbridge, William Galston – might be expected to endorse the analysis of the concept of citizenship as presented in Chapter 2. The strength of their thinking lies in the attention they pay to the first two of the enabling conditions for the practice of citizenship: those concerned with empowering individuals and creating the arenas in which they can act. There is a wealth of thought and recommendation having to do with enhancement of the 'rights' of individuals, and with wholesale dismantling of the capitalist state in both its political and its economic forms, most of which I endorse, and none of which will be replicated here. Democratic theorists are weak, however, on the third condition – the one concerned with motivating individuals to engage in the practice of citizenship.

Much recent democratic theory suggests that if individuals are empowered and given the opportunity to act politically, then a virtuous circle of participation breeding participation will result. Not only is the process educative in itself – the more one participates, the more one develops the attitudes appropriate to a citizen: largeness of mind and an appreciation that the interests of the community are one's own – but the example set by the initial participators will draw ever-widening groups of individuals into the political arena. This is a view which is particularly associated with John Stuart Mill,[2] and it is not difficult to appreciate the appeal that it has. For, in leaving individuals free to choose whether or not to participate, it does not undermine their autonomy. And there can be little doubt that for certain kinds of individual – those who are naturally sociable and confident – the activity of participation does have this educative effect, and that similar individuals can be drawn into the activity by their example.[3] It will be argued, however, that fulfilment of the first two conditions – of empowerment and opportunity – is inadequate to

155

generate either sufficiently widespread participation, or a commitment to the practice of citizenship which goes significantly beyond protection of individual rights and interests, and that what is required is a much broader educative effort to inculcate both knowledge of the duties of citizenship and willingness to perform them. It is here, but not only here, that the civic-republican tradition is strong, and why, therefore, that tradition repays study.

The focus of this chapter is limited. It is concerned with that aspect of the practice of citizenship where recent democratic theory is weak and civic republicanism is strong: namely with what has to be done to motivate individuals to engage in the practice. But first, some attention needs to be given to issues which civic republicanism either does not stress or could not be expected to address.

Preliminaries

The civic-republican tradition does not have much to say about providing individuals with the resources they require to become effective agents in the world – that is, to become citizens. Civic republicanism is not, as has been noted, a rights-based manner of thinking. It has a tendency to assume that citizens possess the knowledge and skills, the level of well-being, amount of time, and the freedoms of speech and association that are all necessary for the practice of citizenship. That potential citizens in the modern world patently do not possess such resources in the required amounts, or possess them very unequally, has occasioned in both Britain and the United States a large body of writing, both at the academic level and at that of political rhetoric, with a concern to give priority to the rights of individuals over the rights of property.[4] Civic republicanism does stress, as we have seen, a rough economic equality among citizens, in clear recognition of the fact that political power can be bought, and that it ought not to be. It did not have to deal, however, as we do today, with such concentrations of economic and political power as question the individual's very autonomy. The breaking down of concentrations of economic power and of the hierarchic and authoritarian structure of the workplace was not, and could not have been, a preoccupation of civic-republican thinking, though both Rousseau and Hegel wrote eloquently about how inimical to any genuine freedom was the master-servant relationship.[5] These issues are too large to tackle adequately here. Fortunately, the ground has been well covered by others.[6]

Civic republicanism did address the problem of size. It was the expansion of the Roman republic that, for Machiavelli, contributed to its downfall. Rousseau's *Social Contract* was written with the small face-to-face community in mind. Both Hegel and Tocqueville were concerned to provide citizens with arenas for activity below the level of the state, in functional or local, territorially defined, communities. But, and this follows on from consideration of the concentration of economic and political power, it did not have to cope with the extent to which the modern world is an interdependent, international world. This refers not just to the existence of a variety of international organizations, both economic and political – multinational corporations and producer cartels, as well as such institutions as the United Nations, the World Bank and the European Community. It refers also to the fact that many of the problems with which the modern world is faced cannot be handled by any state alone – environmental problems like acid rain, oil spills, chlorofluorocarbons; problems of trafficking in drugs; terrorism and hostage-taking; the containment of armed conflict. Just as the centralizing tendencies of the state have to be checked, and reversed wherever possible – Tocqueville's contribution is significant here – in order to provide arenas in which citizens can act, so, too, many tasks have to be at least in part delegated upwards. How this is done is, again, an issue which falls outside the scope of this book, but something must be said about the implications of the greater interconnectedness of the modern world, when compared to the past, for the practice of citizenship.

Faced, as citizens are, with the locality or neighbourhood, the state, and the international arena, this means that their loyalty and commitment are shown on more than one level. Whereas for Machiavelli and Rousseau the citizen's loyalty was singly commanded, by Rome or by the social contract itself, both Hegel and Tocqueville did envisage a double, or even a multiple, attachment. Civic virtue, that inextricable mixture of interest and duty, means having an informed concern about issues and problems that arise in all arenas, including the economic, where citizens earn their living. But no single citizen can engage in the practice of citizenship in all arenas, all at once. This means that citizens can, indeed they must, choose to a certain extent where to be active. The citizen who engages in the practice at the local or neighbourhood level, where practice means both deliberating and judging as well as 'doing', is no more, and no less, a citizen than the one who chooses to be active about national or international issues. What follows, further, from these considerations is that with multiple attachments, citizens are open to conflicting loyalties. There can be no single political community to which they always owe overriding allegiance and, when conflicts arise, citizens will have to use their judgment as to where they pledge their commitment. The most that one can say at any general level is that that community deserves allegiance whose integrity and autonomy, within its sphere, are being threatened or undermined against the will of its members.

These considerations suggest that, aside from the probability of conflicting loyalties, the size and complex interconnectedness of the modern world are less of a problem for the practice of citizenship than might at first sight appear. For what size and complexity do, when issues and problems are handled at appropriate levels, is to multiply the opportunities for citizen involvement and action. Such thoughts also tend to dissolve a further problem which the modern world poses for the practice of citizenship: namely, the much greater mobility of population today compared with the past. This mobility is an accompaniment of size and complexity. People no longer expect to live, work and die in the localities and neighbourhoods, even in the countries, in which they are born. While this may weaken the bond of attachment to any particular locality or neighbourhood, the fact that people move – as they marry, change their jobs, or simply think that the grass is greener on the other side – should not, of itself, lead them to forget that they have duties as citizens. Their locality and neighbourhood will change, but that does not mean that they cannot become active in the new one, or that they have to relinquish their involvement in whatever other arenas they have hitherto been active. The duties of citizenship, besides being multi-faceted, are also portable. The function of bonds of attachment is to remind citizens, if they need reminding, that they do have duties. The fact that the bonds are multiple means that the weakening of any one does not jeopardize the whole enterprise of citizenship.

A conception of citizenship appropriate for the modern world must be somewhat broader than that which is revealed in the civic-republican tradition. It must be one which can accommodate multiple loyalties, and therefore the possibility of conflict, and it must be one which extends beyond the territorial boundaries of the nation-state. Its limits are difficult to state with any strict determinacy at a general level – outside circumstances, that is, that are historically and geographically specific. But, given that the lives of citizens can be affected by what happens in the locality and neighbourhood, the state and internationally – and that citizens ought to have some say in what affects them – then the limits of citizenship are provided by whatever decisions, policies, actions and happenings in all of these arenas have an effect on citizens' lives. It is time to consider what contribution recent democratic thought makes to the question of how a commitment to the practice of citizenship may be generated in individuals.

The test of citizenship

A useful entry point here is the answer that democratic theorists give to the question of what it is that makes the individual a citizen. What, in other words, are the criteria of citizenship? As we have seen, the answer given by civic republicanism is that individuals become citizens by taking their civic duties seriously. Individuals are eligible for the status of citizen by virtue of being born and living within some territory, but they only achieve the status by acting accordingly. A sharp distinction is made in civic republicanism between the public life of the citizen, in which individuals live fuller and more satisfying lives, and the private life of the individual, which is restricted to the immediate concerns of family and friends. Individuals can thus choose whether to be citizens or not, and they can, if they cease to perform their civic duties, cease to be citizens. While Machiavelli does claim that one can lead an honourable life as a private person, the clear thought running through civic republicanism is that the public life of the citizen is both a more complete life – it demonstrates more completely than private living what human beings are capable of when they rouse themselves – and a more honourable life. Civic-republican thinking cannot accommodate the oxymoron, 'private citizen'.

Only rarely does recent democratic writing have this conception of citizenship as a status which is 'earned', and which therefore can be lost. It is true, of course, that citizenship for civic republicans was a status reserved for males, and at least until Rousseau, not all males at that. Only for Machiavelli, however, is maleness built into the very concept of citizen. For others, within civic republicanism, the male orientation of their thought is one that is shared by all Western thought, and signifies no more than that – traditionally – males and females had different social roles. But that distinction is breaking down. It has not been difficult, thus, at least at the level of theory and rhetoric, for liberal-individualist thought to extend rights to women, though it has no doubt been difficult in practice. It does not require too much imagination, either, to extend the concept of 'citizen' to include women. Machiavelli apart, there is nothing aggressively male in the civic-republican conception of the citizen, even if one takes on board the fact that that conception included the idea of the 'citizen-soldier'. There may be a valid distinction between masculine and feminine characteristics and virtues, but it does not correspond to the distinction between male and female. Women, when they have been tried, have shown that they can fight. The practice of citizenship in a political community is an egalitarian practice, and one aspect of that egalitarianism is that the practice is not gender-specific.

There is widespread acceptance in democratic writing that the criterion, the test, of citizenship is the performance of civic duties. Thus Michael Walzer writes that there can be no political community without some shared sense of the 'duties of office' and the 'dues of membership'.[7] Benjamin Barber argues that 'to be a citizen *is* to participate', and makes it clear that citizenship is something that follows from participation: citizenship is 'not a condition of participation but one of participation's richest fruits'.[8] For Richard Dagger, 'citizenship is a public vocation'. This means that 'the (true) citizen plays a full and active part in the affairs of his or her community'. Activities here set the citizen 'apart from those who regard politics as a nuisance to be avoided or a spectacle to be witnessed', and carry with them 'a responsibility to act with the interests of the community in mind', for 'every citizen is in a position of public responsibility'.[9] Wilson Carey McWilliams and Marc Landy write that political participation and citizenship are not the same thing: 'Citizenship is participation with at least some regard for the whole.' Obligations arise here from 'a sense of membership in the city, a feeling, however slight, of being part of a larger whole', and take citizens wherever they 'can serve the city best'.[10] It is clear from the above that citizenship does not reside solely in the individual possession of rights, or even in participation. It crucially involves participation in a specific mode. What characterizes citizen participation is not the protection or advancement of individual rights and interests, but a 'public responsibility': attention to a version of the common good.

The question arises of what to do if 'citizens' do not perform their civic duties. This is the problem of the free rider. It is instructive here to compare the accounts given by Benjamin Barber and William Galston. While territory is 'the primary ground of citizenship' – it is what establishes one's eligibility for citizenship – Barber writes that participation is 'at the center of its definition'. In 'strong democracy', the standard for who is a citizen is the procedural one of involvement in 'dynamic activity'; citizenship ' is a function of *what we do* and thus a matter of activity'. No-one is excluded who participates but, Barber asks, 'if activity is a measure of citizenship, will the lethargic, the apathetic, and the alienated be excluded?' Barber shies away from this conclusion, for it seems to raise the possibility of 'a one-way door through which undesirables are continuously ejected'. He therefore makes activity not *the* measure of citizenship, but 'a measure', alongside 'the traditional legal and national definitions of citizenship'.[11] This is confusing, but before attempting to account for the confusion, let us see what Galston has to say.

Galston remarks that citizenship 'is a sphere of equality', and that this equality 'is linked to the formal characteristic of the claims on citizenship. To have a valid claim on citizenship in a community is to meet all the necessary conditions for citizenship.' He then proceeds to enumerate these conditions, which are that citizens 'must be able to act independently and to assume responsibility for [their] acts'; that they must be able to voice their interests and judge policies; that they must 'recognize and take into account the interests and claims of others'; that they must have 'a basic understanding of the language, beliefs, history, and institutions of [their] community'; and that they must be 'loyal to [their] community'. These conditions, for Galston, naturally exclude children, idiots and the deranged, and criminals, but there is a further conclusion that he draws. For, if these requirements are acknowledged as necessary conditions, 'it follows directly that communities may deprive members who do not – or cease to – fulfill them of citizenship'.[12] But what does it mean to 'deprive' members of citizenship or, in Barber's terms, to 'exclude' them? Galston is not forthcoming, but Barber seems to think that exclusion, as the alternative to citizenship, entails 'defacto servitude'.[13] This he rightly rejects, for any community must have an interest in luring lapsed citizens back into the fold; they must be allowed to see the error of their ways and redeem themselves. Barber's confusion arises from attempting to link a liberal-individualist conception of the citizen as a bearer of rights, with a civic-republican one of the citizen as a performer of duties. One can cease to be a citizen if one no longer performs the duties, but this does not mean that one loses the 'rights' – for the rights, contra the liberal-individualist position, belong not to citizens but to individuals. It is through exercise of the rights in appropriate ways that individuals become citizens; to deprive them of rights, as Galston would seem to wish, because they failed to perform their duties, is to leave them with no means whereby they can resume their duties and thus become, once again, citizens. Philip Green suggests that what free riders need is 'a good talking-to from neighbours';[14] and it is moral suasion that Galston also suggests for 'shirkers': 'the noncontributor who receives the scorn or disapproval of the other members of his group will usually shape up quickly'.[15] Not to perform the duties of citizenship, therefore, is not to lose one's rights, but to lose the esteem of one's fellows. It is to declare that you prefer them to take on the responsibility of politics; it is to abdicate from self-government; it is to cease to be a citizen. But it is not to lose the possibility of becoming a citizen again.

Mœurs

One of the preoccupations of civic republicanism was its effort to devise practices and institutions such that there would be no shirkers or

free riders. Emphasis here was placed on what Rousseau and Tocqueville called '*mœurs*', or morals and manners – the whole panoply
of habits, customs, traditions, moral codes and forms of social intercourse that governed relationships between individuals. Civic
republicanism held that individuals would always be prone to forget
their civic duties – by lapsing into idleness and luxury, by paying
others to represent and fight for them, or simply by allowing their
own private concerns to preoccupy them to the exclusion of all else.
The human species was weak, self-indulgent, and short-sighted, and
it needed supporting in a practice which, though immediately unnatural, would, when engaged in, reveal what its nature could
become. The most important of these supports was the *mœurs* of the
community which, themselves, were underpinned by religious faith.
The duties of citizenship were enjoined by the community's *mœurs*,
and performance of them was subject to divine sanction. One of the
duties of citizenship is to take responsibility for the intergenerational
continuity of the community. Citizens maintain a community's
mœurs by living them, as nearly as they can, and pass these *mœurs* on
to the citizens who are to follow them. Citizenship is thus as much
about practice as it is about memory. For what a community's *mœurs*
are, and what therefore the community is, is revealed by reflection on
and interpretation of its past, in the present. The principal and enduring duty of the practice of citizenship – enduring because, unlike
external threat and natural calamity, it is something that has to be engaged in all the time – is to impart the collective memory, the *mœurs*,
of the community to rising generations, a collective memory which
includes the practice of citizenship itself.

Today's democratic theorists do not write about a community's
mœurs in quite this way. There are a number of separate, but connected, issues here. First, there is the question of whether democratic
writing pays any attention at all to *mœurs*; second, whether it sees
mœurs as being crucially underpinned by some form of religious
faith; and finally, there is the issue of how the habits of citizenship
may be inculcated and sustained among a community's members.

Benjamin Barber rejects 'customs and mores' and a civil religion
as the basis for the habits of citizenship,[16] and his rejection is based
on the nature of what he calls 'unitary democracy'. Unitary democracy is 'inimical to genuine democratic politics', because in large
polities the 'identification of individuals and their interests with a
symbolic collectivity and its interests' runs the almost certain and
'grave risks of monism, conformism, and coercive consensualism'. Individual citizens achieve their civic identity through 'merging' their
selves with the collectivity, 'that is to say, through self-abandon-
ment'.[17] Barber suggests that Rousseau's arguments about customs

and mores, and his advocacy of a civil religion (which he also mistakenly associates with Tocqueville), make it 'the more likely ... that a community will take on the suffocating unitary character of totalistic states'. This, however, is to conflate two separate issues. There is a difference between, on the one hand, the function of customs and mores and a civil religion in motivating individuals to take the duties of citizenship seriously, and, on the other, using them to foist a unitary consensus over substantive issues on an otherwise unwilling citizenry. The virtues of 'loyalty, fraternity, patriotism, neighbourliness, bonding, tradition, mutual affection, and common beliefs', without which 'participatory democracy is reduced to crass proceduralism', do not necessarily lead to the kind of unitary nightmare where 'cohesion' is achieved 'at the expense of individual autonomy, social pluralism, and participatory activity'.[18] The question is how to guide autonomous individuals into the practice of citizenship when they have no prior disposition for it, and it is no answer to say that this can be done by the practice of citizenship itself, as Barber would have it.[19] No doubt, once the practice is engaged in, affective ties between citizens may be reinforced – participation is educative; but some bonding between the individual and the community must exist beforehand, otherwise 'citizens' will only participate for instrumental reasons, reasons which have to do with the private rather than the public self. Such a bonding is provided by a community's *mœurs*, its collective memory: these can teach individuals what the duties of citizenship are, and motivate them to perform them, without that teaching either requiring individuals to abandon their selves to the community, or leading to a forced unanimity on the issues upon which citizens deliberate. The object is both to prompt citizens to use their political judgment and to teach them the ground rules for the use of that judgment, not to create conditions in which not judgment, but only enthusiastic affirmation, is required. To reject customs and mores, and a civil religion, because they can be used to sanction an unpleasant unitary democracy, is to neglect how they can function to support what Barber calls 'strong democracy' – a theory of democracy not too far removed from the analysis of citizenship and community presented in Chapter 2.

Just as Barber distances himself from unitary democracy, so Philip Green distances himself both from 'communitarian ideals which are really attainable only in the small scale', and also from the 'pseudo-democracy' of traditional liberalism. He acknowledges that 'genuine citizenship' is predicated on political equality, but accepts that the pursuit of political equality will not necessarily lead to genuine citizenship. Behind this, 'there must stand ... the development of our capacity to appreciate the existence of a public good that on at least some occasions transcends individual or group interests – even our own'.[20] Like Barber, Green rejects a civil religion as a necessary support for democratic politics, on the grounds that he does not believe there is any 'relationship between religion and democracy .... No religious movement has ever had a consistent political program.' The discourses of religion and politics 'are ultimately alien languages'.[21] Anyone, and everyone, can claim – and has – that God is on their side. Again, this is to condemn one of the forces which could sustain 'genuine citizenship' simply because religion can be, and has been, used for objectionable purposes; because it can sustain immoral practices and corrupt regimes. Green also appears to reject any kind of 'manipulative ... cultural communication, no matter how well-intentioned'.[22] In doing so, he leaves the project of genuine democracy without means for its beginnings. It is true that 'democratic participation has to become a habit if democracy is to be realized, and [that] it can only become a habit if opportunity exists to engage in it habitually',[23] but this is clearly not sufficient to get the project off the ground.

Education and service

The moral character which is appropriate for genuine citizenship does not generate itself; it has to be authoritatively inculcated. This means that minds have to be manipulated. People, starting with children, have to be taught what citizenship means for them, in a political community, in terms of the duties it imposes upon them, and they have to be motivated to perform these duties. This is successful when they perceive that the interests of the community are also their own, which does not mean that the totality of their being is bounded by the community. It means simply recognizing that the community, and its practices and institutions, secure for citizens the possibility of living their own good lives, and that there is therefore a duty to sustain that community in being. In the process of performing their duties, collectively with their fellows, citizens will no doubt find their interests changing. The process is one in which, after all, citizens both constitute and discover their joint purposes and goals,[24] in which, as we saw in Chapter 2, the individual moves from 'I' to 'we', but without losing the distinctiveness that makes the individual unique: without, that is, losing autonomy. Even if religion is not necessary to provide the motivation, some form of moral or civic education is.

This much is recognized by Galston. It is legitimate for the community to 'influence the character of its members through education and training .... Since rational principles of appropriate conduct are neither innate nor invariably comfortable, no community can safely forgo an organized attempt to impart them to its members.'[25] This is beginning to approach what Amy Gutmann calls ' "conscious social reproduction" – the ways in which citizens are or should be empowered to influence the education that in turn shapes the political values, attitudes, and modes of behavior of future citizens'. The emphasis is on conscious social reproduction – 'deliberate instruction' – rather than on a largely unconscious political socialization, for one of the virtues of democratic politics is 'that it authorizes citizens to influence how their society reproduces itself'.[26] The attempt is to create citizens who will be suited to the 'constitution', in an Aristotelian sense, of their society.[27] The commitment of the present generation of citizens is the political one of 'collectively re-creating the society that [they] share'.[28] Much of Gutmann's discussion is devoted to apportioning the responsibility for this task between parents, professionals and the state acting on behalf of citizens, and to establishing the principles which will 'simultaneously support deliberative freedom and communal self-determination' within the rising generation.[29] She insists that it is not a question of moral education or not, for, like it or not, schools do shape moral character. The choice, therefore, is over what kind of moral education will best prepare children for citizenship, with the objective of developing those 'cooperative moral sentiments' that are essential for 'the democratic goal of sharing the rights and responsibilities of citizenship'.[30] In this way a form of 'democratic civil religion' can be fostered: 'a set of secular beliefs, habits, and ways of thinking that support democratic deliberation'. The object of teaching a community's history and politics is not to encourage an unreflective celebration of its past but, on the contrary, to increase 'the ability of students to *reason*, collectively and critically, about politics'.[31] Gutmann does not claim that 'democratic education' is, in itself, sufficient for democratic politics. In particular, authoritarianism in the work environment must be overcome, and centralized political institutions must be dismantled, before the full effects of democratic education can work their influence on democratic politics. Conversely, no amount of additional opportunities for citizens to exercise their political judgment will lead to genuinely democratic politics, unless citizens have first undergone democratic education.[32] Democratic education is ' "political education" – the cultivation of the virtues, knowledge, and skills necessary for political participation'; it prepares citizens 'to participate in consciously reproducing their society',[33] or, to put it in words used earlier, to take on the crucial responsibility for ensuring their society's intergenerational continuity.

Gutmann's argument for the sufficiency of democratic education to generate the required motivation in citizens to take their responsibilities seriously is powerful. Nowhere does she claim that a relig-ious faith may be necessary to sustain the lessons of democratic education. Her cursory reference to a civil religion is a simple rede-scription of the attitudes appropriate to democratic politics. There is no suggestion that God ought to be involved to strengthen the re-solve of citizens. Other democratic theorists are not as sanguine as this but, before considering them, it is worth examining the ideas of Morris Janowitz, whose faith in education as a conduit for the incul-cation of civic duties is somewhat jaundiced.

Janowitz's complaint is against the American educational system since the end of the Second World War, in particular its thraldom to academic social science, especially political science, which has em-phasized the rights, rather than the duties, of citizens.[34] We do not need to follow him here, but rather discuss what he puts in place of education: national service, both military and civilian. His starting point is a declaration of the need to reconstruct patriotism, which he redescribes as 'civic consciousness', in order to escape ideas of chau-vinism and nationalism, for there are responsibilities both to and beyond the nation: 'Collective problem-solving, in a democratic so-ciety ... rests on voluntarism, motivated by a sense of moral responsibility for the collective well-being.'[35] For generating this mo-tivation, Janowitz does not dismiss the role that civic education in schools can play. Thus he argues that it can 'strengthen civic con-sciousness' by 'exposing students to central and enduring political traditions of the nation', by teaching them 'essential knowledge about the organization and operation of contemporary governmen-tal institutions', and by fashioning in them the 'essential identifications and moral sentiments required for performance as ef-fective citizens'.[36] Civic education, however, is unlikely to forge the bonds between citizens that create in them the obligation to perform the duties of citizenship unless it includes military or civilian service. Military service, in particular, is the 'strongest test of civic obligation' and has, in America's past, 'served as a form of effective civic educa-tion',[37] especially the idea of the citizen-soldier during the Revolutionary period and after. But military service is not, in modern circumstances, essential.

For effective civic consciousness, some form of patriotic attach-ment to the nation is essential, though it should be neither aggressive nor xenophobic. In civic education, broadly conceived, 'a sense of group affiliation' must have priority over literacy and numeracy. 'Youngsters need group experiences that rapidly contribute to self-esteem'. This is enhanced 'by immersing them in a social setting that emphasizes work and service in the context of symbols of national (or community) identification'.[38] The civic attitudes and self-esteem that are developed as students are given tasks which they can do without elaborate instruction or academic training will themselves be powerful motivating forces to acquire more traditional skills. Yet, the purpose of such national or community work – 'whether the tasks be conservation, protection of the environment, assistance in the control of natural and man-made disasters, or involvement in educational and social work programs' – is not to enhance the skills of individuals with the idea of personal advancement. It is 'to create "civic discipline" ... to affiliate the individual into the large social structure – to help make citizens out of students'.[39] In Janowitz's view, patriotism, or 'civic consciousness', cannot be reconstructed 'without a system of national service'.[40] The object of national service, which would take place when students are in their late teens, is to break down the dominance of economic goals in students' minds, a dominance which is encouraged by both parents and the existing school system, and to teach 'citizens to perform the tasks that are part of civic obligation' by building upon an already existing attraction that youth has for 'the adventure and moral value of national service'.[41]

Rather surprisingly, in view of the tenor of his argument, Janowitz concludes that such a system of national service would have to be voluntary, not obligatory, on the grounds that 'the political support for an obligatory program does not now exist and is unlikely to develop in the next decade'.[42] He may well be right about the lack of political support for an obligatory programme, but if the object is to create a civic consciousness in those who are not already disposed to take the duties of citizenship seriously, then it would seem that compulsion *is* required. The temptations to renege on the duties, even in full knowledge of what they are and that one is obliged, are too strong. The need for compulsion would be lessened if performance of civic duties were one of the articles of a religious faith, but this is something that Janowitz, like Gutmann, does not consider. It is clear, however, that the arguments of Gutmann and Janowitz on the need to motivate individuals to become citizens represent a significant advance on those of Barber and Green, but for some democratic theorists they still do not go far enough. Besides systems of civic education and national service, and the educative effects of political participation itself, many thinkers maintain, in conformity with the civic-republican tradition, that some form of religious underpinning is required for the practice of citizenship.

Religion

Writing at a time when it was widely claimed that political theory was dead,[43] Dante Germino argued that its major responsibility was 'to elucidate such a set of guiding norms' that political change could be 'orderly, coherent, and intelligent' in coping with what he saw as 'the dangers threatening society's existence': the 'experience of alienation and isolation' consequent upon 'the decline of a sense of community'.[44] To restore this sense, he drew attention to what he called the 'three premises of the great tradition' of Graeco–Christian thought. The first of these was that, contra Hobbes and his successors, 'man is a political animal' with an inclination, aside from any immediate interest, to seek the company of fellow-beings.[45] The second premise was that 'man is a rational animal'. Reason, here, was not the calculative, instrumental means that Hobbes and Hume devised for human beings to select the most efficient means to seek already given ends. Reason, in the tradition of natural law, was that capacity which enabled human beings to know the law appropriate to their nature: 'This "natural law" prescribed that the proper end of man is to live a life of virtue and justice ... it is natural for him to seek to deal equitably with his fellows.'[46] Finally, there was the premise that 'man is a religious animal'. The liberal project of 'the autonomous, "masterless" man', besides being a 'fiction', had cut human beings off from their 'sources of spiritual strength' which alone could assuage their sense of isolation. It was thus necessary to recognize that the solidarity and rationality of human beings were insufficient for the urgent task of 'political reconstruction':[47]

> Only if illumined by the superior knowledge of faith, which perfects but does not annul reason, can the classical idea of man as a social, rational, and moral being be raised to that level of truth which alone is capable of redeeming the human community. Philosophy and theology are not enemies, but friends; their separation, which has been so disastrous for modern man, must be ended.[48]

There have been few voices in recent years that have echoed so clearly this central idea of civic-republican thinking. The most perceptive writing on this theme of the relation between religion and politics has been a series of reflections on the founding and subsequent history of the American republic.[49] It has not always been concerned to claim that experience and history for civic republicanism, but has sometimes seen religious belief as crucial for containing the otherwise fissiparous tendencies of liberal politics. Galston calls this association of religion and politics 'juridical liberalism' and derives it from Locke.[50] He suggests that it was a 'Lockean understanding of the proper relations among morality, religion, and the liberal polity [that] was the orthodox view among the American founders'.[51] Madison, Jefferson and Washington all argued that religious faith was the guardian of the liberties of the people, for it constrained individuals to respect and tolerate others in pursuit of their lives, so long as this was consistent with the maintenance of order. As Galston puts it, for those who are not, or cannot be, persuaded of their philosophic validity, 'religion provides both the *reasons* for believing that liberal principles are correct and the *incentives* for honoring them in practice'.[52] It is Galston's view that this connection between religion and politics has broken down in the United States. This is also the view of Robert Bellah, who for a long time has been most closely associated with the idea of an American civil religion. But whereas Galston's argument is for a restoration of juridical liberalism, Bellah's project is to harness religion to the cause of a revitalized civic republicanism.

It is difficult within a short compass to do justice to the full range and richness of Bellah's understanding of the American experience. His understanding, and that of his recent co-authors, is broadly Tocquevilleian.[53] The American republic started life in the late eighteenth century with biblical and republican traditions already well in place and mutually reinforcing each other,[54] but these traditions were increasingly tested by a growing individualism and materialism (or consumerism) during the nineteenth century and beyond. These latter contributed to what Bellah calls a 'culture of separation ... processes of separation and individuation', the result of which is that the world no longer appears coherent, but 'comes to us in pieces, in fragments, lacking any overall pattern',[55] and personal, material ambition becomes overwhelmingly dominant. Yet the biblical and republican traditions never completely lost their hold on the imagination – and, at times, the political practice – of Americans. Against the 'culture of separation' must be set 'the culture of coherence' which derives from these traditions. Such traditions, Bellah claims, are still operative, and they tell Americans about the nature of their world and society, and who they are as people. Each tradition structures time, in the sense that the year is broken up, 'punctuated by an alternation of the sacred and the profane'. The Fourth of July and Memorial Day remind Americans of their republican inheritance. Thus it is a mistake to think that Americans have ever been 'a collection of private individuals who, except for a conscious contract to create a minimal government, have nothing in common'. If, however, it is the biblical and republican traditions which give meaning to the lives of Americans, the erosion of the traditions must threaten that meaning. Some Americans counter this by a 'profound yearning for the idealized small town' but, though this is 'nostalgia for the irretrievably lost', Bellah invites us to consider 'whether the biblical

169

and republican traditions that [the] small town once embodied can be reappropriated in ways that respond to our present need'.[56] To dismiss these traditions, without thought, is both foolish and irresponsible.

Despite America's impressive technological and material achievements, the future seems to hold only 'international conflict ... [and] internal incoherence'. What has gone wrong, 'what has failed at every level – from the society of nations to the national society to the local community to the family – is integration'. Americans have, according to Bellah, 'committed what to the founders of our nation was the cardinal sin: we have put our own good, as individuals, as groups, as a nation, ahead of the common good'. The political and economic equality of 'classical republican theory from Aristotle to the American founders', however, is somewhat at odds with the 'very private' American dream of ambition crowned with success. What Americans fear above all, Bellah argues,

> and what keeps the new world powerless to be born, is that if we give up our dream of private success for a more genuinely integrated societal community, we will be abandoning our separation and individuation, collapsing into dependence and tyranny. What we find hard to see is that it is the extreme fragmentation of the modern world that really threatens our individuation; that what is best in our separation and individuation, our sense of dignity and autonomy as persons, requires a new integration if it is to be sustained.[57]

The hope of Bellah, and his co-authors is that a 'social movement' similar to the Civil Rights movement of the 1950s and 1960s will develop, and enable Americans to recover socially their ecological balance, by drawing on the biblical and republican traditions which are their inheritance. Such a 'reconstituting' of the social world would have its impact in both economy and polity, allowing Americans 'to link interests with a conception of the common good'. It would 'encourage new initiatives in economic democracy and social responsibility, whether from "private" enterprise or autonomous small- and middle-scale public enterprises', and 'restore the dignity and legitimacy of democratic politics'. But above all what would be required is a change in attitudes, 'a new political atmosphere', in which material success would not be so avidly sought, nor the possibility of being a loser be so inordinately feared. This would mark a 'reappropriation of the idea of vocation or calling, a return in a new way to the idea of work as a contribution to the good of all and not merely as a means to one's own advancement'. The rewards would be the knowledge of excellence achieved, and 'the approbation of one's fellows'. Such a redefinition of work, Bellah argues, 'can contribute to what the founders of our republic called civic virtue. Indeed, in a revived social ecology, it would be a primary form of civic virtue.'[58] People need educating into the possibility of such a world, and they need convincing that its principles are worthwhile, for it involves 'a deep cultural, social, and even psychological transformation'.[59] It is here that education and faith join forces: education, in its 'classic' form, 'to articulate private aspirations with common cultural meanings so that individuals simultaneously become more fully developed people and citizens of a free society';[60] faith, to sustain the enterprise. Such a vision, Bellah and his co-authors claim, is not 'absurdly utopian'[61] for it 'arises not only from the theories of intellectuals, but from the practices of life that Americans are already engaged in'.[62]

Would it work? We do not know, for it has yet to be tried. But perhaps that is the wrong question. Is it intelligible? the answer to this must be 'Yes', at least as intelligible as the civic-republican tradition. And it is intelligible in this way because of the extent to which it draws on civic republicanism. Citizens are to take responsibility for their community, for its economy and its polity, strengthened by that amalgam of the biblical and republican traditions which is the American civil religion.

In the late 1960s, Bellah wrote that American civil religion was undergoing its 'third term of trial'. The first trial had to do with the question of independence, and the second with that of slavery. The third term of trial concerns a coming to terms with the power and responsibility which material and technological 'success' have brought Americans in the period since the end of the Second World War. But, Bellah remarks,

> in the midst of this trend toward a less primitive conception of ourselves and our world, we have somehow, without anyone really intending it, stumbled into a military confrontation where we have come to feel that our honor is at stake. We have in a moment of uncertainty been tempted to rely on our overwhelming physical power rather than on our intelligence, and we have, in part succumbed to this temptation. Bewildered and unnerved when our terrible power fails to bring immediate success, we are at the edge of a chasm the depth of which no man knows.[63]

By the mid-1970s, while America had extricated itself from Vietnam, a level of internal incoherence had been reached such that Bellah could argue that 'today the American civil religion is an empty and broken shell'. That civil religion was always largely an 'external covenant', and such covenants will remain necessary 'until we are all angels', but they are never sufficient for a republic: 'It is of the nature of a republic that its citizens must love it, not merely obey it. The external covenant must become an internal covenant and many times in our history that has happened.' In 1975, it was not so much that America was at another 'low ebb' spiritually, waiting for the external covenant to become once more 'filled with meaning and devotion'. It was rather that 'the external covenant has been betrayed by its most responsible servants and, what is worse, some of them, including the highest of all, do not even seem to understand what has been betrayed'. Richard Nixon was no more wicked than many other Americans, but 'when the leaders of a republic no longer understand its principle it is because of a history of corruption and betrayal that has affected the entire society'.[64]

What this fairly lengthy excursion into Robert Bellah's writing has revealed is to a large extent what we know already: namely, how much civic republicanism depends on 'habits of the heart' for its viability. This is the central teaching of the civic-republican tradition. The phrase 'habits of the heart' belongs to Tocqueville, but it is what Machiavelli meant by good laws, good religion and good examples; what Rousseau meant by *mœurs*; what Hegel meant by ethical understanding. No amount of political participation and economic democracy, no level of civic education or national service, will suffice for the practice of citizenship in a political community – unless and until the external covenant becomes an internal one. This much, civic republicanism recognizes.

The sense of community

A clear idea of citizenship emerges from examination of the civic-republican tradition. It is a practice which involves the performance of duties, and before it can be engaged in a number of conditions need to be met. The emphasis in the discussion undertaken here has been on the need to generate a sufficiency of motivation for the practice, rather than on the needs which people have for resources to be citizens, and for opportunities to perform the duties of the practice. This has been because the issue of motivation has, for the most part, been inadequately tackled in modern democratic theory. It is important for the practice of citizenship that individuals be empowered, and it is important that the concentrations of economic and political power be broken down. It is here that democratic theory is strong. But unless citizens are motivated to use the resources which they acquire or are given, in the arenas which are made available, then one must expect that the only ones who will do so are those who already have the disposition to participate in the practice. The crucial issue is to motivate those who do not already have the disposition. This is where civic republicanism is strong.

While the civic-republican conception of citizenship is clear, it might appear that the issue of community has somewhat disappeared from view. It will be recalled that the promise was held out earlier that if the question of citizenship could be resolved, that of community would dissolve. It is time to make good that promise.

It cannot be the case in the modern world that the nation-state can be a community like the ancient *polis* – a face-to-face society in which everyone knows everyone else, even if only by reputation; the kind of society analyzed by Peter Laslett and explored by Jane Mansbridge in her conception of unitary democracy, which is not the same as that of Benjamin Barber.[65] Size, complexity and heterogeneity all argue against such a position. This does not mean, however, that in times of 'clear and present danger', to use Oliver Wendell Holmes's words – as in Britain in 1940, or in the United States after Pearl Harbor – there cannot emerge a sense of community: the idea that everyone is in the same predicament, and that each owes every other his or her utmost in escaping what is common to them all. Such moments, at the level of the nation-state, are rare.

Size, complexity and heterogeneity all militate against any national consensus except on isolated occasions; what they do mean, on the other hand, is that we have plural societies. Human beings may or may not be sociable animals; the fact is that they live in societies composed of diverse and various social groupings ranging from the semi-formal, like the family, to the highly organized, like the trade union or the political party. No human being can live a fully satisfactory life, indeed a fully human life, without ties to some such groupings. In modern societies there are thus multiple points of entry for individuals. There may not be sufficient of them, or of the right kind, but variety is what characterizes modern society, and greater variety is what modern societies make possible. In such societies as we live in, this is where community is found. Why?

The idea of community has less to do with formal organization than with a sense of belonging and commitment. The commitment is to others who share interests, or positions, or purposes, and it is also to those who, for whatever reason, are unable to look after their own interests or pursue their own purposes. It is to seek the good of others at the same time as, and sometimes in neglect of, one's own good. It is to approach social relationships in an Aristotelian spirit of 'concord'. It is this that creates the sense of community; and it is this that creates citizens.

The argument is therefore that if one creates citizens, one also, and at the same time, creates community. Citizenship, as conceived in civic republicanism, entails community. If the conditions for the practice of citizenship are met, then so, too, are those for the existence of community. There are certain duties that all citizens must perform, such as choosing political leaders and holding them to account, paying taxes and, when called upon, defending political arrangements which, because they create order, make the achievement of other purposes and goals possible. But these do not exhaust the areas of public life where the duties of citizenship may be practised. Because modern societies are plural and heterogeneous, citizens who are properly motivated will find that there is much else that they can do. To a large extent, they will choose where to be active and, when and where they are active, they will create a sense of community. Community is found, therefore, not in formal organization, but wherever there are individuals who take the practice of citizenship seriously. The problem is to generate the commitment, which is what this book has been about.

Notes

Preface

1   Bernard Crick, 'Freedom as Politics', in Peter Laslett and W.G. Runciman (eds) *Philosophy, Politics and Society*, 3rd series, Oxford, Blackwell, 1967.

Chapter one   Introduction: Status or practice, rights or duties?

1   In all of western political thought until well into the nineteenth century, citizenship, however conceived, was a male preserve. Even so, it was not open to all males. During discussion of the civic-republican tradition in Part II, I use the male pronoun throughout in order not to misrepresent the tradition. In all other cases, I attempt to use more neutral language to reflect the position that any consideration of citizenship in the modern world cannot be so gender-specific. This is a moral point: 'human beings' or 'individuals' mean men and women. In particular, I seek to avoid the terms 'man' and 'mankind'. I may not always be successful here but, if not, I am to be understood as referring to both men and women.

2   See Michael J. Sandel, *Liberalism and the Limits of Justice*, Cambridge, Cambridge University Press, 1982, ch. 1, especially pp. 31–3, for a discussion of justice as a 'remedial' value.

3   See the discussion in Archibald Cox, *The Court and the Constitution*, Boston, Houghton Mifflin, 1978, ch. 18, and for a recent assessment of the debate, Ronald Dworkin 'The Great Abortion Case', *New York Review of Books*, 29 June 1989, pp. 49–53.

4   See, for instance, the demands presented in 'Charter 88', *New Statesman and Society*, 2 December 1989, pp. 10–11; for an alternative view, see John McCluskey, 'An Enormous Power', *The Listener*, 4 December 1986, pp. 13–16.

5   For a discussion of the social dimension of individual identity, see Edward R. Portis, 'Citizenship and Personal Identity', *Polity*, 1986, vol. XVIII, no. 3, pp. 457–72.

6   Two recent contributions are: Amy Gutmann, 'Communitarian Critics

of Liberalism', *Philosophy and Public Affairs*, 1985, vol. 14, no. 3, pp. 308–22, and Robert B. Thigpen and Lyle A. Downing, 'Liberalism and the Communitarian Critique', *American Journal of Political Science*, 1987, vol. 31, pp. 637–55.

7   See Raymond Plant, *Community and Ideology*, London, Routledge & Kegan Paul, 1974.

8   R.G. Collingwood, *An Autobiography*, Oxford, Oxford University Press, 1967, p. 62.

Chapter two   The citizen in the political community

1   See R.A. Nisbet, *The Sociological Tradition*, London, Heinemann, 1971, ch. 3; Raymond Plant, *Community and Ideology*, London, Routledge & Kegan Paul, 1974, ch. 2; and Joseph R. Gusfield, *Community: A Critical Response*, Oxford, Blackwell, 1975, ch. 1. For a wider perspective, though within a shorter compass, see Carl J. Friedrich, 'The Concept of Community in the History of Political and Legal Philosophy', in Friedrich (ed.) *Community*, New York, Liberal Arts Press, 1959 (*Nomos*, II), pp. 3–24.

2   Nisbet, op. cit., p. 47

3   S.I. Benn, 'Individuality, Autonomy and Community', in Eugene Kamenka (ed.) *Community as a Social Ideal*, London, Arnold, 1982, p. 49.

4   Richard Tuck, *Natural Rights Theories: Their Origin and Development*, Cambridge, Cambridge University Press, 1981, ch. 1.

5   See Geraint Parry, *John Locke*, London, George Allen & Unwin, 1978, pp. 149–50.

6   Raymond Plant, *Community and Ideology*, London, Routledge & Kegan Paul, 1974, p. 32. Dante Germino puts it even more strongly: 'The necessity for resurrecting community without at the same time burying the individual in some new collectivist idolatry is rapidly becoming, after survival itself, the political problem of our time.' (Dante L. Germino, 'The Crisis in Community: Challenge to Political Theory,' in Friedrich, *Community*, pp. 81–2.)

7   Martin Hollis, *Models of Man*, Cambridge, Cambridge University Press, 1977, p. 15.

8   This issue is considered extensively in William A. Galston, *Justice and the Human Good*, Chicago, University of Chicago Press, 1980; Michael Walzer, *Spheres of Justice*, Oxford, Martin Robertson, 1983; Philip Green, *Retrieving Democracy: In Search of Civic Equality*, London, Methuen, 1985; and Samuel Bowles and Herbert Gintis, *Democracy and Capitalism: Property, Community, and the Contradictions of Modern Social Thought*, New York, Basic Books, 1986.

9   Karl Marx and Friedrich Engels, *The German Ideology* (ed.) R. Pascal, New York, International Publishers, 1963, p. 39.

10 See Steven Lukes, 'Power and Structure', in Lukes, *Essays in Social Theory*, London, Macmillan, 1977, pp. 15–17.

11 V.I. Lenin, *What is to be Done?*, Peking, Foreign Languages Press, 1978, pp. 36–9.
12 Alasdair MacIntyre, *After Virtue*, Notre Dame, University of Notre Dame Press, 2nd edition, 1984, pp. 220–1.
13 ibid., pp. 142–5.
14 Aristotle, *The Politics* (ed.) Ernest Barker, Oxford, Clarendon Press, 1961, p. 40 (1261a).
15 ibid., p. 41 (1261a).
16 Aristotle, *The Ethics* (ed.) Jonathan Barnes, Harmondsworth, Penguin, 1976, p. 172 (1129a).
17 ibid., p. 176 (1130b).
18 ibid., pp. 177–8 (1131a).
19 ibid., pp. 258–9 (1155a).
20 ibid., p. 263 (1156b).
21 ibid., p. 273 (1159b–1160a).
22 ibid., p. 273 (1159b).
23 ibid., p. 296 (1166b).
24 ibid., p. 297 (1167a–b).
25 ibid., p. 298 (1167b).
26 Plant, op. cit., pp. 40–4.
27 ibid., p. 47.
28 Plant's reference is to Peter Winch, 'Authority', in Anthony Quinton (ed.) *Political Philosophy*, Oxford, Oxford University Press, 1967, pp. 97–111.
29 Plant, op. cit., pp. 51–5.
30 G.W.F. Hegel, *The Philosophy of Right* (ed.) T.M. Knox, Oxford, Oxford University Press, 1967, paragraphs 250–6, 265, 289–90 and 308–11.
31 Alexis de Tocqueville, *Democracy in America* (ed.) J.P. Mayer and Max Lerner, London, Collins, 1968, vol. 1, pp. 195–210.
32 Ronald Beiner, *Political Judgment*, London, Methuen, 1983, p. 7.
33 W.J.M. MacKenzie, *Political Identity*, Manchester, Manchester University Press, 1978, p. 12.
34 This sense refers not just to a body of laws assigning political offices, but to a way of life, or system of social ethics. (See Ernest Barker's 'Introduction', to Aristotle, *The Politics*, Oxford, Clarendon Press, 1961, p. lxvi.)

Chapter three   Machiavelli: citizenship and glory

1 Niccolo Machiavelli, *Discourses* (ed.) Bernard Crick, Harmondsworth, Penguin, Book I, ch. x, hereafter cited in the text as: *D*, I, x, to indicate book and chapter numbers; most of Machiavelli's chapters are short enough not to require page references.
2 See above: ch. 2, note 34.
3 Hanna Fenichel Pitkin, *Fortune is a Woman: Gender and Politics in the Thought of Niccolo Machiavelli*, Berkeley, University of California Press, 1984, p. 285.

Notes

4 Niccolo Machiavelli, *The Prince* (ed.) George Bull, Harmondsworth, Penguin, 1981, p. 130, hereafter cited in the text as *P*, 130.
5 Niccolo Machiavelli, *The Art of War* (ed.) Neal Wood, Indianapolis, Bobbs-Merrill, 1977, p. 165, hereafter cited in the text as *AW*, 165.
6 Pitkin, op. cit., p. 306.
7 As indeed factions did in the dispute over the Agrarian Law, for which see below; see also *D*, I, vii.
8 J.G.A. Pocock, *The Machiavellian Moment*, Princeton, Princeton University Press, 1975, p. 201.
9 ibid., p. 213.
10 See Crick's note in *Discourses*, p. 543.

Chapter four   Rousseau: freedom, happiness, and virtue

1 Jean-Jacques Rousseau, *The Social Contract* (ed.) Maurice Cranston, Harmondsworth, Penguin, 1968, Book I, Preface, p. 49. All citations are from this edition. In some cases the translation has been amended, for the sake of consistency with translations of his other works. Thus *'patrie'* has been rendered as 'fatherland', rather than as 'homeland' or 'country', and *'opinion'* as 'opinion' and not 'belief'. Hereafter, citations will be placed in the text in the form *SC*, II, iv, to indicate book and chapter. Rousseau's chapters are short and page numbers are thus not required.
2 See, for instance, his reply to Stanislas, King of Poland, in *Œuvres Compltes de Jean-Jacques Rousseau* (eds.) B. Gagnebin and M. Raymond, Bibliothèque de la Pléiade, Paris, Editions Gallimard, 1964, vol. III, pp. 35–7, hereafter cited as *OC*, III, 1964, pp. 35–7.
3 Jean-Jacques Rousseau, *Confessions*, in *OC*, I, 1959, p.404; c.f.: 'It is certain that all peoples become in the long run what the government makes them.' Jean-Jacques Rousseau, *Discourse on Political Economy* (ed.) G.D.H. Cole, London, Dent, 1973, p. 127.
4 Jean-Jacques Rousseau, *Emile* (ed.) Barbara Foxley, London, Dent, 1974, p. 49.
5 ibid., p. 55.
6 Jean-Jacques Rousseau, *Discourse on the Origins of Inequality* (ed.) Maurice Cranston, Harmondsworth, Penguin, 1984, p. 136.
7 ibid., p. 87.
8 *Emile*, p. 44.
9 *Discourse on the Origins of Inequality*, p. 97.
10 *Emile*, p. 44.
11 ibid., pp. 435–9.
12 *Discourse on the Origins of Inequality*, pp. 57–61.
13 As Allan Bloom notes in his introduction to the *Letter to d'Alembert on the Theatre*, there is no single English word which adequately translates the French *'mœurs'*. It is a term wider than either 'morals' or 'manners', and he suggests rendering it as 'morals and manners'. I have followed him in this, though I have more often simpiy left the French untranslated. See Jean-Jacques Rousseau, *Politics and the*

Arts: *The Letter to d'Alembert on the Theatre* (ed.) Allan Bloom, Glencoe, Ill., Free Press, 1960, p. 149.

14 *Discourse on the Origins of Inequality*, p. 77.

15 *Discourse on Political Economy*, p.120.

16 Robert Derathé, notes to *Du Contrat Social*, in *OC*, III, 1964, p. 1447.

17 Jean-Jacques Rousseau, *Du Contrat Social*, (Premiére Version), in *OC*, III, 1964, p.313.

18 See *Emile*, Book IV, pp. 249–53.

19 ibid., Book I, pp. 6–7.

20 See note 11, above.

21 *Discourse on Political Economy*, p. 136.

22 Jean-Jacques Rousseau, *Considerations on the Government of Poland*, in *OC*, III, 1964, p.966.

23 See *Emile*, Book II.

24 *Considerations on the Government of Poland*, p. 968.

25 *Letter to d'Alembert on the Theatre*, p. 78. The French title has, instead of '*théâtre*', '*spectacles*', which is wider in scope than 'theatre', and means any form of public entertainment or amusement.

26 ibid., p. 26

27 ibid., pp. 50–3.

28 ibid., p. 57.

29 ibid., pp. 125–6.

30 ibid., p. 133.

Chapter five   Hegel: rational freedom in the ethical community

1 See G.W.F. Hegel, *Reason in History* (ed.) Robert S. Hartmann, Indianapolis, Bobbs-Merrill, 1953, pp. 11–20, hereafter cited in the text as *RH*, 11–20. This is a translation of the Introduction to *The Philosophy of History*, more recent than the Sibree translation of that work; see note below.

2 Karl Marx, *Critique of Hegel's 'Philosophy of Right'* (ed.) Joseph O'Malley, Cambridge, Cambridge University Press, 1970, p. 15.

3 G.W.F. Hegel, *The Philosophy of Right* (ed.) T.M. Knox, Oxford, Oxford University Press, 1967, paragraph 147, hereafter cited in the text as *PR*, 147. Hegel often added explanatory remarks to his paragraphs: reference to these is indicated by the suffix 'R'. Further remarks have also been added, derived from the notes of his students; reference to these is indicated by the suffix 'A'.

4 G.W.F. Hegel, *The Philosophy of History* (ed.) J. Sibree, New York, Dover Publications, 1956, p. 253, hereafter cited in the text as *PH*, 253.

5 The phrase 'the unhappy Consciousness' is taken from G.W.F. Hegel, *The Phenomenology of Spirit* (ed.) A.V. Miller, Oxford, Clarendon Press, 1971, paragraph 126.

6 For the role of Luther, see *PH*, 412–6.

7 For Rousseau's thoughts on federalism, see *Considerations on the Government of Poland*, in *Œuvres Complètes de Jean-Jacques*

Rousseau (ed.) B. Gagnebin and M. Raymond, Bibliothque de la
Pléiade, Paris, Editions Gallimard, 1964, vol. III, p. 971.

8 What is translated by Knox as 'mind', in *The Philosophy of Right*, is
translated by Hartmann in *Reason in History*, and by Sibree in *The
Philosophy of History*, as 'spirit'. The German term is '*Geist*'.

9 Quoted in Raymond Plant, *Hegel*, London, Allen & Unwin, 1973,
p. 145.

10 G.W.F. Hegel, 'The German Constitution', in Z.A. Pelczynski (ed.)
Hegel's Political Writings, Oxford, Clarendon Press, 1964, p. 210.

Chapter six   Tocqueville: citizenship in town and state

1 Alexis de Tocqueville, *Journeys to England and Ireland* (ed.) J.P. Mayer,
New Haven, Yale University Press, 1958, p. 117, hereafter cited in
the text as *JEI*, 117.

2 Alexis de Tocqueville, Draft for *Democracy in America*, cited in James
T. Schleifer, 'Tocqueville as Historian: Philosophy and Methodology
in the *Democracy*', in Abraham S. Eisenstadt (ed.) *Reconsidering
Tocqueville's Democracy in America*, New Brunswick, Rutgers
University Press, 1988, p. 163.

3 Alexis de Tocqueville, *Democracy in America* (ed.) J.P. Mayer and
Max Lerner, London, Collins, 1968, pp. 10–11, hereafter cited in the
text as *DA*,10–11.

4 Tocqueville, Draft for *Democracy*, cited in James T. Schleifer, *The
Making of Tocqueville's Democracy*, Chapel Hill, University of North
Carolina Press, 1980, p. 243.

5 Alexis de Tocqueville, *Journey to America* (ed.) J.P. Mayer, New Haven,
Yale University Press, 1962, p. 211, hereafter cited in the text as *JA*,
211.

6 See Seymour Drescher, 'Tocqueville's Two *Democracies*', *Journal of
the History of Ideas*, 1964, vol. 25, pp. 201–16; and Drescher, 'More
than America: Comparison and Synthesis in *Democracy in America*',
in Eisenstadt, op. cit., pp. 77–90. For a response to Drescher, see
Melvin Richter, 'Tocqueville, Napoleon, and Bonapartism', in
Eisenstadt, op. cit., pp. 117–44.

7 See Schleifer, *The Making of Tocqueville's Democracy*, p. 134.

8 Alexander Hamilton, James Madison and John Jay, *The Federalist
Papers* (ed.) Garry Wills, New York, Bantam Books, 1988, p. 40.

9 ibid., p. 41.

10 Alexis de Tocqueville, *The Old Regime and the French Revolution* (ed.)
Stuart Gilbert, New York, Doubleday, 1955, pp. 12–13.

11 See Jack Lively, *The Social and Political Thought of Alexis de
Tocqueville*, Oxford, Clarendon Press, 1961, pp. 52–3; and Schleifer,
The Making of Tocqueville's Democracy, p. 286.

Chapter seven   The modern relevance of the civic-republican tradition

1   Karl Marx, *Critique of Hegel's 'Philosophy of Right'* (ed.) Joseph O'Malley, Cambridge, Cambridge University Press, 1970, pp. 122–3.
2   Pascal's wager was that since the benefits to be derived from belief in God were infinite, and the costs to the individual of believing were minimal, it was rational for the individual to go through the motions of belief in the hope that genuine belief would result. See the discussion in Jon Elster, *Ulysses and the Sirens*, Cambridge, Cambridge University Press, 1988, pp. 47–54.
3   Jean-Jacques Rousseau, *The Social Contract* (ed.) Maurice Cranston, Harmondsworth, Penguin, 1968, Book II, ch. vii.
4   Thomas Hobbes, *Leviathan* (ed.) C.B. Macpherson, Harmondsworth, Penguin, 1982, p. 271.
5   Thomas Hobbes, *De Cive*, in Hobbes, *Man and Citizen* (ed.) Bernard Gert, Humanities Press, 1978, p. 216.

Chapter eight   Citizenship in modern democratic theory

1   The title of an article by Amy Gutmann in *Philosophy and Public Affairs*, 1985, vol. 14, no. 3, pp. 308–22. Since the 'communitarians' to be discussed would not necessarily accept this label, it is proposed to use the term 'democratic theorists'.
2   John Stuart Mill, *Considerations on Representative Government*, New York, Liberal Arts Press, 1958, especially chs. I–III. See the discussion of Mill in Carole Pateman, *Participation and Democratic Theory*, Cambridge, Cambridge University Press, 1970, pp. 28–35.
3   Jane Mansbridge, *Beyond Adversary Democracy* (revised edition), Chicago, Chicago University Press, 1983, is, among other things, a very perceptive analysis of the different experiences of participation that people of different temperaments and characters have.
4   See, for instance, Samuel Bowles and Herbert Gintis, *Democracy and Capitalism: Property, Community, and the Contradictions of Modern Social Thought*, New York, Basic Books, 1986, ch. 2.
5   Jean-Jacques Rousseau, *Discourse on the Origins of Inequality* (ed.) Maurice Cranston, Harmondsworth, Penguin, 1984, Part II; G.W.F. Hegel, *The Phenomenology of Spirit* (ed.) A.V. Miller, Oxford, Clarendon Press, 1977, pp. 111–19.
6   See Philip Green, *Retrieving Democracy: In Search of Civic Equality*, London, Methuen, 1985; Bowles and Gintis, op. cit.; and Benjamin R. Barber, *Strong Democracy: Participatory Politics for a New Age*, Berkeley, University of California Press, 1984.
7   Michael Walzer, *Spheres of Justice*, Oxford, Martin Robertson, 1983, p. 68.
8   Barber, op. cit., pp. 155, 212.
9   Richard Dagger, 'Metropolis, Memory, and Citizenship', *American Journal of Political Science*, 1981, vol. 25, no. 4, p. 718.

10   Wilson Carey McWilliams and Marc Landy, 'On Political Edification, Eloquence and Memory', *PS*, 1984, vol. XVII, no. 2, p. 204.
11   Barber, op. cit., pp. 218–28.
12   William A. Galston, *Justice and Human Good*, Chicago, University of Chicago Press, 1980, pp. 265–9.
13   Barber, op. cit., p. 227.
14   Green, op. cit., p. 71.
15   Galston, op. cit., p. 223.
16   Barber, op. cit., p. 233.
17   ibid., pp. 148–50.
18   ibid., pp. 242–3.
19   ibid., pp. 235–7, 244, 265.
20   Green, op. cit., pp. 270–1.
21   ibid., p. 158.
22   ibid., p. 156.
23   ibid., p. 252.
24   See Bowles and Gintis, op. cit., pp. 150–1; and Michael J. Sandel, *Liberalism and the Limits of Justice*, Cambridge, Cambridge University Press, 1982, p. 150.
25   Galston, op. cit., p. 193.
26   Amy Gutmann, *Democratic Education*, Princeton, Princeton University Press, 1987, pp. 14–15.
27   ibid., p. 19.
28   ibid., p. 39.
29   ibid., p. 46.
30   ibid., p. 61.
31   ibid., pp. 104–6.
32   ibid., pp. 282–4.
33   ibid., p. 287.
34   Morris Janowitz, *The Reconstruction of Patriotism: Education for Civic Consciousness*, Chicago, University of Chicago Press, 1983, pp. 145–50.
35   ibid., pp. x–xii.
36   ibid., p. 12.
37   ibid., p. 14.
38   ibid., pp. 168–9.
39   ibid., pp. 171–2.
40   ibid., p. 194.
41   ibid., pp. 195, 202.
42   ibid., p. 198.
43   See Isaiah Berlin, 'Does Political Theory Still Exist?', in Peter Laslett and W.G. Runciman (eds.) *Philosophy, Politics and Society*, (2nd. series), Oxford, Blackwell, 1969. Berlin's article first appeared in 1961.
44   Dante L. Germino, 'The Crisis in Community: Challenge to Political Theory', in Carl Friedrich (ed.) *Community*, New York, Liberal Arts Press, 1959 (*Nomos, II*), pp. 81–2.
45   ibid., pp. 84–9.
46   ibid., pp. 89–92.

47 ibid., pp. 93–7.
48 ibid., p. 98.
49 See William A. Galston, 'Public Morality and Religion in the Liberal State', *PS*, 1986, vol. XIX, no. 4, pp. 807–24, for a review of this literature.
50 Galston's reference here is to John Locke, *A Letter Concerning Toleration* (ed.) James H. Tully, Indianapolis, Hackett, 1983.
51 Galston, op. cit., p. 810.
52 ibid., p. 811.
53 Robert N. Bellah, Richard Madsen, William M. Sullivan, Ann Swidler and Steven M. Tipton, *Habits of the Heart: Individualism and Commitment in American Life*, Berkeley, University of California Press, 1985. The title, 'Habits of the Heart', is from Alexis de Tocqueville, *Democracy in America* (ed.) J.P. Mayer and Max Lerner, London, Collins, 1968, p. 355.
54 Robert N. Bellah, *The Broken Covenant: American Civil Religion in Time of Trial*, New York, Seabury Press, 1975, ch. 1; see also Forrest McDonald, *Novus Ordo Seclorum: The Intellectual Origins of the Constitution*, Lawrence, University Press of Kansas, 1985, chs. II–III.
55 Bellah et. al., *Habits of the Heart*, p. 277.
56 ibid., pp. 281–3.
57 ibid., pp. 284–6.
58 ibid., pp. 286–8.
59 ibid., p. 289.
60 ibid., p. 293.
61 ibid., p. 286.
62 ibid., p. 296.
63 Robert N. Bellah, 'Civil Religion in America', *Daedalus*, 1967, vol. 96, no. 1, pp. 16–17.
64 Bellah, *The Broken Covenant*, pp. 142–3.
65 Peter Laslett, 'The Face to Face Society', in Laslett (ed.) *Philosophy, Politics and Society*, Oxford, Blackwell, 1967; Mansbridge, op. cit., ch. 3; and Barber, op. cit., pp. 148–50.

Bibliography

This bibliography includes all those references cited in the text, as well as those – not otherwise acknowledged – which were consulted during the preparation of this book.

Arendt, Hannah, *The Human Condition*, New York, Doubleday, 1958.
Aristotle, *Politics* (ed.) Ernest Barker, Oxford, Clarendon Press, 1961.
—— *Ethics* (ed.) Jonathan Barnes, Harmondsworth, Penguin, 1976.
Averini, Shlomo, *Hegel's Theory of the Modern State*, Cambridge, Cambridge University Press, 1979.
Barber, Benjamin R., *Strong Democracy: Participatory Politics for a New Age*, Berkeley, University of California Press, 1984.
Beiner, Ronald, *Political Judgment*, London, Methuen, 1983.
Bellah, Robert N., *The Broken Covenant: American Civil Religion in Time of Trial*, New York, Seabury Press, 1975.
—— 'Civil Religion in America', *Daedalus*, 1967, vol. 96, no. 1, pp. 1–21.
Bellah, Robert N., Madsen, Richard, Sullivan, William M., Swidler, Ann and Tipton, Steven M., *Habits of the Heart: Individualism and Commitment in American Life*, Berkeley, University of California Press, 1985.
Benn, S.I., 'Individuality, Autonomy and Community', in Eugene Kamenka (ed.) *Community and Social Control*, London, Arnold, 1982, pp. 42–61.
Berlin, Isaiah, 'Does Political Theory Still Exist?', in Peter Laslett and W.G. Runciman (eds) *Philosophy, Politics and Society*, (2nd series), Oxford, Blackwell, 1969.
—— 'The Originality of Machiavelli', in I. Berlin, *Against the Current*, New York, Penguin, 1982.
Blunkett, David and Crick, Bernard, *The Labour Party's Aims and Values: An Unofficial Statement*, Nottingham, Spokesman, 1988.
Bowles, Samuel and Gintis, Herbert, *Democracy and Capitalism: Property, Community, and the Contradictions of Modern Social Thought*, New York, Basic Books, 1986.
Bowra, C.M., *The Greek Experience*, London, Weidenfeld & Nicolson, 1957.
Cameron, David, *The Social Thought of Rousseau and Burke*, London,

Weidenfeld & Nicolson, 1973.

Cassirer, Ernst, *The Question of Jean-Jacques Rousseau* (ed.) Peter Gay, Bloomington, Indiana University Press, 1963.

'Charter 88', *New Statesman and Society*, 2 December 1988, pp. 10–11.

Clarke, Barry, 'The Substance of Political Thought', *History of Political Thought*, 1982, vol. III, no. 2, pp. 305–33.

Cobban, Alfred, *Rousseau and the Modern State*, (2nd. ed.), London, George Allen & Unwin, 1964.

Colletti, Lucio, 'Rousseau as Critic of "Civil Society" ', in Colletti, *From Rousseau to Lenin*, New York, Monthly Review Press, 1972, pp. 143–93.

Collingwood, R.G., *An Autobiography*, Oxford, Oxford University Press, 1967.

Cox, Archibald, *The Court and the Constitution*, Boston, Houghton Mifflin, 1987.

Cranston, Maurice, *Freedom*, (3rd ed.), London, Longmans, 1967.

—— *Jean-Jacques: The Early Life and Work of Jean-Jacques Rousseau, 1712–1754*, London, Allen Lane, 1983.

Crick, Bernard, 'Freedom as Politics', in Peter Laslett and W.G. Runciman (eds) *Philosophy, Politics and Society*, (3rd series), Oxford, Blackwell, 1967; also in Crick, *Political Theory and Practice*, London, Allen Lane, 1971.

—— *In Defence of Politics*, London, Weidenfeld & Nicolson, 1962.

Cullen, Bernard, *Hegel's Social and Political Thought*, Dublin, Gill & Macmillan, 1979.

Dagger, Richard, 'Metropolis, Memory, and Citizenship', *American Journal of Political Science*, 1981, vol. 25, no. 4, pp. 715–37.

Dahl, Robert A. and Tufte, Edward R., *Size and Democracy*, Stanford, Stanford University Press, 1974.

Downing, Lyle A. and Thigpen, Robert B., 'Beyond Shared Understandings', *Political Theory*, 1986, vol. 14, no. 3, pp. 451–72.

Drescher, Seymour, 'More than America: Comparison and Synthesis in *Democracy in America*', in Abraham S. Eisenstadt (ed.) *Reconsidering Tocqueville's Democracy in America*, New Brunswick, Rutgers University Press, 1988, pp. 77–90.

—— *Tocqueville and England*, Cambridge, Mass., Harvard University Press, 1964.

—— 'Tocqueville's Two *Democracies*,' *Journal of the History of Ideas*, 1964, vol. 25, pp. 201–16.

Duncan, Graeme (ed.) *Democratic Theory and Practice*, Cambridge, Cambridge University Press, 1983.

Dunn, John, *Western Political Theory in the Face of the Future*, Cambridge, Cambridge University Press, 1979.

Dworkin, Ronald, 'The Great Abortion Case', *New York Review of Books*, 29 June 1989, pp. 49–53.

Ehrenberg, Victor, *The Greek State*, London, Methuen, 1969.

Eisenstadt, Abraham S. (ed.) *Reconsidering Tocqueville's Democracy in America*, New Brunswick, Rutgers University Press, 1988.

Ellenberg, Stephen, *Rousseau's Political Philosophy: An Interpretation from Within*, Ithaca, Cornell University Press, 1976.

Elster, Jon, *Ulysses and the Sirens*, Cambridge, Cambridge University Press, 1988.

Finley, M.I., *The Ancient Greeks*, Harmondsworth, Penguin, 1984.

Flathman, Richard, *The Practice of Rights*, Cambridge, Cambridge University Press, 1976.

Friedrich, Carl J., 'The Concept of Community in the History of Political and Legal Philosophy', in Friedrich (ed.) *Community*, pp. 3–24.

—— (ed.) *Community*, New York, Liberal Arts Press, 1959 (*Nomos II*).

Galston, William A., *Justice and the Human Good*, Chicago, University of Chicago Press, 1980.

—— 'Public Morality and Religion in the Liberal State', *PS*, 1986, vol. XIX, no. 4, pp. 807–24.

Germino, Dante L., 'The Crisis in Community: Challenge to Political Theory', in Carl Friedrich (ed.) *Community*, New York, Liberal Arts Press, 1959 (*Nomos II*).

Gildin, Hilail, *Rousseau's Social Contract: The Design of the Argument*, Chicago, University of Chicago Press, 1983.

Goldstein, Doris S., 'Alexis de Tocqueville's Concept of Citizenship', *Proceedings of the American Philosophical Society*, 1964, vol. 108, no. 1, pp. 39–53.

—— *Trial of Faith: Religion and Politics in Tocqueville's Thought*, New York, Elsevier Press, 1975.

Green, Philip, *Retrieving Democracy: In Search of Civic Equality*, London, Methuen, 1985.

Grimsley, Ronald, 'Introduction,' to Jean-Jacques Rousseau, *Du Contrat Social*, Oxford, Clarendon Press, 1972, pp. 1–95.

—— *The Philosophy of Rousseau*, London, Oxford University Press, 1973.

Gusfield, Joseph, R., *Community: A Critical Response*, Oxford, Blackwell, 1975.

Gutmann, Amy, 'Communitarian Critics of Liberalism', *Philosophy and Public Affairs*, 1985, vol. 14, no. 3, pp. 308–22.

—— *Democratic Education*, Princeton, Princeton University Press, 1987.

Hamilton, Alexander, Madison, James and Jay, John, *The Federalist Papers* (ed.) Garry Wills, New York, Bantam Books, 1988.

Hampshire, Stuart (ed.) *Public and Private Morality*, Cambridge, Cambridge University Press, 1980.

—— *Two Theories of Morality*, Oxford, Oxford University Press, 1977.

Harris, David, 'Returning the social to democracy', in Graeme Duncan (ed.) *Democratic Theory and Practice*, Cambridge, Cambridge University Press, 1983.

Hegel, G.W.F., *The Phenomenology of Spirit* (ed.) A.V. Miller, Oxford, Clarendon Press, 1977.

—— *The Philosophy of History* (ed.) J. Sibree, New York, Dover, 1956.

—— *The Philosophy of Right* (ed.) T.M. Knox, Oxford, Oxford University Press, 1967.

—— *Reason in History* (ed.) Robert S. Hartman, Indianapolis, Library of

Liberal Arts, 1953.

Hereth, Michael, *Alexis de Tocqueville: Threats to Freedom in Democracy*, Durham, Duke University Press, 1986.

Hirsch, H.N. 'The Threnody of Liberalism: Constitutional Liberty and the Renewal of Community', *Political Theory*, 1986, vol. 14, no. 3, pp. 423–49.

Hobbes, Thomas, *De Cive*, in Hobbes, *Man and Citizen* (ed.) Bernard Gert, Humanities Press, 1978.

—— *Leviathan* (ed.) C.B. Macpherson, Harmondsworth, Penguin, 1968.

Hollis, Martin, *Models of Man*, Cambridge, Cambridge University Press, 1977.

Ignatieff, Michael, *The Needs of Strangers*, London, Chatto & Windus, The Hogarth Press, 1984.

Ionescu, Ghita, *Politics and the Pursuit of Happiness*, London, Longman, 1984.

Jacobson, Norman, *Pride and Solace: The Foundations and Limits of Political Theory*, London, Methuen, 1978.

Janowitz, Morris, *The Reconstruction of Patriotism: Education for Civic Consciousness*, Chicago, University of Chicago Press, 1983.

Kamenka, Eugene (ed.) *Community as a Social Ideal*, London, Arnold, 1982.

Kaufmann, Walter (ed.) *Hegel's Political Philosophy*, New York, Atherton Press, 1970.

Laslett, Peter, 'The Face to Face Society', in Laslett (ed.) *Philosophy, Politics and Society*, Oxford, Blackwell, 1967.

—— (ed.) *Philosophy, Politics and Society*, Oxford, Blackwell, 1967.

Laslett, Peter and Runciman, W.G. (ed.) *Philosophy, Politics and Society*, (2nd series), Oxford, Blackwell, 1969.

—— (eds) *Philosophy, Politics and Society*, (3rd series), Oxford, Blackwell, 1967.

Lenin, V.I., *What is to be Done?*, Peking, Foreign Languages Press, 1978.

Levine, Andrew, *The End of the State*, London, Verso, 1987.

Lindley, Richard, *Autonomy*, London, Macmillan, 1986.

Lively, Jack, *The Social and Political Thought of Alexis de Tocqueville*, Oxford, Clarendon Press, 1961.

Lockyer, Andrew, ' "Traditions" as Context in the History of Political Thought', *Political Studies*, 1979, vol. 27, pp. 201–17.

Lukes, Steven, 'Power and Structure,' in Lukes, *Essays in Social Theory*, London, Macmillan, 1977.

Machiavelli, Niccolo, *The Art of War* (ed.) Bobbs-Merrill, Neal Wood, Indianapolis, Bobbs-Merrill, 1977.

—— *Discourses* (ed.) Bernard Crick, Harmondsworth, Penguin, 1970.

—— *The Prince* (ed.) George Bull, Harmondsworth, Penguin, 1981.

McCluskey, John, 'An Enormous Power', *The Listener*, 4 December 1986, pp. 13–16.

McDonald, Forrest, *Novus Ordo Seclorum: The Intellectual Origins of the Constitution*, Lawrence, University Press of Kansas, 1985.

MacIntyre, Alasdair, *After Virtue*, (2nd edition), Notre Dame, University of Notre Dame Press, 1984.

MacKenzie, W.J.M., *Political Identity*, Manchester, Manchester University Press, 1978.

McWilliams, Wilson Carey, *The Idea of Fraternity in America*, Berkeley, University of California Press, 1973.

McWilliams, Wilson Carey, and Landy, Marc, 'On Political Edification, Eloquence and Memory', *PS*, 1984, vol. XVII, no. 2, pp. 203–10.

Mansbridge, Jane, *Beyond Adversary Democracy*, (revised edition), Chicago, University of Chicago Press, 1983.

Masters, Roger D., *The Political Philosophy of Rousseau*, Princeton, Princeton University Press, 1968.

Marx, Karl, *Critique of Hegel's 'Philosophy of Right'* (ed.) Joseph O'Malley, Cambridge, Cambridge University Press, 1970.

Marx, Karl and Engels, Friedrich, *The German Ideology* (ed.) R. Pascal, New York, International Publishers, 1963.

Mill, John Stuart, *Considerations on Representative Government*, New York, Liberal Arts Press, 1958.

Mulgan, R.G., *Aristotle's Political Theory*, Oxford, Clarendon Press, 1977.

Nisbet, R.A., *The Sociological Tradition*, London, Heinemann, 1971.

Oakeshott, Michael, *On Human Conduct*, Oxford, Clarendon Press, 1975.

Parry, Geraint, *John Locke*, George Allen & Unwin, 1978.

Pateman, Carole, *Participation and Democratic Theory*, Cambridge, Cambridge University Press, 1970.

Pelczynski, Z.A. (ed.) *Hegel's Political Philosophy: Problems and Perspectives*, Cambridge, Cambridge University Press, 1970.

—— *Hegel's Political Writings*, Oxford, Clarendon Press, 1964.

—— *The State and Civil Society: Studies in Hegel's Political Philosophy*, Cambridge, Cambridge University Press, 1984.

Pitkin, Hanna Fenichel, *Fortune is a Woman: Gender and Politics in the Thought of Niccolo Machiavelli*, Berkeley, University of California Press, 1984.

Plamenatz, John, *Man and Society*, (2 vols), London, Longman, 1963.

Plant, Raymond, *Community and Ideology*, London, Routledge & Kegan Paul, 1974.

—— *Hegel*, London, Methuen, 1973.

Pocock, J.G.A., *The Machiavellian Moment*, Princeton, Princeton University Press, 1975.

Portis, Edward B., 'Citizenship and Personal Identity', *Polity*, 1986, vol. XVIII, no. 3, pp. 457–72.

Quinton, Anthony (ed.) *Political Philosophy*, Oxford, Oxford University Press, 1967.

Rees, John, *Equality*, London, Macmillan, 1972.

Richter, Melvin, 'Tocqueville, Napoleon, and Bonapartism', in Abraham S. Eisenstadt (ed.) *Reconsidering Tocqueville's Democracy in America*, New Brunswick, Rutgers University Press, 1988.

Rousseau, Jean-Jacques, *Confessions, Œuvres Complètes*, vol. I.

—— *Considerations on the Government of Poland, Œuvres Complètes*, vol. III.

—— *Discourse on the Arts and Sciences* (ed.) G.D.H. Cole, London, Dent, 1973.
—— *Discourse on the Origins of Inequality* (ed.) Maurice Cranston, Harmondsworth, Penguin, 1984.
—— *Discourse on Political Economy* (ed.) G.D.H. Cole, London, Dent, 1973.
—— *Emile* (ed.) Barbara Foxley, London, Dent, 1974.
—— *Œuvres Complètes* (eds.) B. Gagnebin and M. Raymond, Bibliothèque de la Pléiade, Paris, Editions Gallimard, vol. I, 1959, vol. III, 1964.
—— *Politics and the Arts: The Letter to d'Alembert on the Theatre* (ed.) Allan Bloom, Glencoe, Ill., Free Press, 1960.
—— *The Social Contract* (ed.) Maurice Cranston, Harmondsworth, Penguin, 1968.
Sandel, Michael J., *Liberalism and the Limits of Justice*, Cambridge, Cambridge University Press, 1982.
Schleifer, James, T., *The Making of Tocqueville's Democracy*, Chapel Hill, University of North Carolina Press, 1980.
—— 'Tocqueville as Historian: Philosophy and Methodology in the *Democracy*', in Abraham S. Eisenstadt (ed.) *Reconsidering Tocqueville's Democracy in America*, New Brunswick, Rutgers University Press, 1988.
Sennett, Richard, *The Fall of Public Man*, London, Faber & Faber, 1986.
Shklar, Judith, *Freedom and Independence: A Study of the Political Ideas of Hegel's Phenomenology of Mind*, Cambridge, Cambridge University Press, 1976.
—— *Men and Citizens: A Study of Rousseau's Social Theory*, Cambridge, Cambridge University Press, 1969.
Skinner, Quentin, *Machiavelli*, Oxford, Oxford University Press, 1981.
Sniderman, Paul, *A Question of Loyalty*, Berkeley, University of California Press, 1981.
Taylor, Charles, *Hegel and Modern Society*, Cambridge, Cambridge University Press, 1979.
Taylor, Michael, *Community, Anarchy and Liberty*, Cambridge, Cambridge University Press, 1983.
Thigpen, Robert B. and Downing, Lyle A., 'Liberalism and the Communitarian Critique', *American Journal of Political Science*, 1987, vol. 31, pp. 637–55.
Tocqueville, Alexis de, *Democracy in America*, (2 vols) (ed.) J.P. Mayer and Max Lerner, London, Collins, 1968.
—— *Journey to America* (ed.) J.P. Mayer, New Haven, Yale University Press, 1962.
—— *Journeys to England and Ireland* (ed.) J.P. Mayer, New Haven, Yale University Press, 1958.
—— *The Old Regime and the French Revolution* (ed.) Stuart Gilbert, New York, Doubleday, 1955.
Tuck, Richard, *Natural Rights Theories: Their Origin and Development*, Cambridge, Cambridge University Press, 1981.
Urmson, J.O., *Aristotle's Ethics*, Oxford, Blackwell, 1988.

Bibliography

Vincent, Andrew and Plant, Raymond, *Philosophy, Politics and Citizenship*, Oxford, Blackwell, 1984.

Walzer, Michael, *Spheres of Justice*, Oxford, Martin Robertson, 1983.

Weale, Albert, *Political Theory and Social Policy*, London, Macmillan, 1983.

Williams, Bernard, *Ethics and the Limits of Philosophy*, London, Fontana, 1985.

Winch, Peter, 'Authority', in Anthony Quinton (ed.) *Political Philosophy*, Oxford, Oxford University Press, 1967.

Wolin, Sheldon, *Politics and Vision*, Boston, Little Brown, 1960.

Index

The following terms have not been separately indexed: citizen, citizenship, civic republicanism, community, political community.